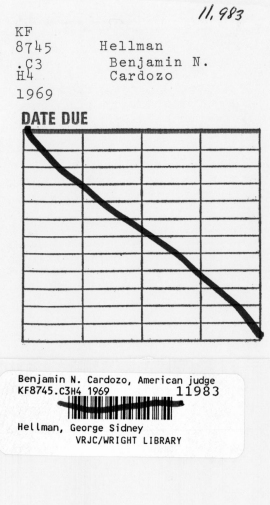

BENJAMIN N. CARDOZO

Associate Justice of the Supreme Court

Benjamin N. Cardozo

AMERICAN JUDGE

by

George S. Hellman

NEW YORK / RUSSELL & RUSSELL

To

I. S. H.

FOREWORD

IN THE comparatively brief time since the death of Justice Cardozo, various volumes have been published, given over, for the most part, to his far-reaching opinions. Here we are concerned primarily with the personality of the man who, indeed, described himself when, in his tribute to John G. Milburn at the Bar Association in 1930, he said: "He thought of his profession in the grand manner and in the grand manner he served it. . . . Not often did he let his voice rise above the modulated level of equitable persuasion. Only some rank injustice, some breach of fundamental safeguards of security or liberty, could stir its quiet depths. He was a gentleman speaking to gentlemen; and gentlemen, he seemed to say, could make their points without need to rant and rave."

Cardozo, in urging that the picture of the great lawyer should not be lost to posterity, continued in these words: "And so this becomes an attempt to clutch at transitory Time before it whirls into oblivion. It is a fond endeavor to retard that hurrying chariot, to grasp at the vanishing shadow. . . . Something of that kind I am feeling here and now when I think of the man, so courtly and so simple, who has gone out of our sight. The vanishing shadow must not elude our clutching hand till some hint of what it meant has been caught out of darkness and written on the scroll of Time. 'Quick thy tablets, Memory!'"

That Cardozo was willing, indeed desired, to be similarly remembered, to have a portrayal of himself made while the tablets of memory were still legible, is apparent in a letter written to his cousin, Maud Nathan. He had been reading the article published in *Fortune* in 1936 wherein pen portraits are given of the members of the Supreme Court. Cardozo was the first to be described, and in terms more laudatory than those accorded to any of the eight other Justices. The lovableness of the man, the brilliancy of his mind, the scholarship, the charm, are dwelt on with the greatest warmth. Presumably it was for this reason that the shy and modest Justice wrote: "I think it is not the kind of article that should be written of the living. . . . When I am dead I shall be glad to have someone write of me as *Fortune* did."

In preparation for a biography whose foremost object is the presentation of a man's character and personality, with the evaluation of his achievements—however important— as the secondary aim, at least four sources must be tapped. The man's public writings and addresses and his private correspondence constitute one source. Contemporary events affecting his thoughts and deeds are the second. What has been written to and of him and said in public addresses, is the third. The recollections and estimates of his family, his friends, and his acquaintances are the fourth. The author has spoken with many of the Justice's associates on the bench and at the bar; with relatives, friends, and compatriots. He has gathered together hundreds of the Justice's letters. He has drawn, as well, on personal recollections of the man who signed himself "Your devoted and faithful friend." Let it, however, be said that there is no pretense of belonging among the intimates of the late Justice. These could be counted on the fingers of a one-armed man. The portals into the very private recesses of his nature were never opened to me, yet in our talks they were approached. So, too, in his conversations and correspondence with other friends and relatives. Indeed, Cardozo's letters, richly drawn upon in the pages following, furnish forth the picture of the man more vividly, more convincingly, than any other words the biographer could summon. Here is revealed the constant loyalty to old family ties. The attributes of mind and character which made Cardozo a great leader are here well indicated. Many of the letters throw off the gray robe of an often sad man and dance with the charm that was his. "Wit is brushwood," we read in the poetry of the Hebrew tradition, "wit is brushwood—judgment is timber. The first makes the brightest flame, but the other gives the most lasting heat." Bright flame of delightful wit, lasting heat of ennobling thought, issue from the letters of Cardozo. They, with the recollections of friends and associates who love to speak of him, love to remember him, provide those personal touches giving vital color to the canvas of biography.

But enough of this Foreword; and "Quick, thy tablets, Memory!"

G. S. H.

There will be one rather feebler than average in build, and yet the God will so crown what he says with a bloom of beauty that all who look on him are moved. When he holds forth in public it is with assurance, yet with so honey-sweet a modesty that it makes him shine out above the ruck of men who gaze at him whenever he walks their city as if he were a god.

From T. E. SHAW's translation
of Homer's *Odyssey*.

BENJAMIN N. CARDOZO

I

*The childhood shows the man as morning
shows the day.*   MILTON

THE year 1870. On West Forty-seventh Street—12, to be exact, was the number of their residence— lived an old New York family of quiet distinction. Its head, Albert Cardozo, a brilliant man, was a justice in the Supreme Court of the State of New York. His wife Rebecca, by all accounts a lovely woman, was noted for her culture, in part the inheritance from a long line of cultured ancestors. To the three young daughters and one son who romped around the spacious house she added, on the twenty-fourth of May, a little girl and a little boy— Emily and Benjamin. A household of fine traditions reaching back to Spain and Portugal, Holland and England, and redolent with memories of active participation in the American War of Independence.

Then came tragedy. Only a few weeks after the birth of Benjamin Nathan Cardozo, the uncle for whom he had been named was murdered. Shock and sorrow to Rebecca and her kin.

From his many-acred country home at Morristown, N. J., Benjamin Nathan had come to town on Thursday, July 28. A Wall Street man of ample fortune, he would visit

[3]

the city only once or twice a week during the summer months. On this occasion not financial affairs, but motives of piety, brought him from across the Hudson. Friday was the anniversary of the death of his mother, Sarah Seixas, wife of Seixas Nathan, both of them, as were their great flock of children, devoted to the rituals of their religion. On all death anniversaries thousand-year-old prayers must be offered to the Lord their God in honor of the dead and for their eternal peace. So Benjamin Nathan came to town.

That afternoon he attended services at the Spanish-Portuguese synagogue—Shearith Israel—whereof he was the president, as his father had been. Then he visited the rabbi, his brother-in-law the Rev. Dr. J. J. Lyons. Remaining till a little after nine, Mr. Nathan then went a few blocks uptown to his home at 12 West Twenty-third Street. The *New York Times* described it as "one of the most elegant and spacious of the private residences in the city." At any rate, a comfortable house, an appropriate home for the wealthy and distinguished citizen who—a colonel on the Governor's staff, a vice-president of the Stock Exchange, president of Mt. Sinai Hospital, a member of the Union Club, the Union League, and the St. Nicholas Society—held in financial, social, and philanthropic circles so prominent a place.

Well, then, before ten o'clock that Thursday night Benjamin Nathan was at home and in bed. At six-thirty the next morning he was due at the synagogue for the prayers of filial piety. When the hour came he lay, a shattered corpse, at the passage between his bedroom and the study wherein stood his safe.

For the first time in the history of the press, the death of a private citizen swept from the front page the news of a European war. That very week, after the formal declaration of war, Napoleon III had proclaimed to the people of France that "Prussia has aroused distrust in all quarters,

[4]

necessitating exaggerated armament and has made of Europe a camp where reign disquiet and fear of the morrow. We wish," the Emperor continued, "to conquer a durable peace, based on the interests of the people, and to assist in abolishing that precarious condition of things where all nations are forced to employ their resources in arming against each other." These words of the vainglorious Napoleon may, in their application to the events of his day, seem not wholly to cover the situation, but for our own times they ring true, with deep and dark prophetic meaning. The clash of arms followed swiftly the echoes of the Emperor's voice. With eager interest the people of America watched the war begin. Yet in the fortnight succeeding the murder of Benjamin Nathan "the war in Europe"—these are the words of the *New York Herald*—"the war in Europe is forgotten and affairs of state and local political topics cease to be commented upon, so great is the interest felt in the latest and most mysterious horror that has ever stirred New Yorkers, and thrilled them with wonder and alarm at the daring of the deed."

The investigation by the coroner's jury, reported in full by the press, led to no results. Equally futile was the work of the detectives on the police force. Some time after the inquest was ended, a burglar named Ellis accused a fellow burglar, Forrester by name, of the murder. Two years went by before the man was arrested, but there was not sufficient evidence against him, and once more the case was dropped. To this day the tragedy remains a mystery. Those who may still care to seek its unraveling will find challenging data in Edmund Pearson's *Studies in Murder*. A burglar, very possibly, as Mr. Nathan's diamond studs and gold watch had been taken. To this day no one knows.

Profound was the suffering of the clan of the Nathans and the Cardozos. A great family, proud and reserved, for the first time in the glare of sensational publicity, in a

[5]

tragedy affecting the earliest colors on the palette of Benjamin Cardozo's life.

A great family, proud and reserved. New York is rich in reminders of Cardozo's kin. Every ship that sails into its port carries men and women whose hearts thrill to the spirit of America at seeing the Statue of Liberty, on whose base, in letters of bronze, appears the noble sonnet of Emma Lazarus, a niece of Cardozo's mother. To the building, in 1711, of the spire of Trinity, New York's historic church, his ancestors contributed with the public spirit of their clan. Fraunces' Tavern, where in 1783 Washington said farewell to his officers, had previously been the house of Phila Franks, a kinswoman. There, in the spacious brick residence at Pearl and Broad streets, she presided over the household lavishly maintained by her husband, General Oliver de Lancey, whose brother, James, was the Governor of the Province of New York. In the cemetery, in the New Bowery, of the Spanish-Portuguese congregation whereof he was the president, the tombstone of her grandfather, Moses Raphael Levy, still remains, though long ago his mansion on his great estate at Rye has paid the price of years. The oldest daughter of this Spanish-born merchant and shipowner, who had come to America in the seventeenth century, married into a family of noted soldiers. There was Colonel Isaac Franks, an officer in the Continental Army, a participant in many battles of the Revolution. There was Colonel David Salisbury Franks, who had proved of such service on the staffs of Washington and of Benedict Arnold that, when the Commander in Chief became the first President of the United States, Colonel Franks was appointed marshal of the day at Washington's Inauguration.

A few in the group of Cardozo's ancestors and their kin retained their allegiance to the King of England. General de Lancey's brother-in-law, another David Franks, was a Loyalist officer. His daughter married in 1822 General Sir Henry Johnson, a direct ancestor of the general of the same name who, as Commander in Chief, headed the British Expeditionary Forces in the World War.

If here and there we find instances of unwillingness on the part of Cardozo's forebears to give up their allegiance to that England from which they came, the preponderant devotion was to the cause of the colonies. To Benjamin's great-grandfather, Moses Seixas, who had been a soldier in the Revolution, George Washington sent his address for the Hebrew Congregation in Newport whereof Seixas, founder of the Bank of Rhode Island, was president. This speech of Washington in 1790 was one of the great liberal pronouncements of our Republic's early years, and fittingly addressed to a member of a family renowned for their patriotism.

When the bicentenary of George Washington's birth led to special services by the New York congregation to which Benjamin Cardozo belonged, the newly appointed Justice of the Supreme Court of the United States listened to the historian Leon Huhner dwell in a learned address on the many contacts of America's first President with men of the Justice's clan.

Not only men. Women also. If one of the clan who fought at the Battle of Long Island was, together with his son, fighting in the army and unable to protect his home in the dubious days of 1779, was not that home burned to the ground by the Tories as punishment for the wife who was determined to give no information of service to her questioners? When "Home, Sweet Home," most beloved of all songs, rises from the heart to the lips, let it be remembered not only that the words were written by a man whose mother belonged to a family allied to Cardozo's. Let there also be thought of the women who sacrificed their homes in the days of liberty's travail.

"The name of Cardozo," the Judge once wrote to a friend, "is or was a very common one in Spain and Portugal. Indeed there was someone of that name who claimed to be the Messiah." We wonder whether that could have been the Cardozo mentioned in a history of the Inquisition, who, as he proudly marched to the flames of torture, chanted the centuried cry of "Hear, O Israel, the Lord is our God, the Lord is One."

The American Cardozos had, as their first ancestor in the Western Hemisphere, a London merchant, Aaron Nunez Cardozo, who came to the colonies in or about the year 1752. According to Captain N. Taylor Phillips, now the president of Shearith Israel, some of the ancestors of Justice Cardozo were Marranos, Judaeo-Christians, who had fled from Portugal during the Inquisition.

They went first to Holland, and then to England before establishing themselves in America, where various of their descendants were to become so prominent in the life of New York, Philadelphia, and Charleston. Aaron's son, Isaac Nunez, after serving in the patriot army from Pennsylvania during the Revolution, was captured by the British and held prisoner of war until he was exchanged. His daughter, Rachel, was the wife of Joseph Phillips, a soldier in the War of 1812, and five years later the Secretary of the Territory of Illinois. His son, Michael Hart Cardozo, was nominated for Justice of the Supreme Court of New York State but died before the election. This was the grandfather of the late Justice of the Supreme Court of the United States.

Benjamin Cardozo belonged, the word is used advisedly, to a clan. Generation after generation there had been in this clan marriages among a small group of families of Spanish, Portuguese, and English descent. Peixotto, Seixas, Nathan, Hart, Frank, Levy, Mendez, Hendricks, Florance, Wolff, Phillips, Gomez, Lazarus—these are names frequently occurring in the family genealogy. In the religious life of their own group, men of these families were, in almost unbroken succession, either the rabbis or the presidents of the Spanish-Portuguese congregation in New York. In the public affairs of America, whether during peace or war, this clan took, and still takes, a prominent part. As early as 1769, after the repeal of the Stamp Act, the second nonimportation agreement was promulgated in further protest against restrictions by the ministers of George III. Among the signers were relatives of Benjamin Cardozo. Sixty years later came the clash of arms at Lexington. New York, even with its many Loyalists, followed in the footsteps of Massachusetts. In the military organization, formed at once in New York to defend the cause of liberty, one of Cardozo's ancestors was an officer. Another, a Southerner, with the rank of colonel, fought at the front until Cornwallis surrendered. Still another was a colonel in the Seventh Regiment of Massachusetts. Aaron Levy, a brother of Zipporah Seixas, was a colonel in the War of 1812. Her son-in-law, Bernard Hart, later the chairman of the New York Stock Exchange, served as a private; her brother, as a captain. Her son Emanuel, a member of Congress and the surveyor of the Port of New York, fought in the Mexican War. As members of the Seventh Regiment of New York, when the city was harassed by the great riots of Civil War days, Frederick and Harmon Nathan, two brothers of Benjamin Cardozo's mother, performed their dangerous duties. In the World War, N. Taylor Phillips, a sometime deputy controller of New York City, served as captain in the United States Army, as did also Michael H. Cardozo, Jr. Another of the cousins of Justice Cardozo was Colonel Arthur R. Wolff

Departing from the military record, one could go on at length with the contributions of this clan to the cultural life of New York. There was the artist, Jacob R. Lazarus,

[9]

who painted five generations of the Astor family. Emma Lazarus, the poet, was the young woman who roused the admiration and won the friendship of the great leaders in American literature of her day, foremost among them Ralph Waldo Emerson. To our own times the literary tradition has been continued in the books of Maud Nathan and Annie Nathan Meyer and, most delightfully of all, in the novels and poems of Robert Nathan.

No wonder, then, that Benjamin Cardozo took quiet pride in his family, which for over two hundred years had so serviceably entered into the life of America. Small wonder that when, as a lad, he came into knowledge of the shadow that dimmed the luster of his clan, his sensitive soul took on the resolve to restore the name of Cardozo to its former honor. Perhaps he never voiced this resolution until in college days, to his classmate, Willard King, he expressed the desire burning within him. It affected with unswerving force the earlier years of boyhood and the later years of manhood.

His father, Albert Cardozo, was, by common consent, one of the most brilliant of the judges in the Supreme Court of New York State. He was the vice-president of the Spanish-Portuguese congregation. He was active in various charities. A man of eloquence and of distinguished manner, his was a high place in the community. But those were the days when Boss Tweed was drawing even judges into his net, and Albert Cardozo did not prove strong enough to resist temptation.

With George G. Barnard and John H. McCann he formed a trio of justices countenancing illegal naturalization. New citizens were created wholesale, not infrequently a thousand in a day; and, of course, the great majority of these naturalized voters supported Tammany at the polls.

An ally of Tweed in various machinations leading to undeserved profits was Jay Gould, the sinister figure in the railroad world. Gould's manipulations of the Erie Railroad are so well known a part of our financial history that repetition of his schemes of wreckage would make a thricetold tale. After, at the behest of Tweed, Albert Cardozo granted the appointment of a receiver for the railroad, his actions on the bench were made, at the request of the Bar Association of New York, a subject of investigation by the Judiciary Committee of the state assembly. Judge Cardozo resigned before the investigation was concluded. Lawyers who have gone deep into the study of the proceedings are of the opinion that he never accepted any money bribe from the Tammany boss, but they agree that the evidence is strong of his having taken orders.

Certainly he showed unprecedented nepotism in assigning refereeships. Out of less than six hundred which Albert Cardozo was authorized to bestow, over three hundred were given to a nephew and over a hundred to the son of Boss Tweed.

The Judge himself maintained that he had been made the victim of politics, but admitted that his value on the bench had been largely destroyed by reason of the accusations at the hearing. His friends stood by him when he resumed the practice of law and his political associates showed their confidence by electing him one of the Grand Sachems of the Tammany Society. Yet the verdict of his own days, as that of later times, is of malfeasance in office. A shadow had fallen on the Cardozo name.

All this took place when, in 1873, Ben was only three years old. Six years later his lovely mother died and grayness settled still more deeply on the home of the Cardozos. Ellen—but always called Nell or Nellie by her kin—became virtually the mother of her sisters and little Ben, and motherly also to her elder brother, Albert. Her life was henceforth devoted to her family, with that special affection for Benjamin which will bring fragrance to later pages of this book. Grace and Lizzie (an invalid from girlhood) were decidedly talented in painting and poetry, and Emily had much charm, but it was Benjamin who even in boyhood showed most brilliancy of mind. Yet brilliancy of mind and brilliancy of talent did little to bring happiness into that now withdrawn and reserved family whose home at 803 Madison Avenue held so many shadowed thoughts. In earlier days, when from the windows of the house on West Forty-seventh Street Albert Cardozo could have looked across the Avenue to the mansion of Jay Gould, horses and carriages, butlers and all the other appurtenances of wealth were part of the family life. Gradually there was a decline in affluence. When the father died in 1885, there was little left of his one-time wealth. The chief inheritance from the father was a religious atmosphere. Sustaining in early youth, but of gradually dissipating force as Benjamin Cardozo approached manhood, it calls for interesting discussion in the peculiar manifestations which affected the Cardozo household.

There is no more unusual evidence of his father's devotion to the laws of his religion than is shown in an episode when Albert Cardozo first ascended the bench. New York City then had only a few justices of the Supreme Court—five in all, we are told. Their work called for meetings on Saturday mornings—a fact not known to Albert Cardozo when he accepted the nomination. So intense was his adherence to those religious decrees which had come down from the days of Moses that his first intention was to resign from the bench rather than depart from the injunction not to do any work on the Sabbath. As vice-president of the Spanish-Portuguese congregation, and brother-in-law of its rabbi, he could not very well turn for unprejudiced advice to his own group. Accordingly, he wrote to London to get counsel from the religious court there—Beth Din, the House of Judgment, the group assembled by the chief rabbi of

[12]

England to pass on questions of this nature. The answer came that public business required by the law of the State took precedence over any Jewish law. Duties to the country must always come first. Whereupon Justice Albert Cardozo, attending the Saturday morning services, not without pain folded up the prayer shawl, put away the books, and left for his court work before the exercises were completed. But in his own home he neglected no detail of ancient ritualistic custom as to prayers, to food, and to special observances of religious holidays.

Albert Cardozo's children were taught to recite the words of the Prophet Micah: "To do justice, to love kindness, and to walk humbly with thy God." They were enjoined to "avoid not the society of your brethren but be firm in faith. Be good citizens and seek the welfare of the community in which you dwell." They were taught, in the words of the rabbi, to "treat the rich and the poor alike, be kind and civil to those in thy employ." They were instructed in the virtue of patience, in the value of speaking mildly.

All these teachings went to mold the character of young Benjamin Cardozo. But after, at the age of thirteen, he had been confirmed by Dr. H. Pereira Mendes in the faith of his fathers, the outreachings of his mind led him away from conviction in the absolute value of such commandments as "marry not with those not of thy faith" and "defile not thy soul by the eating of forbidden food." True, in his own home of later years filial or fraternal sentiment led him to abstain from serving food forbidden by the ancient precepts. In the homes of others he ate what the host provided. Ritualism in itself was alien to his philosophy. Religious in spirit, he abstained from orthodox services while maintaining his status as a member of the congregation and as a hereditary elector therein.

The unwillingness of the father to subject his children to temptations of unorthodox ways interfered with their

[13]

several enjoyments. Seldom did the two boys and the four girls go out to have luncheon or dinner with any save relatives. With the exception of Emily, the youngest daughter, who went to school after her father's death, all received their education within the walls of their home. Ben's tutor was Horatio Alger, who was selected after his twelve years of tutorship of the sons of Joseph Seligman, the founder of the international banking firm. The country homes of the Cardozos and the Seligmans were near each other at Long Branch, then a favorite summer resort of such distinguished men as President Grant and George W. Childs, the Philadelphia philanthropist. Alger, shortly after the Civil War, had come from Massachusetts where he had been a somewhat ineffectual young minister. He was a roly-poly little man, shy, and not at all forceful. But he was devoted to all boys, and all the boys of America avidly read the books he continued to write during his years of tutorship, until finally large royalties placed him in a position of affluence. *Ragged Dick*, *Tattered Tom*, and all those others with the same formula of the poor boy, or the boy starting under adverse circumstances, growing rich, and the bad rich boy ending in disaster—how they swept the country, reaching a sale of millions of copies! They are sneered at nowadays, yet they had their value in the rousing of ambition, in the stirring of imagination, and, it may even be believed, in the strengthening of character. Men now past threescore still remember them with perhaps slightly smiling yet sincere affection. And indubitably they helped to mold the early life of Benjamin Cardozo, perhaps even more than did the easygoing instruction he received from a tutor who could never be strict with his pupils and whose intellect was far inferior to that of the brilliant lad he was teaching. So when the Justice Cardozo of later days was asked by Mr. Milton Halsey Thomas, Curator of Columbiana, for a note concerning his preparation for college, he replied that it was the work of Horatio Alger, adding: "He did not do as successful a job for me as he did with the careers of his newsboy heroes."

Horatio Alger, whose finest claim to remembrance rests on his warm-hearted benefactions to newsboys and bootblacks and many poverty-stricken men of the Bowery in old days, was, in his own estimation, a poet. He had enough imagination to dream of a time when he might be elected to the presidency of the United States—an office for which he was named in a speech by one of his admirers. A dear, absurd man—one remembers him well. He was absurd enough to publish an entire volume satirizing American society in an interminable poem. All its pages contained less wit than is found in a single stanza of William Allen Butler's satire where "Miss Flora McFlimsey, of Madison Square," has so pathetically, despite her extravagant wardrobe, "nothing to wear." Yet Horatio really was fond of poetry and in some measure communicated his liking for fine literature to his young pupil. Shakespeare and Browning, and especially Shelley, were early favorites of Ben.

He himself had a talent for verse. There lies before us the Album that Ben's grandfather, the first Michael H. Cardozo, had given to his "beloved daughter Adeline" in 1845, her eleventh year—"that this small memento of her fond Father will cause her to recollect with pleasure the days of her childhood, when *he* shall have gone to 'that bourne from which no traveller returns.'" As time went on many poems by members of the family were inscribed in the pages of this old red morocco volume with its floral gold tooling. Fluent enough, these verses by Albert Cardozo and Sarah Peixotto and all the others, but conventional, and generally with the thought—not overjolly—that, while Adeline was really an attractive girl, she, like the rest of humanity, had better not count on much happiness until

[15]

she arrived in heaven. Young Ben, however, not interested in moralizing, contributed at the age of less than ten the one imaginative poem. As the earliest of his literary compositions extant, and because of the interest of the unwitting prophecy of its final line, we give, in its original—very original—spelling

THE DREAM

As I slept t'other night in the old arm chair
A little black spirit to me did appear
And as he kept hovering over my head
He spoke a few words and thus to me said
Come arouse thee get up for by the bright sun
I sware, you shall write in Ad's album
There is no use in saying you haven't the time
For I am here now and will help you to rhyme
Then out of his pocket he drew forth a pen
And handing it to me said Sir—now begin
Seizing hold of the pen, for I never knew fear
The subject said he Sir said I the New Year,
Begin Sir—
Each coming year brings new delight
—What now is that, twas Aunty said goodnight.
Aunty I wish you had not said goodnight
You have arroused me from a worlds delight
Both sprits & dreams have flown away
Perhaps to come some other day
And when they do I promise truly then
You shall heare more from
                                    Master Ben

Yes, indeed, we have heard more from "Master Ben." Spirits and dreams returned to him, and made him their own. A man with a vision, and in himself "a worlds delight."

Well, then, in their common interest in poetry, in their love for the classics, in the enjoyment beyond the hours of study and recitation, of reading the works of Thackeray and Dickens and George Eliot with which the young boy was so happily at home, Horatio Alger was a companion not without value to his pupil. Perhaps Alger's lesson of kindness was the best fruit from that curious little tree whose arms stretched out so timorously yet so eagerly to the world about him. But Ben's enthusiasm for his studies preparatory to entering Columbia had deeper roots than any Horatio Alger could provide. It went far back to the most noted and notable of his forebears.

The Rev. Dr. Gershom Mendez Seixas, Cardozo's greatgranduncle, had shown in boyhood the spirit of leadership and a brilliant love for learning. At the age of twenty-one he became the minister of the Spanish-Portuguese synagogue. Ten years later the British fleet sailed into New York harbor. The forces of Sir Henry Clinton, of General Howe, and his brother the Admiral, were threatening the city—their soldiers outnumbering almost two to one the republican army composed mainly of inexperienced militia. Yet the ministers of the King were willing to pardon the civilian adherents of the Revolution if the terms for peace to be advanced by the British government should be unconditionally accepted. Citizens who were Loyalists and citizens who returned to the fold had little more than incidental disturbances to fear from the invasion into their city of the British and Hessian troops. But the Liberty Bell had rung and the Declaration of Independence had been proclaimed and Gershom Seixas had become an American forever. If his city was now to be ruled by the British, it should no longer be his home, nor the place of his ministrations, until the flag of the enemy should be hauled down. In August, 1776, Gershom Seixas delivered a patriotic sermon. Let his congregation be disbanded, if God so willed. But let not his congregation be untrue to the tenets of George Washington, or sound a discordant note in opposition to the challenging and inspiring music of the Liberty Bell. The words of their spiritual guide were obeyed by his flock.

The lights of the house of worship were put out, the doors locked. Taking with him the Scrolls of the Law, Gershom Seixas went first to Connecticut. Later he went to Philadelphia, whither a considerable portion of his congregation had preceded him. After four years of ministrations there, his synagogue was reestablished in New York, the Treaty of Peace between England and the United States having been consummated.

The patriot minister was so greatly esteemed by his brothers of the cloth that exchange of sermons with the Episcopal clergy was no unusual event. One of Gershom Seixas's first sermons was delivered at St. Paul's. In 1787 he was elected to the Board of Trustees of Columbia College, whose former name of King's College had been jubilantly discarded. Two years later, on the morning of the last day of April, his congregation, among others, was assembled "to invoke heaven's blessing upon the new government" and "success and acceptance to General Washington's administration." Gershom Seixas was chosen as one of fourteen clergymen to attend the Inauguration.

Among the guests of honor, Gershom Seixas was one of the most thrilled. Here was the hour of reward for the years when his brothers had gone into battle, and he himself had given up home and pulpit for those principles of freedom personified in George Washington. "The great Constitutional Charter," to which the new President paid homage in his address in the Senate Chamber immediately after his induction into office, was both the wall of protection and the path of advance far beyond the dreams of Gershom Seixas's ancestors when they had been driven forth, centuries earlier, from the Iberian peninsula. In November, 1789, the first national Thanksgiving sermon preached in the State of New York was by Gershom Seixas.

II

*Education is an ornament in prosperity and
a refuge in adversity.*   ARISTOTLE

THE year 1883 was of great significance for the boy of thirteen, by reason of his confirmation in the faith of his fathers. His mind was in ferment, busied with questions of religion and occupied with secular studies. Add to this his perennial interest in the life of New York, the city of his ancestors, the city with which he ever found his own life so intimately and affectionately interwoven.

The structural marvel in an age of mechanical development rose before wondering eyes when the Brooklyn Bridge was formally opened. The lad, already devoted to the serious reading of contemporary English thought, could follow in the newspapers personal accounts of Matthew Arnold, who arrived in America that year. The boy, so talented that his piano teacher suggested he make music his career, read the papers with special eagerness when the Metropolitan Opera House first opened its doors with a performance of Gounod's *Faust*. But assuredly, of all the local affairs of 1883, the one which held the most sentimental interest for Ben was the Centennial Anniversary of Washington's farewell to his officers at Fraunces' Tavern, the former residence of a member of the Nathan clan.

[19]

The following year, in which Ben brilliantly passed his preliminary college entrance examinations, witnessed various events of significant interest to him. There was a slight earthquake in August of that year, but its reverberations were mild compared with those of the defeat, three months later, of James G. Blaine. During that presidential campaign Ben had his first lesson in the danger of religious animosity in political contests, for it was the inadvertent use of the phrase "Rum, Romanism, and Rebellion" that led to Cleveland's victory by the narrowest of margins in the State of New York and carried the Democratic candidate into the White House

In the realm of music, the great event was the introduction of German Opera, with Leopold Damrosch conducting *Tannhäuser* as the initial performance. Ben Cardozo was one of the earliest devotees of the Wagnerian operas. His classmate, George Odell, has told us how Ben and Hamilton Odell (no relative of George) broke into his room during the long intermission of *Parsifal*, aflame with enthusiasm.

Even so, the event of the year 1884 most intimately related to young Cardozo's family was one which, like the Centennial Anniversary of the previous year, was associated with American history and ideals. On October 5 the cornerstone of the pedestal for the Statue of Liberty had been laid at Bedloe's Island with notable ceremonies. On the base of the Statue, in letters of bronze, is the sonnet written by Emma Lazarus, a niece of Benjamin Nathan, the uncle for whom Benjamin Nathan Cardozo had been named. Thus, as long as bronze shall endure, the verses of Justice Cardozo's cousin will urge America to be generous toward the wretched of Europe, "yearning to be free." Alas, that in our own day America does not proclaim:

> Send these, the homeless, tempest-tost to me,
> I lift my lamp beside the golden door!

The Columbia of fifty years ago was in many ways even more different from the great University of today than from the little institution near the Battery. Now the University counts the beneficiaries of its courses by the tens of thousands, and many hundreds enter the Freshman class of the college. In Cardozo's time the entering class averaged about sixty, with the graduating number less than forty. There were no dormitories and many of the boys went home for luncheon. There was, indeed, a fair amount of extracurricular activity, but by and large the life there was a continuation of school days. The boys came mainly from New York families. The contacts with boys from different parts of the country were thus insignificant as compared with those at Harvard, Yale, and Princeton, the three other major American colleges of the day.

From letters of Cardozo's classmates emerges a vivid picture of Ben during his collegiate period. We see him descending the steps of the home at 803 Madison Avenue, laden with books. Serious-looking, frail of physique, in pleasant weather he walks the separating mile to Hamilton Hall. In inclement weather he takes the car whose two horses amble down the Avenue, stopping at every corner where the conductor is hailed.

When Cardozo entered Columbia, Dr. Frederick A. P. Barnard was still the President, soon to be succeeded by Seth Low, who in turn made way, on being elected to the mayoralty, for Nicholas Murray Butler. Dr. Butler was already expounding Logic and Philosophy to the youthful mind, and he remembers how Ben sat in the front row "desperately serious." The young student did not ask many questions but those he did ask were searching ones. In later life, when Dr. Butler complimented Cardozo on the profound logic of his opinions, the Judge "laughed and said, 'You taught me.'" Yet while this rejoinder was deserved by a master of clarity in exposition, the evidence

[21]

of classmates shows that, even in his teens, Ben Cardozo had little need for instruction in the fields of accurate thinking and elucidation.

He belonged to the Barnard Literary Association, a debating society named in honor of Columbia's President. "We recognized," writes a fellow member, "that once granted to Cardozo the premises he claimed—all was lost in the strict logic of his arguments." "While he was one of our most logical debaters and eloquent speakers," writes another, "he would never take part in one of the joint debates with the other societies or in any way force himself into the limelight. With the exception of Dr. Butler, he seemed to me to be easily the ablest and broadest scholar in the '80s and '90s." "I recall," writes a third, "how all the members were amazed and sometimes awed at the readiness with which Cardozo, when he presided, standing up and small of stature and looking like a mere boy, sized up the arguments, calling attention to their strong and weak points and doing it all without notes. He showed then his remarkable ability to remember all the important things said, and his résumé was delivered with the utmost ease and smoothness. It was a treat in itself to watch, and no other presiding officer that I heard ever equalled him in that ability. Even the sophisticated students looked on these addresses with wonder."

Still another classmate remembers what may have been Cardozo's first discussion concerning the Constitution of the United States, the document which, in his closing years, was to lead to perhaps his most far-reaching judicial opinions. The debate was entitled: "Resolved that the Missouri Compromise was Unconstitutional." Although Cardozo's side, which took the affirmative, was defeated, "he was credited as having made the ablest speech of the debate."

Ben, by common opinion, was easily the foremost member of his class in almost every study. For special excellence

Ben and Emily

Allie and Lizzie

Honors were awarded at the end of each year. From Freshman year until he graduated, Cardozo gathered in these Honors in Latin, Greek, and other studies, sometimes with the perfect score of a hundred. It became the habit of some of his classmates to ask him what Honors he was trying for. All save two or three preeminent students would continue in or drop out of the competition according to his reply. But when it came to Fellowships which, in contradistinction to Honors, carried financial awards, Ben Cardozo stood aside. His feeling was that money should go to those who needed it more than he did, or to those, perhaps, who had less unhappy recollections associated with the power of money. The shadow of dishonor, indeed, affected Ben with unabating force from the earliest years of boyhood until his own achievements had lessened its effect.

In regard to Ben's attitude in connection with the Fellowships, one recalls the modest statement of his classmate, George Odell, now the distinguished Columbia professor whose monumental history of the New York stage has added luster to the publications of the Columbia University Press. "In a manner of speaking," the Professor said, "I owe my career to Ben Cardozo." He called it a blessing that Ben did not try for the Fellowship in Letters which, for three years, carried $500 a year. "Ben," said George Odell, "never tried for money prizes, contenting himself with trying for Honors." He could, in his friend's opinion, easily have won the Fellowship, in which case Dr. Odell's professorial career might not have eventuated.

These two friends were devoted to Greek. In Senior year, when students were allowed to choose their courses, they became members of the class of six whereof Willard King, a brilliant student of the classics, was one. The readings and discussions were given up to the odes of Pindar, a poet more than once quoted by Cardozo in his addresses at Yale and Columbia in later years. The course, through the

[23]

Professor's comments and through their own collateral study, gave them a fine insight into the life of ancient Greece. The culture of that life, the high plane on which moved its protagonists in philosophy, in law, in literature, and in art, made permanent appeal to Cardozo. To the very end of his years he had recourse to the atmosphere of Plato and Aristotle, and it is significant that his last recorded gift of a book to a friend should have been a history of Grecian civilization.

The student who heads his class in Greek is not necessarily, indeed not frequently, exceptionally proficient in Mathematics. Yet here's a story we have from Professor Thomas B. Fiske: "When I first became Professor Van Amringe's assistant, at the initial lesson of the year I sat beside him. 'Van Am,' as you know, liked to frighten the Freshmen a little. So he began with a difficult question. One after another the boys failed to answer, until it was the turn of a frail lad—fourteen or fifteen years old. I can still see him rising quietly, hardly more than a child. I remember his voice—a soprano voice like that of a choir boy. It was Bennie Cardozo, giving the correct answer. . . . You know," added Professor Fiske, "I said to myself then, as I observed both his poise and his modest demeanor: 'That boy will go far.'"

"When we entered Columbia in the fall of 1885," writes Mr. Remsen Johnson, a classmate of Ben's, "I remember Cardozo as a clean-cut, modest stripling. I think I am correct in saying he was the youngest of us all, between fifteen and sixteen years of age. His first name was well chosen for he was the Benjamin of the class. We were all very fond of him, but he was too young to enjoy our social activities, a fact that he appreciated and regretted in later years. Intellectually, however, he was head and shoulders above us all. In our time it was currently stated that he and Professor Abraham Valentine Williams Jackson ('83) had the highest standing of any student that had ever matriculated at the College. Unlike Cardozo, however, Jackson, while an undergraduate, was a social light and was in great demand as a cotillion leader. To meet his social requirements and to maintain his wonderful standing as a student, every minute was precious and it was said that, when he ate at home, his mother at meal times would read to him on subjects pertinent to his studies. We all idolized Dr. Jackson. He had us in a certain subject and he was wont to give the fairly good students a mark of 100 plus. And so to Cardozo he must have given 100 to the fifth degree."

One could go on at length with tributes to Cardozo in letters from classmates. Though shy and keeping considerably to himself, with the reading of books on philosophy as his chief recreation, the handsome boy, wholesome-looking despite his frailty—he weighed only about a hundred pounds when he entered Columbia—increasingly won the admiration of his classmates, who numbered, among other men of future distinction, James W. Gerard and Robert F. Cutting. Evidence of this appreciation is found in many Columbia publications of those days, with, here and there, as in the *Columbiad* for 1888, a teasing comment in accordance with the tradition of that Junior publication. In its page headed "Bets," the wager is made: "Dollars to pennies that Cardozo has been eating snowballs again," which E. H. Hornbostel of the class of 1890 explains as referring to Cardozo's "placidity and calmness and poise." When, at the end of Senior year, the Class Book of '89 was issued, Ben was voted the cleverest man and the second most modest. In the Prophecy by Edward Bright, Jr., appeared these lines:

Cardozo's scholarly fervor and zeal
Will hurry him on towards the legal ideal,
Where he'll snatch all the buns from the Bar he can freeze on,
Thus proving his size is no gauge for his reason.

The Class Poem continues the evidence of how the boy of nineteen was appreciated by his fellows. In these verses by George Odell, the first to be mentioned is Ben.

A score of faces rises to our view,
Stamped with Learning's pale and thoughtful hue,
And lined with many a problem hard and deep,
Whose strange solution has a pledge to keep,
That high and bright their life will be. This hope
And day-dream tender as May evening's slope
Toward darkness and a fair and perfect day.
Among these faces in the morning's ray
Two we distinguished seemed for lofty prize,
Who, linked by honors, rise before our eyes—
Cardozo, Pfister, to them may all esteen
Of glory that from noblest deeds may stream
Accrue forever. We can only take
Their hands in ours and, for affection's sake,
Wish them God-speed.

Professor Odell seemed to have quite forgotten these youthful verses when recently they were brought to his attention. But he added the comment: "We all recognized Cardozo as the star spirit of our class."

In accentuating the brilliancy of Cardozo's student years and the reserve of the shy lad, there is a danger of portraying him as indifferent to undergraduate activities. It is true that Ben had little if any part in athletics, and his name is not to be found among the members of the Card Club whose officers bore such interesting titles as Calculator of Probabilities, Protector of the Kitty, Dispenser of the Ivories, Supervisor of the Counter, Engrosser of the I.O.U.'s, and Tender of the Pap. His intense application to his books left no time for participation with banjo, guitar, or the dramatics. But he was one of the ten members of the Moustache Club, where, as an officer, he held the title of Herald. There seems to be no survivor to provide information concerning the purpose and doings of this little group, nor does one know where they got their name, though the opinion has been hazarded that it was derived from a song about moustaches in one of the Sophomore Shows.

No doubt, Ben smiled his very charming smile when he found himself described in a group of "Hits" at the end of the *Columbiad* as:

> 'Tis he, 'tis Nathan, thanks to the Almighty.
> Women and men he strove alike to shun,
> And hurried homeward when his tasks were done.

The use here of Cardozo's middle name carried a reference to Lessing's famous play, *Nathan the Wise*, for young Ben was already esteemed for his wisdom. Yet if he generally held himself aloof, he joined his classmates in the most dangerous task of undergraduate life. There, with the determination which was as much a part of him as his gentleness, he acquitted himself in characteristic fashion. All of us who are old Columbia graduates know that not even in the football days when the flying wedge was the battering ram sometimes fatal in its consequences was anything more dangerous to life and limb than the Cane Rush. Here the entire Freshman and Sophomore classes would engage in the struggle at whose conclusion hands were counted. A long broomstick theoretically became the cane. If Freshman hands on it exceeded in number those of the Sophomores, the entering class would be allowed certain privileges otherwise withheld. The pummeling, the tearing at faces, the gasping for breath under the writhing mass of over a hundred boys were so intense that casualties were ever likely to result.

In the eighties one lad died from his injuries and the Cane Rush was temporarily abolished until, after its resumption in the nineties, a second fatality led to its being permanently placed under the ban of the college authorities. But no danger ever prevented Ben Cardozo from using strength of mind and body in seeking to achieve. When hands were counted in the Cane Rush of his Sophomore year, his frail and delicate fingers were wound firmly around the broomstick.

By Senior year Ben had come richly into his own in the affection as well as the admiration of his classmates. They elected him as their vice-president for life and chose him as the first orator at the 135th Commencement of Columbia College, celebrated on June 12, 1889, at the Metropolitan Opera House. His subject was "The Altruist in Politics." Fifty years have gone by since this address was published in the Class Book. Practically unknown, it has so much interest for the present when Communism threatens those principles of democracy so dear to Cardozo, that it would be a pity to omit it from this record. We see the clear-minded, idealistic, handsome young fellow standing on the stage of the Opera House before an audience resplendent in evening dress—for those were the days when New York was a city of New Yorkers and when formality of attire was the attractive custom at concerts and theater and opera. From one of the boxes his sisters and his cousin, Addie Cardozo, with other members of the family looked proudly down at the young Bachelor of Arts.

He began with a sentence prophetic of that attitude toward law as a living thing which was to guide many of his decisions as Chief Judge of the Court of Appeals of New York State and as Associate Justice of the Supreme Court of the United States: "There comes not seldom a crisis in the life of men, of nations, and of worlds when the old forms seem ready to decay and the old rules of action have lost their binding force." Then, as the young fellow went on, he showed, with his lasting sympathy for the oppressed, the danger of Communism as a solution for social ills.

[28]

"The evils of existing systems," he maintained, "obscure the blessings that attend them; and, where reform is needed, the cry is raised for subversion. The cause of such phenomena is not far to seek. 'It used to appear to me,' writes Count Tolstoy, in a significant passage, 'it used to appear to me that the small number of cultivated, rich, and idle men, of whom I was one, composed the whole of humanity, and that the millions and millions of other men who had lived and are still living were not in reality men at all.' It is this spirit—the spirit that sees the whole of humanity in the few, and throws into the background the millions and millions of other men—it is this spirit that has aroused the antagonism of reformers, and made the decay of the old forms, the rupture of the old restrictions, the ideal of them and of their followers. When wealth and poverty meet each other face to face, the one the master and the other the dependent, the one exalted and the other debased, it is perhaps hardly matter for surprise that the dependent and debased and powerless faction, in envy of their opponents' supremacy, should demand, not simply reform, but absolute community and equality of wealth. That cry for Communism is no new one in the history of mankind. Thousands of years ago it was heard and acted on; and, in the lapse of centuries, its reverberations have but swelled in volume. Again and again, the altruist has arisen in politics, has bidden us share with others the product of our toil, and has proclaimed the communistic dogma as the panacea for our social ills. So today, amid the buried hopes and buried projects of the past, the doctrine of Communism still lives in the minds of men. Under stress of misfortune, or in dread of tyranny, it still is preached in modern times as Plato preached it in the world of the Greeks.

"Yet it is indeed doubtful whether, in the history of mankind, a doctrine was ever taught more impracticable or more false to the principles it professes than this very doctrine of Communism. In a world where self-interest is avowedly the ruling motive, it seeks to establish at once an all-reaching and all-controlling altruism. In a world where every man is pushing and fighting to outstrip his fellows, it would make him toil with like vigor for their common welfare. In a world where a man's activity is measured by the nearness of reward, it would hold up a prospective recompense as an equal stimulant to labor. 'The more bitterly we feel,' writes George Eliot, 'the more bitterly we feel the folly, ignorance, neglect, or self-seeking of those who at different times have wielded power, the stronger is the obligation we lay on ourselves to beware lest we also, by a too hasty wresting of measures which seem to promise immediate relief, make a worse time of it for our own generation, and leave a bad inheritance for our children.' In the future, when the remoteness of his reward shall have weakened the laborer's zeal, we shall be able to judge more fairly of the blessings that the communist offers. Instead of the present world, where some at least are well to do and happy, the communist holds before us a world where all alike are poor. For the activity, the push, the vigor of our modern life, his substitute is a life aimless and unbroken. And so we have to say to communists what George Eliot might have said: Be not blinded by the passions of the moment, but when you prate about your own wrongs and the sufferings of your offspring, take heed lest in the long run you make a worse time of it for your own generation, and leave a bad inheritance for your children.

"Little thought has been taken by these altruistic reformers for the application of the doctrines they uphold. To the question how one kind of labor can be measured against another, how the labor of the artisan can be measured against the labor of the artist, how the labor of the strong can be measured against the labor of the weak, the communists can give no answer. Absorbed as they are in the principle of equality, they have still forgotten the equality of work in the equality of pay; they have forgotten that reward, to be really equal, must be proportionate to effort; and they and *all* socialists have forgotten that we cannot make an arithmetic of human thought and feeling; and that for all our crude attempts to balance recompense against toil, for all our crude attempts to determine the relative severity of different kinds of toil, for all our crude attempts to determine the relative strain on different persons of the same kind of toil, yet not only will the ratio, dealing, as it does, with our subjective feelings, be a blundering one, but a system based upon it will involve inequalities greater, because more insidious, than those of the present system that it would discard.

"Instances, indeed, are not wanting to substantiate the claim that Communism, by unduly exalting our altruistic impulses, proceeds upon a false psychological basis. Yet if an instance is to be chosen, it would be hard to find one more suggestive than that afforded by the efforts of Robert Owen. The year 1824 saw the rise of Owen's little community of New Harmony, and the year 1828 saw the community's final disruption. Individuals had appropriated to themselves the property designed for all; and even Owen, who had given to the enterprise his money and his life, was obliged to admit that men were not yet fitted for the communistic stage, and that the moment of transition from individualism to Communism had not yet arrived. Men trained under the old system, with its eager rivalry, its selfish interests, could not quite yet enter into the spirit of self-renunciation that Communism demands. And Owen, therefore, was led to put his trust in education as the great molder of the minds of men. Through this agency, he hoped, the eager rivalry, the selfish interests, the sordid love of gain, might be lost in higher, purer, more disinterested ends; and, animated by that hope—the hope that in the fullness of time another New Harmony, free from the contention and the disappointments of the old one, might serve to immortalize his name—animated by that hope, Owen passed the last thirty years of his life; and with that hope still before his eyes he died.

"But years now have passed since Owen lived; the second New Harmony has not yet been seen; the so-called rational system of education has not yet transformed the impulses or the aims of men; and the communist of today, with a history of two thousand years of failure behind him, in the same pathetic confidence still looks for the realization of his dreams to the Communism of the future.

"And yet, granting that Communism were practicable, granting that Owen's hopes had some prospect of fulfillment, the doctrine still embodies evils that must make it forever inexpedient. The readers of Mr. Matthew Arnold's works must have noticed the emphasis with which he dwells on the instinct of expansion as a factor in human progress. It is the refutation alike of Communism and of Socialism that they thwart the instinct of expansion; that they substitute for human personality the blind, mechanical power of the State. The one system, as the other, marks the end of individualism. The one system, as the other, would make each man the image of his neighbor. The one system, as the other, would hold back the progressive, and, by uniformity of reward, gain uniformity of type.

"I can look forward to no blissful prospect for a race of men that, under the domination of the State, at the cost of all freedom of action, at the cost, indeed, of their own true selves, shall enjoy, if one will, a fair abundance of the material blessings of life. Some Matthew Arnold of the future would inevitably say of them in phrase like that applied to the Puritans of old: 'They entered the prison of Socialism and had the key turned upon their spirit, there for hundreds of years.' Into that prison of Socialism, with broken enterprise and broken energy, as serfs under the mastery of the State, while human personality is preferred to unreasoning mechanism, mankind must hesitate to step. When they shall once have entered within it, when the key shall have been turned upon their spirit and have confined them in narrower straits than even Puritanism could have done, it will be left for them to find, in their blind obedience and passive submission, the recompense for the singleness of character, the foresight, and the energy, that they have left behind them.

"In almost every phase of life, this doctrine of political altruists is equally impracticable and pernicious. In its social results, it involves the substitution of the community in the family's present position. In its political aspects, it involves the absolute domination of the State over the actions and the property of its subjects. Thus, though claiming to be an exaltation of the so-called natural rights of liberty and equality, it is in reality their emphatic debasement. It teaches that thoughtless docility is a recompense for stunted enterprise. It magnifies material good at the cost of every rational endowment. It inculcates a self-denial that must result in dwarfing the individual to a mere instrument in the hands of the State for the benefit of his fellows. No such organization of society—no organization that fails to take note of the fact that man must have scope for the exercise and development of his faculties—no such organization of society can ever reach a permanent success. However beneficent its motives, the hypothesis with which it starts can never be realized. The aphorism of Emerson, 'Churches have been built, not upon principles, but upon tropes,' is as true in the field of politics as it is in the field of religion. In a like figurative spirit, the followers of Communism have reared their edifice; and, looking back upon the finished structure, seeking to discern the base on which it rests, the critic finds, not principles, but tropes. The builders have appealed to laws whose truth they took for granted; they have appealed to a future that has no warrant in the past; and fixing their gaze upon the distant dreamland, captivated

[33]

by the vision there beheld, entranced by its ideal effulgence, their eyes were blinded to the real conditions of the human problem they had set before them. Their enemies have not been slow to note such weakness and mistake; and perhaps it may serve to clear up misconceptions, perhaps it may serve to lessen cant and open the way for fresh and vigorous thought; if we shall once convince ourselves that altruism *cannot* be the rule of life; that its logical result is the dwarfing of the individual man; and that not by the death of human personality can we hope to banish the evils of our day, and to realize the ideal of all existence, a nobler or a purer life."

This address followed studies revealed in greater detail in Cardozo's thesis, submitted for his degree of Bachelor of Arts. The suggestion has from time to time been made that this thesis, still extant in his autograph in the files of Columbia, should be published as his most important early essay. Cardozo himself regarded it as a rather callow performance, smilingly commenting on the cocksureness of youth. Yet important are its many evidences that both Communism and Socialism were alien, even in boyhood, to the philosophy of the aristocratic jurist devoted to democratic principles.

A few passages from the essay itself follow:

"It was by no means a unique phenomenon that was presented to the world when Carlyle, in professing to narrate the history of clothes, set forth a theory of metaphysics. Such incongruity between results and their occasions finds its parallel in almost every sphere of human research. The radical element of the world's population is seldom slow in carrying to fantastic lengths doctrines that, in their inception, were rational enough. That there *is* a certain bond uniting humanity, and that this bond should be guarded and maintained, are truths the appreciation of which demands, indeed, no marked lucidity of mind. But, like other feelings, this feeling of benevolence has been imposed upon. In recognizing that there is a tie between man and man, enthusiasts have made the mistake of supposing that it is in every case of equal strength; in their horror of egoistic impulses, they have sought to thrust upon mankind their own untempered altruism; and in their conviction that excessive individualism would make life intolerable, they have raised the standard of an all-reaching and unconditioned Communism. . . .

"It would seem almost inevitable that many persons should prefer comparative idleness and a bare competency to the slightly increased remuneration that would be the result of increased effort. It would seem that, unless Communism is going to change human nature, work under such a system must often be slow, heartless, and ineffectual. It would seem that Communism has no adequate substitute to offer for the fear of dismissal, which, notwithstanding the lack of any personal interest in the work, may be shown now to actuate the laborer; and finally, it would seem that the not inconsiderable class of peasant proprietors and of individual producers, who *have* a direct interest in their work, would, under a communistic system, cease to exist. . . .

"That Communism is directly opposed to the instincts of our nature; that it stunts individual enterprise and individual development; that it leads to the formation of one common type of man, passive, heartless, and mechanical in its actions; that it marks the dawn of a new serfdom in which all men will be the serfs and government the master; that it would gradually decay into a condition of common poverty and common squalor—this is the prospect that any believer in the dignity and the personality of the individual man must see before him in a communistic state. No organization of society that radically contravenes the essential impulses of our human constitution, that fails to take note of the fact that man must have scope for the exercise and development of his faculties—no such organization of society

[35]

can ever reach a permanent success. In a noble passage of his *Essay on Liberty*, Mr. John Stuart Mill, treating of Socialism, writes: 'A government cannot have too much of the kind of activity which does not impede, but aids and stimulates, individual exertion and development. The mischief begins when, instead of calling forth the activity and powers of individuals and bodies, it substitutes its own activity for theirs; when instead of informing, advising, and, upon occasion, denouncing, it makes them work in fetters or bids them stand aside, and does their work instead of them. The worth of a state in the long run is the worth of the individuals composing it; and a state which postpones the interest of *their* mental expansion and elevation to a little more administrative skill or that semblance of it which practice gives in the details of business, a state which dwarfs its men in order that they may be more docile instruments in its hands even for beneficial purposes, will find that with small men no great thing can really be accomplished; and that the perfection of machinery to which it has sacrificed everything will, in the end, avail it nothing, for want of the vital power, which, in order that the machine might work more smoothly, it has preferred to banish.' Communism and Socialism alike find their refutation in these words of Mill. The one system, as the other, marks the end of individualism. The one system, as the other, would make each man the image of his neighbor. The one system, as the other, would hold back the progressive, and, by uniformity of reward, gain uniformity of type."

As in the Commencement Address, there is here obvious the emphasis on the value of individual exertion, free of excessive governmental control. Young Cardozo, however much he was, in his closing years, to feel sympathy with many of the objectives of Franklin D. Roosevelt, had already taken his stand with John Stuart Mill in relation to the liberty of the individual.

After the orations at the Commencement exercises came the announcements of Honors, with Cardozo again leading the list of the thirty-five graduating Seniors from the College and fifty-four from the School of Mines. With his Bachelor of Arts parchment safely bestowed and the key of Phi Beta Kappa dangling from his watch chain, Cardozo continued his studies at Columbia. The year after graduation he got his degree of Master of Arts. In the School of Law he had a two-year course which he did not complete. In a letter to his cousin, Ernest A. Cardozo, written in 1932, the Supreme Court Justice gives the explanation for his failure to go through the Law School.

"Just about the middle of the second year when a man had received the same instruction that had led to an LL.B. in the past, the Trustees tacked on a third year. I was anxious to go out into the world and make my living, so I never came back for the third year. It wasn't of much value, for it had not yet been coordinated with other courses of instruction, but represented a lot of extras. Of course, later on it became an integrated part of the Law School scheme. A good many of my classmates did as I did. So I never received an LL.B., though I left in good standing, and have no reason to doubt that I could have had it if I had been willing to stay."

III

Toil, says the proverb, is the sire of fame.

EURIPIDES

THROUGHOUT the years the grief of family circumstances colored the life of Benjamin Cardozo. The Madison Avenue house was a house of sorrow—the home of aristocrats dwelling in the shadow of sad memories and of present circumstances tinged with grief. Proud reserve, fine spirituality, and natural affection bound those brothers and sisters together in a home where gaiety seldom entered and whose strongest cement was sorrow. Father and mother were dead, then Grace, one of the sisters, died, as did Allie, Benjamin's only brother, in comparative youth. Lizzie was an invalid until death brought release. Then his twin sister Emily, the one high-spirited member of the family, who has been described by her cousin, William B. Cardozo, as the gayest, loveliest girl he had ever known. Emily was the only one of the four sisters who married. But her marriage out of the ancestral faith brought little joy to her kin, though it never lessened her brother Ben's love for her. Finally, he and Nell alone remained of the group that had lived in the Madison Avenue home.

Ellen, the oldest—Ben's beloved Nell—was from girlhood the mother of the brood. What she meant to all the younger

[38]

ones, and how profound was the tie of family melancholy, verses of Elizabeth ("Lizzie") tenderly make evident.

Close is the tie of flesh that binds us twain,
But closer yet the soul-tie, for I see
The Lamp of Solace, burning steadily,
Raised by your hand, when through the wastes of Pain
My way was set; and as I look again,
Lo, the old play-name now comes back to me,
Fraught with new readings of love's mystery,—
My "mother-sister," runs the old refrain.
Yet most I own the tie for tears we shed
Together; well I mind me of a day
When you and I and she who might not stay
Long mourning with us, wept our newly-dead . . .
Oh, joy and pain may fade throughout the years,
But not the tie was forged of those shed tears!

Lizzie, who never quite overcame a spinal affliction, had more than that facility in the writing of verse belonging to various of her relatives. In her case it made itself manifest in the volume of poems entitled *Salvage* and dedicated to her cousin, Josephine Lazarus. During the early years of the century she studied art with Kenneth Hayes Miller, who gives a remarkable picture of her. She was an "extraordinary personality, so acute, so distinguished." She gave one the impression of being "the end of a long line of aristocrats. She looked like a feminine edition of Dante. Eyes so dark and intense, the aquiline, aristocratic nose." Lizzie was extremely neurotic, and there were times when she had fantasies on the borderline of hallucinations. Her talent was only mediocre, but she was fairly successful with portrait heads done in pastel. Her verses were far better than her drawings, and as a conversationalist she was always stimulating. "A lovely nature," says Mr. Miller, "detached, so pleasant, so pleasant."

[39]

The frustration which brought Lizzie unhappiness brought corresponding tribulation to Cardozo. No one ever heard him complain. His love and sympathy for his ailing sister were unbounded. Yet the burden was there, borne with generosity.

This unfailing consideration displayed itself in regard to various distant relatives as well as Cardozo's immediate family. "As a child," writes his cousin, Annie Nathan Meyer, "I was always trying to tread a path warily through the maze of family feuds. 'Was it Aunt Becky or Aunt Rachel,' I would ask myself, 'who didn't speak to Uncle John?' 'Which aunt was it with whom Mama had quarreled?' These perplexing feuds always had their start in the failure of some relative to ask after one of the family. There were fourteen aunts and uncles—almost all with numerous progeny—so some slight, quite unintentional lapse might easily have been pardoned. But not in our family. It was the crime of crimes. It was with us as the laws of the Medes and Persians that on meeting a relative (particularly an 'in-law') however fortuitously, however pressed for time, one must inquire meticulously into the state of health of each and every member of that particular family. Any deviation, any temporary forgetfulness was set down as a deliberate slight, to be resented as such. In this respect, I am certain that my beloved cousin, Mr. Justice Cardozo, would never be caught napping."

Ben was still at Columbia the winter a young woman came uptown to continue at the Cardozo home her professional duties in the field of medicine. Kate Tracy was a trained nurse at St. Vincent's Hospital when the superintendent of Bellevue sent word to her asking whether she would wish to have, as her first private patient, Miss Elizabeth Cardozo. The Cardozos, she was informed, were "a wonderful family to be with." Eagerly she rode up to their home and was discomfited when—it was a slippery day—

she fell into the gutter as she got out of the car. Her trim clothes got muddy. A fine way to make a first entrance into a distinguished household! But Lizzie Cardozo, smiling at her apologies, made Miss Tracy immediately feel at home. The friendship thus launched between her and Kate Tracy, her constant attendant till death parted them, was a devoted one on both sides. A short while before her death, Lizzie told Kate that she intended to leave to her the cottage in Connecticut where the two women had long lived. Miss Tracy thought this would not be fair to the family, especially to Ben, who had been the main support of his sister. But the Judge insisted on having the cottage left to the devoted companion and, further, paid all bills for keeping it up until it became rented.

The maintenance of the Madison Avenue home depended to a considerable extent on the earnings of Cardozo. In spite of the scant two years of law education he had no difficulty in passing his bar examinations. It was a very handsome young fellow who left the college halls to pore over books in the law firm where his brother Albert, ten years his senior, was already active. Slender, tall enough, dark eyed, wavy haired, a fine nose, a chin that spoke determination, he was a youth of distinction. His was that spiritual quality which led his cousin Annie to associate his looks with those of Shelley. His very hands were instinct with sensitivity. See for yourself what manner of hands they were. Go to the gallery of his friend Pirie MacDonald whose walls are covered with photographs of authors and artists, of statesmen. Ask to see the pictures of Justice Cardozo.

You will see few other hands like his—the delicate hands of the poet and the aristocrat. And then go back to the chin. One must never forget Cardozo's chin. The hands and the chin—they tell the story. The eyes and the brow will serve as guides to the intellect of the man; but for the temperament and the character, the hands and the chin. In observ-

[41]

ing them, one begins to understand how this shy, this terribly shy person could emerge from his reticence and take immovable stand on the grounds of principle. His words, like those of the poet whose "Ode to the West Wind" he so admired, remain "inextinguishable sparks."

It is exceedingly interesting to study these looks from infancy to the close of life. They are already shy and reserved when Ben is a baby in his mother's arms. Intelligence is written in his eyes, but it is the reserve that is most striking. In the daguerreotype showing him at the age of five with his twin sister, little Ben seems again to draw back from the world in keen and questioning reserve.

So it was a distinguished-looking young man who went downtown to help his brother support their sisters, for the father had left an inheritance of less than $100,000 to six children who had formerly lived in considerable affluence. But on what should he immediately set at work—this lad who had not even finished the courses at the Law School? At least, he could be kept out of mischief and out of the way of his busy elders. So, half in jest, half in earnest, one of these elders proposed that Ben should read a set of volumes dealing with torts—a special branch of the law. Ben took the suggestion seriously. Page after page, volume after volume, he went through the books, making notes and developing that faculty of memory which was to become one of the most amazing assets in his subsequent career at the bar and on the bench. Page after page, volume after volume, as no one in that office had ever before read those books. When he had finished them he was such an authority on their subject that all questions relating to it were thenceforth referred to him.

The late Stephen C. Baldwin (the father of Faith Baldwin, the novelist) was a clerk in the same office with Cardozo. They were always great friends and Baldwin had the warmest admiration and affection for Cardozo. Cardozo as a young law clerk, he said, lived almost the life of a hermit, spending all his spare time in the library.

So swiftly did he make his way that, soon after graduation, he became his brother's partner. In 1903 they gave up their firm name of Cardozo Brothers, joining the older firm of Simpson and Werner, with offices at 52 Broadway. On January 4, 1909, Albert Cardozo, Jr., died. That April the firm took new offices in the Trinity Building at 111 Broadway. The name of Simpson, Werner and Cardozo was changed to Simpson and Cardozo on the retirement of Mr. Werner. Mr. George H. Engelhard became a member in 1912. The next year, on the retirement of Mr. Simpson, the name was again changed, this time to Cardozo and Engelhard.

Because Benjamin had to be the main pillar of support for the family, money-making was necessary; but nearer to his heart—indeed, next to his heart—remained the desire so to achieve as to restore the family name. Those early years as a lawyer were a period of toil devoid of almost all the usual pastimes of youth. "Work, work, work" was its daily refrain. Early in the morning he was at his office in lower Broadway. The hurried luncheon of an ever-rapid eater broke into Cardozo's daylong hours of conferences, research, and the writing of briefs. Then back to the Madison Avenue house for the family dinner. Sometimes this was followed by a brief respite at the piano, playing four-handed with Nell; or there might be an occasional evening at concert or opera —rarely at the theater. Work was almost invariably the order of the night, as of the day.

Cardozo had no time for cards, no time for dancing, even when his sister Emily or his girl cousins tried to coax him into accompanying them as escort. His eyes were fixed on a difficult goal and could not be averted.

For a little more than a score of years Benjamin Cardozo toiled in his law offices. From the very beginning his conscientiousness and his brilliancy made themselves apparent.

Gradually judges took more and more notice of the cogency of his briefs. Commercial firms, banking firms, and frequently individuals brought him their cases. Legal firms increasingly found it expedient to call Cardozo into consultation. If an appeal was to be made, who, they asked themselves, could more effectively advise them, in connection with the brief to be presented to the higher court, than this quiet young man, so thoroughly versed in the common law, and already so greatly respected by the bench? In case after case he was called in as counsel. He came to be known as a "lawyers' lawyer."

An acecdote related by Charles H. Tuttle, the Republican candidate for the governorship of New York when Franklin D. Roosevelt was his successful opponent, shows there were limits to Cardozo's interest in pleasing clients. One of the chief attorneys of the Shuberts invited Cardozo, then a consulting lawyer of those theater managers, to attend a Shubert production where glamorous girls were the main attraction. There was, for Cardozo's taste, too much frankness in words of the songs and in the exposure of feminine beauty. He offered no criticism beyond saying to the Shubert lawyer: "Very interesting, very interesting indeed." At the first entr'acte he rose to leave. He explained to his companion that he had much work to do before morning.

After Cardozo was elected to the Supreme Court of New York, he suggested that Mr. Tuttle should succeed him as consultant for the Shuberts. The younger Columbia graduate was also taken to a similar show produced by his new clients. He admits to having sat through the nonpuritanic performance. Mr. Tuttle's demur was entered when he was asked whether he would care to go backstage to meet some of the charming young ladies.

Judge Learned Hand relates an incident which indicates the early age at which Cardozo was appreciated by judges. While he was still at the bar a vacancy occurred in the

United States District Court. Cardozo was leaving the courthouse as Hand ran after him and asked him whether he would consider taking a position in the court. The salary was then only $6,000 and Cardozo, after reflection, declined it.

After Cardozo had left the bar he presented to the Library of St. John's Law School in Brooklyn the records of his cases as a lawyer, the many volumes of his briefs. A study of these is beyond the scope of this biography, beyond the capacity of its author. Moreover, the general nature of the cases—commercial in most instances—does not provide the human interest and the great social significance of Cardozo's opinions as a judge. These opinions have already been made the subject of volumes from the pens of Mr. Beryl H. Levy, Mr. A. L. Lainer, and Mr. Joseph P. Pollard. Perhaps someday a writer on law may care to make thorough research into the volumes now at St. John's Law School. Mr. William H. Freese, Justice Cardozo's friend and executor, and for many years associated with him in the law, would doubtless make available the index he has retained of these legal cases, these early briefs. Such a study should result in a work of value for the legal fraternity of our own day and of succeeding generations. We, for our part, shall draw upon the period prior to Cardozo's ascendance to the bench primarily to illustrate not the ability of the writer of briefs but the nature of the man.

There was the case which had to do with litigation about closing highways in the Bronx. Opposed as counsels were two lawyers who eventually were to sit side by side in the Supreme Court of the United States—Harlan F. Stone and Benjamin N. Cardozo. "He licked me," said Justice Stone in speaking of the case, in a tone of such cordial satisfaction that the words throw a lovely light on both friends.

Cardozo's success at the bar was in part due to his being, as Charles E. Hughes, Jr., has said, "a walking encyclopedia of the law." His memory was amazing. Melville Cane has related the circumstances of a case when his firm had asked Cardozo to be associated as counsel. Cardozo, on having the case outlined to him, immediately said that in no New York State case had there been an adequate adjustment of the question involved. Then he went on to refer Mr. Cane to a Chancery case in England before the Queen's Bench. "It seems to me," he said, "that if you will look up volume so-and-so, about page so-and-so, you will find the decision which has direct bearing upon your case." The reference was looked up, the point established. Mr. Cane's firm won. Cardozo sent in a bill for his services so moderate that the slight sum occasioned surprise. He insisted, however, with his customary modesty that it was quite sufficient.

In another case involving a great amount of money, where one of the most famous of New York's legal firms, headed by the late William D. Guthrie, was involved, there was an unusual circumstance. Mr. Abraham Tulin, associated with the Guthrie firm, suggested that Cardozo should be called into consultation. The Appellate Division of the Supreme Court had, in reversing a decision, at the same time granted a sum of over $600,000 to Guthrie's client. In those years the Appellate Division did not have the right to adjudicate damages. Mr. Tulin pointed this out to Mr. Guthrie. What should be done? Inform the Justices that they had acted unconstitutionally? Obtain, as a consequence, perhaps a smaller amount for the client? Cardozo's advice led to rectification. Though the final damages awarded were considerably less than those named in the first verdict, they still reached a high figure. Cardozo's fee of $250 was considered so absurdly inadequate that Mr. Guthrie insisted on doubling it. In this instance Cardozo was persuaded to accept the larger amount as it was coming from lawyers whose own remuneration would be exceedingly great.

In still another case Cardozo showed, together with a wide-ranging knowledge of the common law, his ability in breaking into new ground, in affecting future cases by the decisions he won. A stock exchange house had gone bankrupt and a very able lawyer, James N. Rosenberg, was counsel for the trustees in bankruptcy. Cardozo was the counsel for a client who had sent $1,500 to the brokerage house, not knowing that it was bankrupt. In the lower court the case went against the client, but the other court reversed the decision. Cardozo had in his brief forcefully dwelt on the point that, if payment had been made by mistake, the funds, if they could definitely be traced, should be returned. The amount involved was small, but Cardozo gave it the same extraordinary care that would have been given had millions been at stake.

The opinions of Cardozo on the bench in New York and on the Supreme Court at Washington show his aversion from any judgment essentially unethical, humanly unfair. At the same time, his respect for the law as a whole never abated, and so he was frequently wrestling with problems involved in this duel between legalism and the higher justice. Probably no jurist of our day has cut Gordian knots with more conservative wisdom gathered from the past and more liberal sympathies leading to precedents for future application. If in his years as a lawyer he ever availed himself of technicalities, one may be very sure that Cardozo felt justice as well as legalism to be on the side of his client.

Evidence appears again and again to witness to the ever-modest fees of Cardozo throughout his ever-increasing success as a lawyer. Emphasis is laid on this point as it illustrates the noncommercial aspect of a man on whom financial responsibilities lay heavily enough. Cardozo's were not only the self-imposed obligations to be the chief maintenance of the Madison Avenue home. He had, throughout those years, to aid in the support of the country home, first on Long Island and later in Connecticut, where his invalid sister Lizzie lived.

One vacation of several months Cardozo was persuaded to allow himself, when, in 1907, he went to Europe with his partner, Angel Simpson. They visited England, Paris, Venice, and Switzerland, Nuremberg and Berlin. But Cardozo enjoyed most his days on the Thames. Those days, he once said, were the happiest of his life.

These European weeks were the lengthiest of all the vacations of his younger years. When they ended, Cardozo went back to take up again his almost incessant labor.

For all his deep concentration on his work, he was never so completely absorbed as to forget his gentle humanitarianism, never too busy for acts of kindness, never too hurried for sympathy. There was a young girl who had lived in a rooming house next door to the Cardozo home. The two often saw each other as they both left at the same early hour to go to work. However, they never spoke until one day when Cardozo, desiring fresh air, was on the platform of the elevated train where the girl was also standing. Having seen her so often, he ventured the remark: "Isn't it very early for you to start out? School doesn't begin for some time yet." She answered that she didn't go to school; she had a job. Although she was fifteen years old at the time, the girl was small and looked much younger. "A little child to go to work!" exclaimed Cardozo. "Oh, what a pity!"

Cardozo's tenderness and gentleness are recognized by all who knew him. They are qualities bringing up the thought of the one great omission in the Justice's life that his friends continue to regret. This man made to love and be loved went his way with disciplined abnegation, shutting the door to the happiness of wife, of sons and daughters, of grandchildren. Was it because of the obligation to aid in

[48]

support of his sisters that Cardozo in his earlier years kept away from marriage? In later life, when Nellie and he were all that were left of the brothers and sisters, he dismissed all thought—or at least all intention—of taking a wife. Nellie's entire life was wrapped up in her devotion to him. She had taken the place of a mother to Ben when, as a lad of nine, he had lost his mother. He knew all that he meant to her—the jealousy as well as the depth of her affection. He made allowances for the jealousy; he was grateful for the affection. To a cousin, who brought up the question of his marrying, he answered, "I can never put Nell in second place."

One evening, at the home of one of his associates in the Court of Appeals, Cardozo was seated next to a young married woman.

"Won't you tell me, Judge Cardozo," she asked, "whether you were ever in love?"

The Judge, taken by surprise, answered, "Once."

It was a query that no one had ever before ventured to address to the sensitive and very private gentleman. He displayed no resentment, but by immediately changing the topic he showed that he did not care to have the subject pursued further. As it is, however, a subject that has been discussed by many of his family and his friends—the answer still remaining problematic—the theory may be advanced that Benjamin Cardozo never married in his earlier years because marriage might have interfered with the great passion of his lifetime. As a college boy he had set his goal. As a young lawyer he was working toward it. As a judge he arrived. No devotion to wife, no thought for children (though he loved children) must hinder the arrival at the goal. Cardozo, for all his gentleness, had a stubborn will. The solution to the riddle of Cardozo's bachelorhood may be approached from various directions. The chief clues remain in his proud and pious passion to redeem the Cardozo name and in his devotion to his sister Nell.

Cardozo knew with Justice Oliver Wendell Holmes that "man must face the loneliness of original work." Yet with the close of his career at the bar, and with increasing contacts as a public officer and as a recipient of university honors, the loneliness of Cardozo was somewhat to abate.

This, in the year 1913.

IV

Ring in the nobler modes of life with sweeter manners, purer laws.   TENNYSON

URING Cardozo's years as a lawyer he showed not only keenness, but specialized knowledge in his ever-courteous questioning of witnesses. Constantly, through his varied reading, he added to his information, and thus was qualified to elicit replies on subjects often technical. But it was in appellate work, in his briefs before the higher courts, that he shone most brilliantly. In New York, at Albany, in Washington, judges appreciated the lawyer's contribution in facilitating their decisions.

Judge Samuel Seabury relates that during his first year as a justice of the New York Supreme Court a case came up in his court in which a woman sued the brokerage firm of D. White & Co. Cardozo, representing the brokers, was opposed by James Osborne, a prominent lawyer of those days. In Osborne's summing-up address to the jury he had made an emotional appeal—with what Judge Seabury called hurrah features—on the theme of the poor widow and the rich brokers. Cardozo made a quiet, reasoned address.

Seabury, fearing that unfair prejudice might affect the jury, determined on a "special verdict." Such a verdict is preceded by the justice's asking questions of the jury to determine their understanding of questions of fact. After he had done this, Seabury inquired of Cardozo whether he cared to take any exceptions. Cardozo had no exceptions to take. Seabury then asked Osborne, "Have you?" Osborne complimented the judge on his address and answered, "No exceptions." After the jury had brought in a verdict for Cardozo's clients, Osborne, surprised that his appeal to sentiment had failed, asked Seabury whether he might not now take an exception so that an appeal could be made to a higher court. Seabury smilingly answered, "If you can get Mr. Cardozo's consent." This, of course, was not forthcoming; and as in such circumstances no exceptions can be granted without the consent of both counsels, the case ended there.

Judge Seabury commented on the fact that, though Cardozo was at his best as a lawyer's lawyer, advising and preparing briefs for other legal firms, here was an instance where the quiet ways and the fine logic of the man were far more effective than the emotional oratory of his opponent.

But Cardozo's career was not to continue for long as a practicing lawyer.

New York was having one of its periodic fits of moral indignation. An easygoing community had borne with Tammany rule until in the summer of 1912 the murder of Herman Rosenthal dramatized the association of the police force with the criminal elements. A gambler's assassination by thugs was in itself a matter of no special moment, but the revelations throughout the following year of how Police Lieutenant Charles Becker had instigated the crime in order to prevent disclosures involving presumably not alone himself were sufficient to suggest the infamy of the civic situation. A crusade against Tammany rule was soon in progress. John Purroy Mitchel, a fearless and upright lawyer, then not quite forty years old, was nominated for the mayoralty.

In November intermittent virtue triumphed, while vice went snarling into temporary background.

Mitchel and Cardozo admired each other, though one can hardly visualize two men more different in temperament and in the casual ways of life. While the elder Columbia graduate kept to his well-nigh monastic life, his junior by ten years—the youngest man ever to become Mayor of New York City—similarly a hard worker during the day, found time for many social enjoyments at night. Indeed, his pleasure in associating with the wealthy élite and his dancing at night clubs were made the target for many gibes in the Hearst newspapers.

The campaign of 1913 that brought Mitchel to the mayoralty saw Cardozo elected to the Supreme Court of New York State. The Anti-Tammany Committee proposing candidates for the Judiciary was headed by Charles Burlingham, long president of the New York Welfare Council.

Walter H. Pollak (who in later years acted as counsel in the Supreme Court of the United States when the Scottsboro case was appealed and the lives saved of Negroes unjustly charged with rape) arranged the details of Cardozo's campaign. Or one might better say the campaign of his supporters, for Cardozo himself held aloof.

Stanley M. Isaacs made the nominating speech when on August 20, 1913, the Progressive party named Cardozo. After briefly outlining Cardozo's career as a lawyer, and after dwelling on the "ability, integrity, and courtesy" of the man, the speaker went on: "We must not have as our candidate even an able lawyer who is so schooled in the precedents of the past as to forget the needs of the present; who is so immersed in his books as to be completely out of touch with the living forces around him; or who is so imbued with the dignity and aloofness of his office that he draws closely about him his judicial robes so that neither contaminated nor distracted by the sordid facts of present day life he can continue to at-

[53]

tempt to solve current problems with an eye fixed on the dead and settled issues of the past.

"We must elect judges who will decide in a progressive spirit, looking not to what was determined a hundred years ago, but looking forward to the effect of their decisions, to their influence on present-day conditions and on the future development of our political and social life. Such a man is Benjamin N. Cardozo. He has stated to me that he believes that the general doctrines which are at the root of our Constitution and of our social system need recasting in every generation; that a lawyer must interpret in the light of surrounding conditions and in accordance with the ethical sense of the generation in which he lives, the written formulas laid down many generations ago. He believes in emphasizing the conditions of the day; he believes in adapting and modifying the fundamental concepts of the law so that they accord with the present views of a live and active community. Society is in a constant state of flux. The ideas of one generation are sometimes directly opposed to the ideas of the next. A decision right twenty-five or fifty years ago is frequently wrong if repeated twenty-five or fifty years later. Mr. Cardozo is a man of the present day; his active practice has kept alive his interest in present-day needs and present-day problems, and if you wish to put upon the bench a judge who will at once dignify it by his legal attainments and ability and at the same time liberalize it by his humane personality, you will nominate Benjamin N. Cardozo."

When Cardozo received a copy of the address, he wrote: "I do not recognize myself at all in your picture, but it paints me as I would wish to be, and so it may be useful as holding an ideal before me. . . . Believe me, I am deeply grateful to you for all that you have so generously said. I will try to be worthy of it."

Mr. Burlingham, Walter Meyer, Mr. Pollak, and other

[54]

In his mother's arms

His mother as a younger woman

prominent lawyers were among the most active campaigners. When B. Aymar Sands looked at the list of the distinguished men of the bar who were urging Cardozo's election, "Since the 1860's," said he, "I have been familiar with these endorsement lists, and this is the best list that has ever been prepared."

"The undersigned members of the bar," the endorsement read, "irrespective of party, wish to call to the attention of the public the eminent fitness of Benjamin N. Cardozo for the office of Justice of the Supreme Court, and to ask the voters of Manhattan and the Bronx to support his candidacy at the polls. Mr. Cardozo's great learning, ability, and devotion to the highest ideals of his profession have won for him in remarkable degree the confidence of the courts and the respect of the bar. His nomination came to him unsought and as a spontaneous recognition of his qualifications. It has been pronounced by many members of the bar to be one of the finest nominations for judicial office made in recent years, and in that judgment we concur.

"We believe that our fellow members of the bar can render helpful service in this campaign by bringing Mr. Cardozo's qualifications to the notice of voters, and we urge them to do so."

The list was headed by Joseph H. Choate. Among the 130 signers were Henry W. Taft, Louis Marshall, Harlan F. Stone, Charles H. Tuttle, Charles E. Hughes, Jr., Elihu Root, Jr., Bainbridge Colby, Harold Nathan, William Travers Jerome, Henry L. Stimson.

But Cardozo would not allow the statement to be published in the newspapers. He would not go further than consenting to have the list shown to lawyers, who might then, if they cared to, speak about it in private conversation with their friends—all of which seems a bit quixotic and even, perhaps, illogical. But the sensitiveness of the man, the sense of privacy, remain apparent.

[55]

Cardozo's supporters could thus not get much aid from the candidate himself. The chief influence working against them was the Hearst press, at that time very powerful. Hearst was giving qualified support to Mitchel, but opposed George McAneny and William A. Prendergast, respectively candidates for the presidency of the Board of Aldermen and the comptrollership. He endorsed Francis B. Weeks against Cardozo in the First Judicial District, where Tammany was strongest. All the other newspapers, with the exception of the *Sun*, came out immediately in favor of Cardozo. The *Sun* was strategically important. The public for the most part didn't (and doesn't) pay much attention in voting for candidates for the bench. They cast their ballots rather automatically along party lines. But the *Sun* in especial was read by the intelligentsia. Could not its influence be swung to Cardozo?

Walter Pollak was on very friendly terms with Chauncey Garver. The young man's father, John Anson Garver, was the partner of James M. Beck. These two influential lawyers were the counselors for the *Sun*. They were admirers of Cardozo who, as counsel for the *Globe*, had more than once discussed with them matters in connection with libel suits against the press. Mr. Garver was persuaded by Mr. Pollak to intercede with the *Sun*. The voting would presumably be close. Every vote was worth obtaining.

A week before election the *Sun* came out with an editorial advising its readers to vote for Cardozo. The election was, indeed, close. A swing of 1,400 votes would have defeated him. The *Sun's* editorial had doubtless proved of value, although Cardozo humorously attributed his success to another cause. The First Judicial District had many Italians. The name Cardozo has an Italian sound. That might have been the explanation of his election. At least Mr. George R. Farnum, formerly Assistant Attorney General of the United States, records that Cardozo, in conversation on the vagaries of chance, said to him, "I would never have been elected had I not received the support of a group of Italian-Americans who voted for me on the supposition that since my name ended in 'o' I was one of their race."

Cardozo's career as a lawyer came characteristically to a close. During the summer months of 1913 Walter Pollak was with him at Allenhurst, N. J., working on briefs for the opening of the fall court. Cardozo gave the easier briefs to the young man who was soon to succeed him as George Engelhard's partner. October came, with Cardozo still in New Jersey. His physician, Dr. Woolley, had suggested as long a vacation and as much country air as possible. Mr. Pollak went to the law office and reminded Miss Miller, Cardozo's secretary, that Cardozo's briefs were now due.

"They are already in," said Miss Miller.

"How can that be?" she was asked. "He didn't have the reference books of cases at his country house."

Miss Miller then explained that Cardozo, without any books to resort to, had put into his briefs the names of cases and the numbers of the volumes in which they appeared.

Mr. Pollak recalled also the occasion when, over the telephone, Cardozo had given a reference to be looked up in connection with the construction of a statute. He had read the case years ago and could give the name on the spur of the moment. Three days' search led to finding no other case that applied. This was remarkable enough—but how much more amazing the mastery of memory implied in those references included in all the briefs written by Cardozo at Allenhurst!

There are many illustrations of this almost magic retention of wide readings. Judge Learned Hand tells of a consultation among judges at Albany. In discussing a reference, Cardozo said that it could be found in the New York State Reports, Vol. 157. "By God," said Judge Kellogg, "he's forgotten the page!"

Charles E. Hughes, Jr., Cardozo's law secretary during January and February of 1914, recalls how the Justice, as he was leaving his chambers to sit on the bench, handed him a brief and gave him the exact names of the cases to which reference should be made. Going further in his research, Mr. Hughes found that Cardozo's remark, "They'll give you a start," might well have been accompanied by a statement to the effect that, "They'll be all you need."

In the campaign which had led to Cardozo's election as a justice, Seabury was defeated as a candidate on the Progressive ticket for the Court of Appeals. He had made speeches wherein he freely criticized the reactionary tendencies of the Court of Appeals, yet Governor Glynn thought highly of him. When, early in 1914, a vacancy occurred, the Governor, thinking of designating him, telephoned to Seabury, saying, "Clear your desk; you may have news before long." Obviously opposition developed, and a little later Cardozo received a similar message from the Governor. Seabury and Cardozo joshed each other about these messages. As the days went by one would say to to the other, "It looks as if I were going to get it." Then, finally, Cardozo was appointed, and Judge Seabury expressed his opinion that "there could be no better choice."

An order by a justice of the Supreme Court of New York State bears the initials J.S.C. under the blank line for his signature. One day, after Cardozo had signed an order, young Hughes made some remark about it—some comment on the rightness of that particular order. Thereupon Cardozo jestingly said: "J.S.C. means Justice's Secretary Concurs." But when the anecdote got abroad, and people smiled at its wit, Cardozo—departing from his usual veracity—always maintained that it was his law secretary who had thus interpreted the initials. "It was," says Mr. Hughes, "one of his favorite cracks."

The friendship between Charles E. Hughes, Jr., and

Judge Cardozo never lessened. When, in 1924, the younger man was appointed Solicitor General, one of the warmest letters of congratulation came from the man whose law secretary, ten years previously, he had been. "If I had to express my feeling for Judge Cardozo," Charles E. Hughes, Jr., has told us, "the word that I should use is 'reverence.' Of course, I felt deep affection for him and great admiration for his mind, but above all this was my lasting reverence for his spiritual qualities."

Such was the lawyer who put on the robe of judgeship on January 1, 1914. The ambition of Cardozo's lifetime was now fulfilled. He was now a justice on the Supreme Court from which his father had resigned. In conversations with Mayor Mitchel and Governor Whitman, Cardozo told what this meant to him. His—one recalls the phrase of Edmund Burke—"his was that chastity of honor which felt a stain like a wound."

Hardly had a month gone by when Governor Glynn designated Cardozo to serve on the Court of Appeals. In those years not more than four such appointments could be made to relieve congestion. It was unprecedented that a man should be chosen who had so recently been elected to the bench. When Governor Glynn asked the other judges to suggest the appointee they desired, they unanimously named Cardozo. The Governor made no assent to their first request. He suggested other men. Whereupon all the judges of the Supreme Court respectfully repeated their original request. A prayer from such a source had the moral weight of a justified demand. The Governor appointed Cardozo. In later years Governor Glynn said that this was the finest act of his life.

"[Cardozo] brought to the Bench," Mr. George R. Farnum has written in *Lights and Shadows*, "a knowledge of legal history, an understanding of legal principles, and a familiarity with judicial precedents comparable to Story's."

Fittingly, then, Governor Whitman showed less hesitation than was displayed by his predecessor, when, in 1917, the Republican Governor made the Democrat Cardozo a permanent member of the Court of Appeals. Charles S. Whitman was elected to the governorship largely because of his brilliant prosecution, as district attorney, of Police Lieutenant Charles Becker and his confederates in the murder of Herman Rosenthal. The cold-blooded shooting of a gambler by thugs under order of a police officer had, as has already been said, much to do with the popular indignation sweeping Mitchel and Cardozo into office. Vagaries of chance, indeed! Three fine public servants assisted in their careers by the bullets shot into a gambler by "Whitey Lewis," "Dago Frank," "Leftie Louie," and "Gyp the Blood"!

The four assassins were executed in April, 1914, and Becker followed them to the chair in July, 1915, after his appeal had failed before the court in which Cardozo was one of the judges. Becker's lawyer was Martin T. Manton, whose later career as Federal Circuit judge was to end so disastrously. Manton had succeeded in obtaining a second trial for Becker on the contention that Justice Goff had not been fair to the accused. A second conviction resulted from the trial presided over by Justice Seabury. When the case went up to the state's highest court, Cardozo agreed with his associates under the leadership of Chief Judge Bartlett that the technicalities advanced by Manton carried no weight. Despite the dying statement of one of the gunmen, the chain of evidence led directly to Becker by way of his accomplices, notorious gamblers who were in his power. The gentle Cardozo was not gentle when patent murder called for the sword of justice.

It took a little while for Ben Cardozo to find himself at Albany, his shyness and modesty, and the briefness of the time that he had sat as a judge, leading him to refrain from expressing himself with much force at the beginning of his career on the bench. But before long his influence made itself decidedly felt and in later years Cardozo became not only the beloved friend, but the adviser and leader of all the judges in his court.

According to Judge Hand, who knew him well, Cardozo was always a sad man, yet he liked to laugh and had a joyous laugh. In some ways he was very defenseless. He seemed to have no power to protect himself from bores and sycophants. He put up with people who forced themselves on him. It is difficult to say whether this was in part a lack of forcefulness or whether it was another manifestation of his essential gentleness, his unwillingness to hurt anyone.

During the weekdays Cardozo made his home at the Hotel Ten Eyck, spending his week ends at his home in New York. But even in Albany he was constantly in touch with Nell, calling her frequently and, when work was not too urgent, running down to New York during the week, knowing how lonely she was without him.

His ways of instinctive courtesy were most happy when directed toward youth. His cousin Annie cites one such instance. "He accepted at once," she says, "when I told him a young lawyer was anxious to meet him, and suggested that he come to tea one day when he was down from Albany. My young friend was lifted to the seventh heaven. Imagine his feelings when the Judge, tall, eagle-eyed, an impressive, distinguished figure, stood in the doorway and remarked that he was frightfully afraid of meeting young lawyers—they knew such a terrifying amount of law!"

John F. Brosman relates another instance of Cardozo's kindliness. "In our neighborhood," he tells us, "there died several years ago a poor Irish-American who, by dint of honest labor, had succeeded in raising and educating a family of eight children. I had played with some of the boys and therefore, upon hearing of his death, went to the home for the purpose of expressing my sympathy. The oldest son with conscious pride showed me a letter which his mother had just received. It was written in longhand and the writer stated that, having just heard of her husband's death, he hastened to extend his sincerest sympathy, stated that he had respected and admired her husband for many years and that in his death he knew that she had lost a fond husband, the children a good father, and the community a worthy citizen. He added, however, that they would always have and be able to cherish the heritage which such a life had left to them, and then concluded by placing his services at her disposal. The writer of that letter was Benjamin N. Cardozo, then Chief Judge of the Court of Appeals of New York, and the decedent had for many years tended the furnace in the Judge's city home."

At Albany, as later in Washington, constitutional problems frequently presented difficult knots cut by Cardozo with what might be termed a sword of wide justice. Cardozo's character and personality, combined with the scholar's knowledge of the law, resulted in that "dominant influence" which, to quote former Attorney General Cummings, made the New York Court of Appeals "the second tribunal in the land." How this court functioned is described by Judge Frederick E. Crane, who succeeded Cardozo as Chief Judge. In his tribute to his predecessor, at the opening of the court session on October 1, 1938, Judge Crane said: "The method of our work and the conditions under which we live probably bring us into closer fellowship than is customary with other courts. During the four weeks' session of each term we live here in Albany. The majority of us dine together every day of the session. Every Tuesday, Wednesday, and Thursday we·are in consultation from half past nine in the morning until one, followed by the court session from two until six. In the evening it has been customary for members of the court to work in their chambers in the courthouse until late at night. It will thus be seen that while the court is in session, the judges are together most of the day and evening. We get to know each other very well, indeed. Virtues and faults cannot be hidden.

"By tradition the consultations of the court are an outstanding feature of main importance to the work. They are quite formal. The judge to whom a case has fallen is expected to report fully upon all questions involved, and while making his report it is the duty of the Chief Judge to see that he is not interrupted, no matter how long he may take. When he is through, the matter then passes to the next associate in rank, who is accorded like treatment.

"By this method it has been found that every man is afforded full opportunity for self-expression and the indulgence of his own peculiar method of approach or attack. He is not cramped or frightened or dismayed by constant or boisterous interruption. The calmness of the discussions which, never in my twenty-one years of experience, have exceeded parliamentary language, affords reason its proper domain. Excitement, feelings and emotions, experience has taught us, are apt to deter good judgment. I speak of these things in order that we, his associates, may pay tribute to that quality of Judge Cardozo's work which might not be known unless we mention it.

"He was of a gentle, highly sensitive nature. He needed such an atmosphere as I have described, within which to do his best work. It was in these consultations that he excelled. His power of analysis, of clear and precise statement, and ability to apply the authorities to the point involved were delightful to listen to and frequently removed the doubts under which his associates labored after careful study. . . .

"I talk of Judge Cardozo's work as though this was the principal thing which impresses us—not so! The man himself was greater than anything he did or produced. His gentleness, his kindness, his helpfulness, his consideration for the feelings of others, the moderation of his language, made him at all times and under all circumstances the gentleman, and endeared him to all his associates. His aims and ideals have been an inspiration to all who met him. The body may perish, but this personal influence which uplifts and animates has in it a species of immortality." For fifteen years Judge Crane had sat with Cardozo in the Court of Appeals. His pen picture of his associate has the weight and confirmation of all those years at Albany.

Henry Uterhart, in referring to the friendly relations which existed among the judges of the Court of Appeals, says of Cardozo: "I recall one other talk I once had with him during the depression and he said that the judges of the Court of Appeals were talking one day as to the possibility of the Court of Appeals being abolished in the interests of economy. This, of course, was a joke. However, Judge Andrews said, 'Do not worry, my brethren. I have a large farm up the state with horses, and cows, and pigs, and chickens, and all the other things that go with a farm. If necessary, we can all go up and live there.' " Said Judge Cardozo, "The difficulty was that every member of the court knew something about farming except me, so I don't see what use I would be there." "You can be the philosopher," Mr. Uterhart told him. But, he said, "What good would a philosopher be on a farm?" "Well," pointed out Mr. Uterhart, "wasn't Emerson the philosopher of Brook Farm?"

Another who has reported concerning these Albany years is Filan T. Ryan, the manager of the Hotel Ten Eyck. "With other judges of the Court of Appeals," he says, "including Chief Judge Pound, Chief Judge Crane, Judge Irving Lehman, Judge Kellogg of Plattsburg, Judge O'Brien and others, he dined regularly at a large table in the main dining room."

"His habits were apparently calculated to the minute.

He arrived from his room for breakfast every morning at precisely five minutes of seven o'clock. He returned at noon for luncheon and dined at six or six-thirty. Breakfast always consisted of orange juice, cereal and coffee. Luncheon also was a light meal—usually of soup, rye bread toasted, and milk. The evening meal, similarly simple, generally consisted of roast beef, baked potato, and milk. He rarely departed from these menus. Even at dinner there were no extras beyond the single dish. He drank coffee only in the morning."

"Judge Cardozo," wrote Mr. Ryan, with special knowledge, "was the quietest of all the judges. He listened to everything that was said, but had very little to say himself. I never saw him when he was not calm. He seemed to be greatly interested in everything that went on. He was always gracious and friendly and everybody without exception respected him. You could tell that by the way people regarded him whenever he appeared about the hotel."

"After luncheon, according to Chris Bogiages, the maître d'hôtel, Judge Cardozo immediately returned to the Court of Appeals. After dinner he took a short walk, often with Judge Hiscock, up the State Street hill and around the Capitol or farther, going back to the courthouse until ten-thirty or eleven o'clock at night. He returned quietly to the hotel, slipping in often unobserved, to arise early the next morning. He rarely dined out, attending few functions except for the annual dinners given by the Governor to the Court of Appeals."

Cardozo ever remained simple in his wants, as to food and drink as in other ways. Yet he was the last to criticize those who differed from him and who found satisfaction in the pleasures of the flesh. While not averse from a glass of sherry or the lighter wines, he adhered to the Prohibition Amendment after it went into effect in 1920. When some of his friends at private parties chose to disregard it, the Judge refrained from embarrassing his host by any objection or comment.

Reflecting upon these conversations with and letters from those who knew Judge Cardozo, there arises a Latin phrase which may be regarded as a cornerstone in the structure of Benjamin Cardozo's social intercourse. *Amicorum magis quam tuam ipsius laudem praedice.* In the perfect translation of a Cambridge scholar: "Enlarge upon the praises of your friends rather than on your own." It was Cardozo's nature to do this; it was his second nature; it was his delight. He carried this approach so far, because of his generosity and his self-deprecatory modesty, that the recipients of his praise must, indeed, have been blind did they not realize that they were being offered a gift beyond their deserts. In his valuation of others, his judgments were at times those of the gracious gentleman rather than of the profound judge. His heart in these instances took precedence over his mind.

And yet one wonders whether a philosophy did not to some extent underlie the charming words flowing so naturally in his correspondence and in his conversation. Call them flattery, if you will, because at times they gave more than one's due; and flattery connotes undue praise. Recall, if you will, that Cardozo once smilingly admitted to a friend that he enjoyed flattery—the term he used for any high praise directed toward himself. Any touch of weakness brings him in welcome manner into the circle of imperfect human nature. And surely we can accept with a happy smile that care for appearance which might lead him to exchange his spectacles for the more becoming pince-nez at the approach of some visitor. We recall how some one or other of his woman cousins would tease him if a hair was out of place. But this vanity—the word is perhaps excessive, yet let it stay—was mainly the punctiliousness of a gentleman of the old school.

[66]

In overpraising others there was no self-seeking, no selfish object to be gained. He could be quietly stern with offenders, withholding no criticism when criticism served a purpose. A tricky lawyer was rebuked by Judge Cardozo with the admonition: "Mr. Blank, that is not the way things are done in this court." A loud-mouthed attorney would be turned down with a phrase subtly ironical yet sufficiently courteous. A more serious offender might be subjected to a touch of shining acid on the rapier of Cardozo's speech. Only when the innate graciousness of the man—the desire to give pleasure to others—led him to abstain from critical comment did he relinquish the keenness of his judgment in favor of however friendly overpraise. This remains, in our opinion, intellectually a fault, though such "flattery" may well be defended, not only by reason of its kindliness.

Essentially Cardozo remained the same through boyhood and later life. His character and personality did not alter in any fundamental way. Life impinges on many characters, contracts or expands them. Not so in his case. True, he rose from achievement as a matter of family honor to achievement as a matter of public service. True, the man of solitary inclinations became the center of a circle of friends. But basically he remained the same throughout his life.

He had humor, Judge Hand said of him, what the French call *malice*, a kind of sly humor which is not so easily appreciated. He could, indeed, handle the scalpel, but so painlessly that the subject would not know he was being dissected.

On one occasion, after lunching together, both of us wished to look up something in the New York Public Library. The volume I was after was an exceedingly rare one, kept under lock and key. I happened to tell the Judge that, rather than go through the routine of obtaining such an item, it was my custom to go to the director's office, and ask to have an attendant bring it to me.

The Judge, his voice ever courteous and without any criticism in his glance, said quietly, "Do you?"

"Yes, to save time. Do you disapprove?"

The Judge smiled. "I wait in line," he said.

"Your time is too valuable for the public," I countered.

"I don't know about that," answered the Judge. "As a citizen I take my turn."

V

A Daniel come to judgment! Yea, a Daniel!

SHAKESPEARE

A FEW months after Cardozo's appointment to the
Court of Appeals, Seabury became an associate
judge of the same court where he served until
August, 1916, resigning then to accept the nomination by
the Democratic party for the governorship of New York
State. During his score of months at Albany, Seabury
observed with admiring interest the gracious and tactful
ways of Cardozo as contrasted with his own forceful manner of expressing himself. There was in particular one instance when a minority opinion of Seabury's had been
opposed by practically all the other judges in their discussion around the table. Cardozo had had at first some misgivings about the constitutional points involved, but when
he came over to Seabury's way of thinking his conciliatory
methods brought the other judges into line after Seabury
had willingly consented to have his own original forthright
opinion not filed.

Judge Seabury told me of another occasion when he
especially admired Cardozo for his handling of a difficult
situation. William B. Guthrie had suggested changes in
connection with admission to the bar—changes in which

Judge Seabury and many other leaders of the law agreed. However, there were many opponents to such changes, many who thought that "the little red schoolhouse" was almost sufficient education for candidates. The Court of Appeals controls the rules of admission to the bar. Cardozo was at the time presiding over the Court of Appeals. In the generally sparsely attended courthouse at Albany there was now a throng that filled the room. Bar Associations of various states had sent members to attend. In the audience were several belligerent lawyers who were constantly interrupting the proceedings. "It was a pleasure to see," says Judge Seabury, "how Cardozo handled them—quietly but forcefully—putting each one in his place without antagonizing any."

The year following Cardozo's appointment as Justice saw two unusual cases of crime come up for the consideration of the Court of Appeals. Mr. Pollard, in his book on Cardozo, relates them at some length. One had to do with the shooting of young Rizzo by another young Italian, Shilitano. The latter's father had been knocked down and beaten by Rizzo in a poolroom quarrel. The evidence of various witnesses was sufficient to convince the jury that the son had committed a murder of revenge. But after he had been sentenced to the chair at Sing Sing, the witnesses received from the convicted man's gang such dire threats that they recanted. Martin W. Littleton, Shilitano's lawyer, thereupon asked for a new trial. It was refused by the judge of the lower court. The Court of Appeals sustained him. "I am unable to say," Cardozo wrote in his opinion, "that the trial judge made a mistake when he held that he was dealing, not with an honest recantation, but with a criminal alliance to release a guilty man."

Again in 1916 an Italian murder case came before the judges in Albany. Two brothers by the name of Galbo were suspected of having killed Marzella, a blackmailer.

His headless and legless body was found in a barrel at the bottom of a ravine near Rochester. Only one of the brothers, Domenico, was captured and brought to trial. But Domenico was a cripple, a man without legs. Circumstantial evidence pointed clearly to his having been at the scene of the murder and he had presumably aided his brother in disposing of the corpse. But could he have taken part in the killing itself? Was it fair to accuse him of more than being an accessory after the crime? If not, a new trial should be ordered, and a different charge be made against Domenico.

"If the circumstances," wrote Cardozo in his opinion, "make one inference just as reasonable as the other, we must give the defendent the benefit of the conclusion that would mitigate his guilt. In this case, a legless cripple is charged to have murdered a strong man. The murder followed a fierce fight in which the strong man was beaten and wounded. It seems certain that the wounds were inflicted and the head severed as parts of a single combat. We cannot with reason say that the cripple did these things. Least of all can we say that he was able to do them and escape without a scratch or a blood stain. . . . If all that he did was to help the murderer to escape, he was not a principal, but an accessory, and the jury under the charge required to acquit him. The charge is sound, but it propounded to the jury a problem incapable of reasoned solution. . . . In considering him as a principal, conjecture has filled the gaps left open by the evidence, and the presumption of innocence has yielded to a presumption of guilt."

Cardozo's entire opinion should be studied as an essay on judgment in relation to crime. It is subtle as well as profound; it is deeply conscientious; and then, too, it is such excellent English! In his opinion that conviction should be reversed and a new trial ordered, his associates, Bartlett and Hiscock and Chase, Collin and Seabury and Hogan, unanimously agreed.

Of course, trials involving murder, kidnaping, robbery, adultery, or the malpractices of public officials are exciting meat for the appetite of the vast majority of newspaper readers. Most of us are less interested in those unsensational cases which often more essentially, more widely, affect the public welfare. As we follow Cardozo's career during his first four years on the bench, we shall see him rendering many opinions remote from the sphere of crime, but invaluable in the march of social justice. While our Expeditionary Force was seeking to make the "world safe for democracy," he and his associates were construing with new vision the processes of law whereby the ideals of democracy might, under changing conditions, best be brought into effect.

There is no attempt here, no desire, to exaggerate the importance of Cardozo in that series of decisions which began in 1914 to make the Court of Appeals in New York State the increasingly significant court in the United States. Yet his fine group of associates became ever more profoundly influenced by the student and philosopher of the law, this conservator of the past who looked with liberal yet practical eye at the present, and with a poet's imagination toward the future. Then, too, one must not overlook that rare, well-nigh indefinable quality which men call charm. Ben Cardozo had charm.

To resume briefly, then, some of the cases whose liberal effect was to benefit the people of the United States. In 1917 the New York court had voted as unconstitutional a law which would have limited the working hours of women in factories. In 1915, after factory conditions had been reported to the legislature by Robert F. Wagner, the Court of Appeals confirmed a statute protecting women from work late at night and in the early morning hours. In reversing

[72]

its decision of ten years earlier, the Albany court had turned around the hand on the signpost. It was no longer to point to any narrow construction of "due process" whereby the employer might benefit at the cost of women's health. It pointed now to that avenue whereon the power of the state might constitutionally safeguard public welfare coming into conflict with personal profit or so-called "personal liberty."

In the same year, Cardozo wrote an opinion on a question which had arisen as to whether the State of New York could give preference to its citizens in the construction of public works. Was such discrimination in opposition to aliens' rights? Cardozo decided that "if doubt exists whether there is a conflict between the statute and the constitution, the statute must prevail." Doubt obviously did exist. The state did not owe equal obligations to citizens and aliens and in the use of its funds might, in Cardozo's opinion, "consult the welfare of its own citizens rather than that of aliens."

For us, in the study of the Justice as a man, the chief interest in this case rests in what is implied by the various phrases in Cardozo's opinion. "It is not enough," he says in reference to the statute voted by the legislature, "that it may seem to us to be impolitic or even oppressive. It is not enough that in its making, great and historic traditions of generosity have been ignored. We do not assume to pass judgment upon the wisdom of the legislature. Our duty is done when we ascertain that it has kept within its power."

Another pregnant phrase in this same opinion is to be found in the sentence where Cardozo refers to "an expanding consciousness in the modern state that relief against unemployment, both after the event and before it, is part of the state's function." Workmen's Compensation Acts were already being passed, but we were then merely on the threshold of that advance in social welfare through legislation which made such enormous strides in the subsequent quarter century. With his sympathy for the poor, and his admiration for every sincere workman, Cardozo was one of many liberal judges to forward this advance.

Toward men who violated in mean manner the ethics of their profession, Cardozo was adamant. There was the case, in 1917, of a lawyer who fought disbarment on the contention that he had acted as witness in a trial whose proceedings disclosed his own derelictions. Cardozo discussed the claim of immunity in these memorable words: "If the exemption protects lawyers, it must equally protect physicians, whose licenses have long been subject to revocation for misconduct. Two great and honorable professions have in that view been denied the right to purify their membership and vindicate their honor. The charlatan and rogue may assume to heal the sick. The knave and criminal may pose as a minister of justice. Such things cannot have been intended, and will not be allowed."

Another sentence frequently quoted belongs to an opinion of the year 1916. A well-known motorcar company was being sued by a Mr. MacPherson who had bought a car that turned out to have a defective wheel. The Company's defense was that they had not sold the car to the complainant. He had purchased it from a dealer. There was no proof that the manufacturers had known of the defect. Yet the car had collapsed when it was being driven at a speed of eight miles an hour.

"Beyond all question," wrote Cardozo, "the nature of an automobile gives warning of probable danger if its construction is defective. This automobile was designed to go fifty miles an hour. Unless its wheels were sound and strong, injury was almost certain. It was as much a thing of danger as a defective engine for a railroad. The defendant knew the danger." Cardozo then went on to state that the company in supplying its cars to dealers knowingly supplied them for the use of purchasers. The contention that the Company's only legal responsibility was to dealers was contrary to equity. "The Law," said the Judge, "does not lead us to so inconsequent a conclusion." Then followed the famous phrase, the metaphor which President Roosevelt approximated when, some twenty years later, he spoke of "the horse and buggy days." "Precedents drawn from the days of travel by stagecoach," said Cardozo, "do not fit the conditions of travel today. The principle that the danger must be imminent does not change, but the things subject to the principle do change. They are whatever the needs of life in a developing civilization require them to be."

One could go on at length drawing on cases during Cardozo's years at Albany, to illustrate that passion for equity leading him, where the law was either too vague or too universal, now to protect, now to condemn, according to his sense of the profounder justice. We see him, for instance, maintaining that legal wrong is not necessarily moral wrong and that medical science should hold up its shield to save the life of the criminal insane. Thirteen years prior to his famous address on "What Medicine Can Do for Law," Cardozo was already advocating the humanitarian and the scientific advance that has borne fruit in court decisions and in prison reform.

To his few opinions already selected from the years 1914–1917, let there be added just one from 1918, the final year of the Great War. A cigar packer by the name of Grieb had, at the request of his employer, started out to deliver some boxes of cigars, for which he was told to collect payment. He stumbled on the staircase and fell. His injuries proved fatal. The accident had not taken place during working hours. Grieb, for what reason is unknown, had returned to the factory during the evening. Were, then, his widow and child entitled to the death benefit provided for in the Workmen's Compensation Law?

The employer contended that he was not legally responsible for what had occurred. Grieb was not in his employ in the nighttime. Said Cardozo: "Grieb's service, if it had been rendered during working hours, would have been incidental to his employment. To overturn this award, it is necessary to hold that the service ceased to be incidental because rendered after hours. That will never do. The law does not insist that an employee shall work with his eye upon the clock. Services rendered in a spirit of helpful loyalty, after closing time has come, have the same protection as the services of the drone or the laggard. . . . What Grieb then undertook to do with his employer's approval was just as much a part of the business as if it had been done in the noonday sun. . . . It was not mere friendship, it was the relation of employer and employee, that led the one to request the service and the other to render it. If such a service is not incidental to the employment within the meaning of this statute, loyalty and helpfulness have earned a poor reward."

Absorbed as he was in his court activities and in the rigid routine of his days, which left little leisure for social life, a circle of warm friends grew, nonetheless, about the hitherto solitary man, and at the same time honors came to him unsought.

In the spring of 1915 Nicholas Murray Butler, President of Columbia University, advised Cardozo that the degree of Doctor of Laws, *honoris causa*, was to be conferred upon him—the first of the many honorary degrees that were to be given to him during his career. Later, Yale University followed the example of Columbia. Professor William Lyon Phelps gave the citation, saying of Cardozo: "He is an honor to his profession and the pattern of judicial learning and judicial temper in the leading law schools of our country. He is so frequently quoted that he is a spiritual member of many university faculties."

[76]

The University of Michigan added to the growing list of honorary degrees of the "jurist of eminent distinction, an author of learned and authoritative books in the field of legal science, widely recognized by his associates at the bar as one of America's leading scholars." Harvard joined the procession of sister institutions eager to confer an honorary degree on the New York jurist. In a letter to his cousin Maud, Cardozo remarked that "after strutting about the Harvard campus in the torrid heat of Commencement —all accoutered in the traditional Harvard garb of cutaway coat and silk hat," he felt he had earned the honorary degree "by the sweat of my brow if not otherwise." That same season the Alumni Association of the Columbia Law School gave Cardozo a testimonial dinner at the Hotel Astor.

Cardozo received his sixth honorary degree from St. John's College in Brooklyn, whose law school was having its first annual Commencement. Cardozo had been asked to give the Commencement Address. "Our Lady of the Common Law," he told his hearers "—I say it with the humility that is due from an old and faithful servant—Our Lady in these days is no longer an easy one to please. She has become insatiate in her demands. Not law alone, but almost every branch of human knowledge, has been brought within her ken, and so within the range of sacrifice exacted of her votaries. Those who would earn her best rewards must make their knowledge as deep as the science and as broad and universal as the culture of their day. She will not be satisfied with less."

Cardozo followed these words with comment on the relation of law to life. He accused himself of "rehearsing ancient platitudes," adding that he did not mean by that epithet to cheapen or deride them. "We are wont to call things platitudes when we know them to be truths but have a disagreeable sense that we have failed to live up to them

[77]

altogether in the conduct of our lives." He accused himself of being a bore on account of these platitudes, but suggested that "Socrates was considered by the Athenians to be a horrid old bore who deserved nothing better than his hemlock," yet had won immortality. Boswell was a bore who had been snubbed by "the man he was exalting." Yet he had won immortality for both Samuel Johnson and himself. If his hearers thought that, "like Socrates and other bores," he had earned the draught of hemlock, they were at liberty to pass him the cup.

With all the lightness of touch characterizing this address, there was even more emphasis on the value of character than on the worth of knowledge. "Character," said Cardozo, "includes many things—industry and fidelity as well as conscience and honor." He stressed the value of "individual freedom and the inner life above all things"—the "invisible and imponderable."

As the address drew to its close he recited the oath still administered to the grand jurors of the county, the vow which he compared in beauty to the famous Hippocratic Oath that all physicians must take:

"You shall diligently inquire and true presentment make, of all such matters and things as shall be given you in charge; the counsel of the people of this State, your fellows' and your own, you shall keep secret; you shall present no person from envy, hatred or malice; nor shall you leave anyone unpresented through fear, favor, affection or reward, or hope thereof; but you shall present all things truly as they come to your knowledge, according to the best of your understanding. So help you God!"

"I summon you, the new recruits," he told them, "to do your part in this unending struggle, the charge on the redoubts of fear and hatred and prejudice and passion and the injustice that is born of them. You will need to know much more than the piffle paffle of procedure. You will need to know much more than law, or rather till you know many other things not often ranked as law, you will find that law itself is in reality unknown. As in any other fight, you will hear the call for patience and skill and courage and firmness and endurance. I have faith you will not fail us."

Many more graduating classes of American institutions of learning saw Benjamin Cardozo crowned with academic laurels. Universities in New York, Massachusetts, New Jersey, Pennsylvania; Brown, Chicago, Williams, Yeshiva, joined in high tributes to the Justice. The St. Lawrence University at Canton, N. Y., led the way when Cardozo was its guest at the seventieth annual Commencement. The degree of Doctor of Laws, conferred upon him by President Richard Eddy Sykes, was preceded by a citation wherein Cardozo was addressed: "Modest and cultured gentleman at home in the world of art, philosophy, and literature, but especially distinguished as the legal scholar and jurist whose written opinions are models of substance and style, universally trusted as a man of wisdom, equity, and mercy, lover and friend of mankind, whose character, personality, and authority inspire confidence and give a sense of security in these troublous times."

At the luncheon which followed the graduation exercises, Cardozo gave an informal talk in which he used a phrase in reference to himself which has often been quoted—too modest a phrase, yet indicative of that course of incessant and undeviating labor which eventually brought him to the seats of the mighty jurists whose decisions often maintained our nation's welfare. "I am a mere plodding mediocrity," he said. "I say plodding mediocrity, for a mere mediocrity cannot go far, but a plodding one can go quite a distance."

A few days went by and Cardozo was at Williamstown, gathering in another degree of Doctor of Laws. "We are our own miracles," he told the graduating class, "and we are not to stand aside in hopeful expectation that the miracles we look for will be wrought by others." The avalanche of academic honors went on, heaped upon the man whom institutions of learning sought with delight to honor. A week after the Williams College degree, Cardozo went to Princeton where, in conferring the honorary degree, Dean Trowbridge presented Cardozo: "Master of the clear literary style and with the talent for incisive statement, expert for the promotion of judicial opinion, his pen is the perfect instrument of his candor and discernment."

Among the other recipients of honorary degrees that day was Norman Thomas. Norman Thomas, a Princeton graduate of the class of 1905, had twice been the Socialist candidate for the mayoralty of New York, once for the governorship of the state, and was, at the time, the nominee for the Presidency. In 1930 his book entitled *America's Way Out! a Program for Democracy* had again confirmed that literary reputation established many years earlier when he was an associate editor of the *Nation*. Very fittingly Dean Trowbridge, in writing the citation which was to precede the conferring of a degree of Doctor of Letters, had spoken of him as "the fair and upright advocate of change in the social order" and had added: "Irrespective of party preferences, we join to honor this valiant and distinguished son of Princeton." Not so fittingly, however, the good old Dean had made the slip which Norman Thomas himself has recounted. His letter lies before us.

"I knew Judge Cardozo slightly—I wish I had known him better. There was no event that I recall on the day that we both received honorary degrees at Princeton which would be of significance to your biography. He was, according to custom as the most outstanding of the recipients of honorary degrees, to have received his last. The Dean of the Graduate School in presenting candidates for degrees

[80]

managed to get my citation clipped with some other citation and so passed me over. Thus he reached Judge Cardozo's name, which he prefaced by saying 'And finally' without having read my citation. This caused some flurry and resulted in my being presented as a kind of postscript. The Dean later blamed a Capitalist Clip and Judge Cardozo laughed at the rather amusing situation but made no particularly significant comment of any sort, as I remember. Our talk was of more or less indifferent things. At an earlier period at a small dinner at a friend's house, I had heard Judge Cardozo discuss a great many matters, including capital punishment. I remember, among other things, his vigorous expression of horror at the penal system which led to the serious prison riots at Auburn. He and other judges of the New York Court of Appeals had had to confirm the sentences imposed on the rioters but he was outspoken in his expression of belief that behind it was a system which would have led him or any other man to riot. Doubtless you have further information and more extensive information on this point. He was, as you know, strongly opposed to capital punishment."

Norman Thomas was not the only Princeton graduate to be honored on the day that Cardozo received his degree. There were two others. One of them was Ernest T. Carter, the composer and teacher of music. The other was Robert C. Clothier, formerly the President of Rutgers University. After the degrees had been conferred, Justice Cardozo and President Clothier were engaged in conversation. One of the other guests of Princeton joined them. He was smoking a cigarette. Opening his case, he offered cigarettes to the two men. The Justice declined with thanks.

"I suppose," said President Clothier, turning to Cardozo with a smile, "that Justices of the Supreme Court have no bad habits." Cardozo replied, "None that people know of." But, of course, the Justice never considered smoking or drinking or card playing a bad habit. These were for him merely questions of inclination or of leisure.

The Supreme Court Justice, going the rounds of the universities eager to honor him, might now be regarded as a Circuit Judge. On June 20 he sat on the stands at Williams, and the next day at Princeton. On June 22, with Massacusetts and New Jersey left behind, he attended the Commencement exercises in Philadelphia. There was a very particular pleasure for Cardozo when he was presented with the honorary degree of Doctor of Laws by the University of Pennsylvania. The candidates were presented not by the Dean or by a professor, but by various distinguished alumni. In Cardozo's case, Justice Owen J. Roberts, Cardozo's colleague in the Supreme Court, had been chosen to present him. Justice Roberts had more than once disagreed with Cardozo in Washington decisions during the early months of Mr. Roosevelt's presidency, but it was with cordiality and full sincerity that he said: "Benjamin Nathan Cardozo, distinguished alumnus of an honored sister institution, scholar, lawyer, jurist; instinct with the traditions and aspirations of the American people, student of their institutions and so a just interpreter of their Constitution and laws, your life has been nobly dedicated to the great cause of administering and perfecting justice among men without taint or stain of any motive, private or selfish; the purity of your character and the great talents you have devoted to the service of your fellows, evoke the admiration and gratitude of all men."

This presentation may have been unique in Commencements. Certainly, in the record of American universities, there has been no finer tribute from one Supreme Court Justice to another. Equally certainly the phrase which brought Cardozo the most quiet pride was that in which Justice Roberts characterized him as "instinct with the traditions and aspirations of the American people."

Cardozo was immensely pleased by all these honors from many institutions of learning. Profoundly a scholar, recognition by the world of scholarship delighted him, though in his private correspondence he treated himself with humor and levity as if he were a kind of traveling salesman, or rather a traveling collector of degrees. He liked to joke about his honors, but he was far from regarding them as light matters. They were the very acceptable rewards of a scholar's career.

But of all the honors which came to Cardozo from great institutions of learnings, there was none which gave him the gratification he felt the day he received the following letter:

My dear Chief Judge

Nothing has given me more pleasure and satisfaction in years than the prospect of your unanimous election on Monday next to be a Trustee of Columbia University taking the place long and honorably held by the late Dr. Walter B. James. We look upon you as our most distinguished Columbia contribution to public life during your academic generation and we shall value more than I can say your intimate cooperation in shaping the policies and reaching out toward the ideals of the Columbia that you know and love so well. With warmest regard, I am,

Sincerely yours,
NICHOLAS MURRAY BUTLER.

The next day Cardozo replied: "Your letter brings me pride and pleasure. I hold it a great honor to be a Trustee of Columbia, and one peculiarly gratifying to one of her loyal sons. I doubt my ability to contribute any considerable service, but I will do the best I can. The service, however slight, will be a joy, which will be emphasized by the fact that I shall be serving as your aide."

Cardozo's acceptance thus confirmed, he became, a few days later, chosen for an office held by his great-granduncle, Rabbi Seixas, in the days of George Washington.

To Mrs. E.R.A. Seligman, Cardozo wrote: "I feel very proud of my new title, though I am as ignorant as anyone can be of matters pedagogical. . . . Perhaps the consciousness of such ignorance is not a bad qualification for a university trustee. He is the more likely to keep his hands off, and submit to the judgment of the faculty."

How instructors throughout the universities of our land will enjoy these words!

Cardozo's name added distinction to the Board of Trustees but his services were not onerous. When in New York, his attendance at its meetings were faithful. He served on a few committees, one of them appropriately being the Committee on Honors. His most important work was as chairman of the committee advising the trustees in regard to legal affairs. Inexperienced as to the curricular and executive matters of a university, he listened far more than he spoke at the discussions of the trustees. His comments were to the point, but they were few. He was devoted to Columbia, but his significant work was still at Albany.

VI

*All the charm of all the Muses often
flowering in a lonely word.*   TENNYSON

THE War in Europe was in progress. In November, 1918, the Armistice was declared and, two months later, the Peace Conference began its sessions at Versailles. At the close of the conflict the Court of Appeals at Albany was faced with legal problems new to the judges. These problems, many of them arising directly from the War, and others from economic conditions which were the aftermath of the conflict, influenced decisions that could not always lean heavily on precedents.

There was, for instance, the case of Sarah Techt who was suing her sister, Elizabeth Hughes, in order to obtain some New York City real estate that had belonged to their father, James J. Hannigan. Sarah, the daughter of an American, had married an Austrian. According to law, she had taken on the nationality of her husband. Hannigan had died intestate and Elizabeth claimed that, as her sister was legally an alien, she could not inherit the property. The technical point was in her favor as far as statute law was concerned. But what about international law—the law of treaties? Cardozo in rendering judgment declared: "The courts, in refusing to give effect to treaties, should limit their refusal to the needs of the occasion."

[85]

The War, in his judgment, had not nullified the entire treaty between Austria-Hungary and the United States. Portions of it, dealing with the rights of aliens, maintained their central value. Very clearly the Judge pointed out how, while treaties of alliance fall by reason of war, treaties of boundary, treaties regulating the conduct of hostilities, do not fall. "The efficacy of treaties during wartime is lost only if the execution is incompatible with war."

Cardozo saw no justice in refusing to give her father's property to an American-born woman living in America, a woman who, like her husband, had never by act or word been disloyal to her country. As there was no "rigid formula" to nullify all or nothing of our treaty with Austria, the courts, said Cardozo, "in determining whether this treaty survived the coming of war, are free to make choice of the conclusion which shall seem the most in keeping with the traditions of the law, the policy of the statutes, the dictates of fair dealing and the honor of the nation."

In this case, decided in 1920, there was no dissenting voice among the members of the Court of Appeals. A year later, however, Cardozo was almost alone in his dissent in a case again having to do with the World War. Judge Cuthbert Pound was the only other dissenter, his objection being briefly stated, while Cardozo's went to considerable length. The point at issue was whether New York State might constitutionally issue bonds to be sold for the purposes of bonuses to soldiers and sailors who had been honorably discharged. Cardozo began his dissent with a sentence taken from the Constitution of New York.

"The credit of the state shall not in any manner be given or loaned to, or in aid of, any individual, association, or corporation." These words, the other judges thought, were applicable to the proposed bonus. Cardozo's contention was that such payments, though in one sense gifts, were more profoundly "voluntary assumption of liabilities"

The Dream

As I slept t'other nights in the old arm chair
A little black spirit to me did appear.
And as he kept hovering over my head
He spoke a few words and thus to me said
Come arouse thee get up for by the bright Sun
I sware, you shall write in Ad's album
There is no use in saying you have'nt the time
For I am here now and will help you to rhyme
Then out of his pocket he drew forth a pen
And handing it to me said sir now begin
Seizing hold of the pen, for I never knew fear
The subject said he sir said I the New Year,

Begin Sir
          Each coming year brings new delights
     What now is that-, twas Aunty said good night

Aunty I wish you had not said good night
You have aroused me from a worlds delight.
Both spirits & dreams have flown away
Perhaps to come some other days
And when they do I promise truly then
     You shall hear more from
                              Master Ben

Verses as a young boy to his Aunt Adeline

whose "animating purpose is not benefaction but requital."
After pages of argument, not without reference to precedents, the Judge wrote: "If the soldiers had not suffered
and the sole purpose of the bonus were to reward them
above others, the reward might be said to have no basis
except gratitude, a free offering of thanksgiving untouched
by the admixture of any sentiment of justice." He concluded: "Their service has been coupled with sacrifice,
and from the union of the two there is born the equity that
prompts to reparation."

The opinions drawn upon in the immediately preceding
pages belong to the years 1920 and 1921. Cardozo had now
reached the semicentennial of his birth. At fifty his reputation as a judge was widespread. His opinions were widely
discussed in academic circles and among lawyers. Two
years earlier he had handed down an opinion in the case
of *De Cicco v. Schweizer*—a case, incidentally, which was
later adapted by Arthur Train for a story in the *Saturday
Evening Post*. Professor Corbin of Yale discussed the Judge's
opinion in the *Yale Law Journal*, taking issue with some of
Cardozo's points, and Cardozo wrote to him:

"I cannot avoid the belief that there is more importance
than you seem to discover in the distinction between a
promise made to induce *A* not to *break* his contract and a
promise to induce *A* and *B* not to *rescind* by joint consent.
If Count Gulinelli on the morning of the wedding, as the
wedding party was entering the church, had told his future
father-in-law that unless he got $100,000 he would humili-
ate the daughter by making a hasty exit, I think we should
all be looking for some way to nullify a promise thus ex-
torted. We should then have what you yourself call a black-
mail contract, using the word, of course, in a popular or
loose sense. Between such a contract and a contract not to
rescind, I find a wide difference. It is important, however,
not to treat the mere form of the promise as controlling.

Otherwise, the blackmailer could attain his end through ready means of evasion. We must look to the substance of the transaction. In determining what the substance was, I think it is an important consideration that the promise was for the benefit not of one party, but of both. There is nothing in the case in question to suggest the probability that the Count had threatened to break his promise. The implication rather is that the father appreciated the fact that husband and wife would need some aid in the battle of life, and that he promised this aid to them to induce them to proceed.

"When I read the many and divergent articles in law reviews for many years past on this branch of the law, I am not surprised that there should be disagreement about my opinion and about the line of argument which it follows. I am consoled by the thought that its essential justice cannot be doubted. It seems a monstrous thing to say that at such a crisis in the lives of others, one may throw dust in their eyes, may blind their vision of the future, and their insight into its difficulties and dangers, and yet be heard to say thereafter that the inducement must count for nothing."

Not many months after this defense by Cardozo of his opinion, Professor Corbin and the other editors of the *Law Journal* asked Cardozo to give the Storrs Lectures at Yale. Cardozo declined the invitation, saying that he had no message to deliver, but asked for permission to call upon the faculty at the Law School and get acquainted. "We immediately invited him to come," relates Professor Corbin, "and very soon there was a delightful discussion with him in Dean Swan's office in old Hendrie Hall. Again Cardozo said that he had no subject on which to lecture, that he had 'no message to deliver.' Thereupon I said to him this: 'Can't you tell our students how you decide cases, the sources to which you go, and the process by which you arrive at a decision?' He cocked his head to one side for a

moment, and then replied: 'I believe that I could do that.'
. . .

"He entitled his lectures, 'The Nature of the Judicial Process'; and he delivered them during the year 1920 in the college lecture hall known as Lampson Lyceum, containing perhaps 500 seats. . . . The first lecture was attended by substantially our whole student body and faculty, with not many outsiders. At the end of that lecture, Judge Cardozo smiled, closed his manuscript, and sat down. The entire audience rose and stood, vigorously applauding. After a moment, Cardozo rose and bowed, with his charming deprecatory smile, and again sat down. Not a man moved in his tracks; and the applause continued with no abatement. The Judge saw that he would have to make the first move. With the same brilliant smile, evidently greatly surprised and greatly pleased, he left the platform and departed through a side door with members of the faculty. Not until after his departure did the applause cease or any man in the audience leave the room.

"This identical performance was repeated after each of the three succeeding lectures, culminating with greater intensity at the last one. At each lecture the audience had increased in size, until at the final one the room was crowded to the doors."

Cardozo began his lectures with a series of questions. "What is it that I do when I decide a case? To what sources of information do I appeal for guidance? To what proportions do I permit them to contribute to the result? To what proportions ought they to contribute? If a precedent is applicable, when do I refuse to follow it? If no precedent is applicable, how do I reach the rule that will make a precedent for the future? If I am seeking logical consistency, the symmetry of the legal structure, how far shall I seek it? At what point shall the quest be halted by some discrepant custom, by some consideration of the social welfare, by my

[89]

own or the common standards of justice and morals? Into that strange compound which is brewed daily in the caldron of the courts, all these ingredients enter in varying proportions. . . .

"We may," said Cardozo, "try to see things as objectively as we please. None the less, we can never see them with any eyes except our own. To that test they are all brought—a form of pleading or an act of Parliament, the wrongs of paupers or the rights of princes, a village ordinance or a nation's charter."

Further on, we come to the philosopher's eternal statement that nothing is stable, nothing absolute. "All is fluid and changeable. There is an endless 'becoming.' We are back with Heraclitus." Yet if nothing remains in its original form, the perpetual flux cannot wash away the intangibles. The spirit of man persists through and above and beyond annihilating waves of time. And with the spirit of man, the obligations of men. A weary logic may point to the futility of human effort, but Cardozo still felt commanded to the search for "the essential and the permanent" in the field of justice.

In addressing a group of young men there would have been too great a self-denial had Cardozo not allowed himself some play of wit. "Judges," he told them, "differ greatly in their reverence for the illustrations and comments and side-remarks of their predecessors, to make no mention of their own. All agree that there may be dissent when the opinion is filed. Some would seem to hold that there must be none a moment thereafter. Plenary inspiration has then descended upon the work of the majority. No one, of course, avows such a belief, and yet sometimes there is an approach to it in conduct." Then, after referring to "crevices and loopholes" he had with "due contrition" discovered on rereading his own opinions, Cardozo added: "The persuasion that one's own infallibility is a myth leads by easy stages and with somewhat greater satisfaction to a refusal to ascribe infallibility to others."

The introductory observations in the first of the lectures at Yale flowed on without break into "The Method of Philosophy," as applied to the judicial process. This method based on analogy, or—to quote the dictionary—a resemblance of relations, similarity without identity, Cardozo differentiated from other methods he was later to discuss. They included evolution, or historical development; tradition, or the fruitage of custom; and sociology, the method interested primarily in "justice, morals, and social welfare."

While agreeing with Holmes that experience, and not logic, is the life of the law, Cardozo impressed upon his hearers that, "in default of other tests," the method of analogy must be followed so that favoritism and chance might be excluded and decisions be reached, when possible, with "serene and impartial uniformity." He illustrated by specific cases the theories advanced as his discussion proceeded. There was, for instance, the murderer who "lost the legacy for which the murder was committed because the social interest served by refusing to permit the criminal to profit by his crime is greater than that served by the preservation and enforcement of legal rights of ownership." Here a "compelling sentiment of justice" dictated the decision of the court.

But history, tradition, and sociology, the second of these Yale lectures insists, should play their parts in arriving at judicial opinions. Historical research explains and lightens "the pressure that the past must exercise on the present, and the present upon the future." Cardozo's study of history, his familiarity with the writings of countless authors on law and sociology and philosophy, left him aware that "there are vogues and fashions in jurisprudence as in literature and art and dress." Yet there ever remains "a standard of right conduct" conditioned by the habits and beliefs of living men and women. "Life casts the molds of conduct, which will someday become fixed as law. Law preserves the molds, which have taken form and shape from life."

If anyone of any political party in America still regards Benjamin Cardozo as even remotely a "radical" or too liberally a "liberal," let him study the Yale addresses. Cardozo had reverence for the past. He was, it must not be forgotten, an aristocrat by descent. Certainty, order, coherence, that make for the "symmetry of the law," meant to him much what a sonnet means to a poet. He had the Greek love for form. But form may degenerate into formalism. "There is an old legend," he told his audience, "that on one occasion God prayed, and his prayer was 'Be it my will that my justice be ruled by my mercy.' That is a prayer which we all need to utter at times when the demon of formalism tempts the intellect with the lure of scientific order."

Following in the footsteps of Holmes, Cardozo would not allow any fixed and formalistic interpretation of the Constitution to pervert his understanding of the essential meaning of the word "liberty" in the Fourteenth Amendment. Yet nowhere is the conservative value of the Constitution more eloquently set forth than where Cardozo says: "The great ideals of liberty and equality are preserved against the assaults of opportunism, the expediency of the passing hour, the erosion of small encroachments, the scorn and derision of those who have no patience with general principles, by enshrining them in constitutions, and consecrating to the task of their protection a body of defenders. By conscious or subconscious influence, the presence of this restraining power, aloof in the background, but none the less always in reserve, tends to stabilize and rationalize the legislative judgment, to infuse it with the glow of principle, to hold the standard aloft and visible for those who must run the race and keep the faith."

This is English in the grand manner. At the time that Cardozo was giving this lecture at Yale, a Harvard man who had studied law at Columbia was practicing his profession in New York City. Eight years later he became the Governor of the state. Another four years, and he was elected to the presidency. One can visualize Franklin D. Roosevelt, when still a lawyer, reading and pondering Cardozo's address. It closes with these words: "The law is yet in the making or, better perhaps, in the remaking. We cannot doubt that its newer form will bear an impress of social needs and values which are emerging even now to recognition and to power."

In Cardozo's audience were young men who had fought in the Great War so recently ended. Many of them, doubtless, had felt the flame of President Wilson's idealism, urging them to their soldier's task. But the League of Nations was not progressing in safeguarding democracy for the world. America had withheld its cooperation. Wilson was no longer the leader, the hope, almost the idol in a war-torn world. A pathetic yet noble figure, the discarded paralytic knew that his immediate successor in the White House was a friend of predatory interests blocking the path of social advance. Reaction in high places was in progress during that postwar period when the youth of America, after the hateful and disillusioning life of the trenches, were still looking forward to a finer order of things in the national life. How natural, then, that the young fellows at Yale felt the inspiration of Cardozo's address! Here was clarity; here was practicability; and here, exciting and inciting them with the supreme magic of words, was spirituality. Small wonder that the hall was thronged when the third lecture took place.

After further emphasis on the value of the sociological approach, after illustrations of how logical consistency can fail to result equitably, Cardozo took up the question of the judge as a legislator. "We do not pick our rules of law full-blossomed from the trees. Every judge consulting his own experience," said Cardozo, "must be conscious of times when a freer exercise of will, directed of set purpose to the furtherance of the common good, determined the form and tendency of a rule which at that moment took its origin in one creative act. . . . The mind of the judge should be directed to the attainment of the moral and its embodiment in legal forms . . . The standards or patterns of utility and morals will be found by the judge in the life of the community."

To think from the minds of others, to try to feel with the feelings of others—this is the way of intelligence and generosity. Cardozo's mind was never shut to this truth. Like Holmes, he was unwilling to allow his own predilections, his own traditions, his personal attitude, to be the determining factors in his decisions. However subconsciously a man is affected by such considerations, the function of the judge is "to enforce by his decree the customary morality of right-minded men and women." Similar should be the approach in the enactment of statutes. "Experience and study and reflection" should guide judge and legislator alike in the exercise of their duties. The judge "legislates only between gaps. He fills the open spaces in the law . . . Within the confines of these open spaces and those of precedent and tradition, choice moves with a freedom which stamps its action as creative. The law which is the resulting product, is not found, but made."

There is nowhere a suggestion that the judge is an entirely free agent, entitled to overthrow statutes or to disregard precedents. He is an exponent and interpreter whose judgments may make imperative new codes of social advance. "He is not to innovate at pleasure," Cardozo said, in concluding his third lecture. "He is not a knight-errant, roaming at will in pursuit of his own ideal of beauty or of goodness. He is to draw his inspiration from consecrated principles. He is not to yield to spasmodic sentiment, to vague and unregulated benevolence. He is to exercise a discretion informed by tradition, methodized by analogy, disciplined by system, and subordinated to 'the primordial necessity of order in the social life.' Wide enough in all conscience is the field of discretion that remains."

In the fourth and last of these Yale lectures Cardozo discusses adherence to precedent, and the subconscious element in the judicial process. Here was closer revelation of the speaker himself. A clear expositor, a judge whose opinions have been studied with admiration by the entire legal profession, now characteristically confesses his own misgivings and uncertainties. He says, in one of those frequently quoted passages which cannot be omitted in a portrayal of Cardozo: "Reason plausible and fairly persuasive might be found for one conclusion or another. Here comes into play that balancing of judgment, that testing and sorting of considerations of analogy and logic and utility and fairness, which I have been trying to describe. Here it is that the judge assumes the function of a lawgiver. I was much troubled in spirit, in my first years upon the bench, to find how trackless was the ocean on which I had embarked. I sought for certainty. I was oppressed and disheartened when I found that the quest for it was futile. I was trying to reach land, the solid land of fixed and settled rules, the paradise of a justice that would declare itself by tokens plainer and more commanding than its pale and glimmering reflections in my own vacillating mind and conscience. I found with the voyagers in Browning's 'Paracelsus' that the real heaven was always beyond. As the years have gone by, and as I have reflected more and more upon the nature of the judicial process, I have become reconciled to the uncertainty, because I have grown to see it as inevitable. I have grown to see that the process in its highest reaches is not discovery, but creation; and that the doubts and misgivings, the hopes and fears, are part of the travail of mind, the pangs of death and the pangs of birth, in which principles that have served their day expire, and new principles are born."

Cardozo knew that "the real heaven was always beyond." But he knew, too, as Browning knew:

> Ah, but a man's reach should exceed his grasp
> Or what's a heaven for?

VII

*The law hath not been dead, though it hath
slept.*   SHAKESPEARE

CARDOZO was amused to find in his mail one morning a
letter which read: "Dear Judge Cardozo, I read in
the newspapers that you are a liberal judge. Will
you send me ten dollars, as I'm really very hard up."

However the writer of the letter may have interpreted
the meaning of the word "liberal," Cardozo himself much
distrusted labels of any sort, partly because they tend to
become fixed and rigid in their connotation, partly because
his intelligence was broad enough to realize that truth cannot be pinned down to a single category. Passionate convictions were, he knew, the special prerogative of youth; yet
in commenting to Judge Hand on the paper he had written
on Socialism for his degree of Bachelor of Arts, Cardozo
said, smiling, there was nothing left of Socialism when he
had finished the paper. "Conceited young snips," he added,
"who dispose in this manner of important questions."

Cardozo's skepticism, Judge Hand remarked, was one of
the great things about his wisdom. "You think," said
Judge Hand, "that something is the a priori truth and then
it comes back to you in another setting. Ben Cardozo could
not endure imposing upon the quivering flesh of humanity

[97]

an iron mold. I have seen him, again and again, shying away from a commitment in general terms. In the fluidity of his ideas he was a child of his time as few judges are. As with Holmes, there was no absolute for him."

This man whom William Lyon Phelps had referred to at Yale as "the pattern of judicial learning and judicial temper in the leading law schools of our country" was beginning to pay increasing attention to the business of justice as it was being administered by the courts and taught in the law schools. The good ship *American Jurisprudence* had some unworthy timber, relics of the past. There were leaks through which tricky waters could enter. Crafty hands might use the technique of legalism to affect the compass. In various ways justice might be deflected from its true course. But a truce to our metaphors. The point is, American law was in need of restatement.

In December, 1921, the Association of American Law Schools held in Chicago a meeting that was to have far-reaching importance. Its purpose was to set in progress an investigation of how, through the cooperation of all the elements in legal spheres, the administration of justice might be advanced. On invitation of the committee then formed, another meeting was held the following year in New York where a group of representative judges and teachers of the law, together with a few distinguished lawyers, decided to establish a permanent organization.

A committee headed by Elihu Root, with George W. Wickersham as vice-chairman and William Draper Lewis as secretary, immediately engaged on an investigation financed through the generosity of the Carnegie Corporation of New York. During the summer months of 1922 study and discussions continued. Among those taking part were deans of the various university law schools and such famous judges or lawyers as Charles A. Boston, Charles C. Burlingham, Benjamin N. Cardozo, Frederick R. Coudert, John W.

Davis, William D. Guthrie, Julian W. Mack, John G. Milburn, Cuthbert W. Pound and Roscoe Pound, Harlan F. Stone and Henry W. Taft. Judges, teachers, lawyers—all were aware that much was amiss with the administration of justice. Through its uncertainty in many instances, through its complexity in others, it not only frequently baffled, annoyed, or angered the members of the bar and the bench but, in leading to essential injustice, frequently became a public danger. Disrespect for the law had become aroused not in radical groups alone, but generally. This disrespect might easily become, in the words of the committee, "the cornerstone of revolution."

Unnecessary litigation, delay, the expense of lawsuits— all these were defects in addition to the fundamental defects of frequent uncertainty and complexity in the law itself. If legal ethics were to be kept to the standard which these high-minded men had in view, all lawyers should be encouraged to develop recognition of the public function that was theirs to perform "in relation to the improvement of the law and its administration." All teachers of the law should, through their knowledge and experience, aid judges as well as lawyers.

"Justice Benjamin N. Cardozo," explains Dr. William Draper Lewis, "was a member of the Committee on the Establishment of a Permanent Organization for the Improvement of the Law, which led to the organization of the American Law Institute. Justice Cardozo became a member of the Institute, a member of the Council, a member of the Executive Committee, and also vice-president at the organization meeting in February, 1923 . . . He spent a great deal of time over the development of the most difficult chapter in the Conflict of Laws, namely, that which relates to the administration of estates."

The American Law Institute was Dr. Lewis's idea, although "practicability," he states, "was put into it by Elihu

Root." Of all the advisers, Dr. Lewis considered Cardozo the most important. His mastery of the law of torts and his interest in the conflict of laws were of fruitful service in both the earlier and the later stages of the Institute's work. Cardozo, through his skepticism, contributed to the discussions a caution that was important in preventing over-generalizations of the law. His first guesses were almost always right. He would follow these with analysis and reflection, but when once Cardozo had reached a decision, it was almost impossible to budge him. Friendly discussions he enjoyed. During the conflict of minds, while others at the meetings might say "bosh" or "nonsense" or "all wrong" to the observations of their fellows, Cardozo was ever conciliatory and courteous; but this did not render him less stubborn when his mind had finally been made up. However, his quiet manner frequently calmed troubled waters when discussion became excited.

February 23, 1923, saw the establishment of the American Law Institute. A notable gathering of judges, lawyers, deans of law schools, and other teachers of the law met at Washington. The Institute was founded with Dr. Lewis as the Director. Elihu Root was chosen as its Honorary President. George W. Wickersham became the President, Cardozo the Vice-President, and George W. Murray the Treasurer. Nineteen men, distinguished at the bar or on the bench, were elected to the Council. Among them were Harlan F. Stone, Learned Hand, John W. Davis, John G. Milburn. This group of leaders in association with a score of distinguished professors—Bates, Bohlen, Williston among them, have during the last sixteen years clarified the processes of law and strengthened the cause of justice through the publications of the Institute.

While valuable results were foreshadowed from the outset, the Institute did not escape criticism in its incipiency. Cardozo, who throughout the summer of 1923 had worked hard on the project, replied to this criticism both lightly and seriously at the dinner in Washington on February 23, 1924. Introduced by the Chief Justice, William Howard Taft, Cardozo began in light vein:

"We come here," he said, "to commemorate not a death but a birth. A year ago today our infant Institute was born into the world with such a host of indulgent godfathers as would have spoiled a child of weaker fiber. At once upon his coming the great things that he would do were foretold in the family circle and straightway published to the world. Learned doctors of law, as many it would seem as ever gathered under a single roof, inspected him, measured him, weighed him, and forthwith declared that given ten years of life with proper training of the mind and nourishment of the body he would be ready at the end of the decade to relieve lawyers of the need of studying, judges of the need of thinking, and suitors of the need of worrying—if not altogether, at least in some appreciable degree. Needless to say, this forecast was received with loud acclaim. The greatest masters in the universities were at once retained with instructions to come together, fight out their differences in private, and impart to the infant the strained and clear residuum of undiluted truth that would survive these high contentions. Guides and mentors and critics and advisers were selected to hold the masters in check and to receive reports at frequent intervals of the progress of the prodigy. Never since the days of the younger Mill was there a scheme of education so considered, so comprehensive, so exacting, so intensive.

"Well, a year has gone by and the child is still alive. Its character has not been spoiled by adulation, its temper has not been soured, even though at times it may have heard an echo of the wrangling of its masters, and tonight its guides and mentors, surveying the reports of work already done, of progress already made, mindful that nearly a year of the fateful decade has gone by, look forward to the decade's end with hope and faith and loyalty undimmed. If these men whom we heard today and whose inspiring report has filled us all with a sense of mastery and power, if these men are incapable of restating the law, then the law is incapable of being restated by anyone.

"What is it they are trying to do? What is it that this Institute, if it even faintly realizes the purpose of its godfathers, may be expected to accomplish? I find among its critics—for critics are not lacking—a curious insistence upon contradictory grounds of opposition. Some tell us that its touch will blight. It will sterilize and wither. It will absorb the native juices that make for healthy growth. The books that it writes will be not only closed but clasped. The law, in yielding to its embraces, will be turned into a statute, perfect but immobile. The prophecy is cheerless, yet at least we must say that it is a tribute to our power. We need not fear, if this be true, that our infant, arriving at maturity, will descend to the position of a harmless drudge, a negligible nobody, to be forgotten or ignored. A second band of critics attacks us from another flank. The arrows with which they have armed themselves have been dipped in the poison of contempt. What troubles them is not that the Institute will do too much. They pity us for all our effort and hubbub and commotion, for they foresee with assurance that in the end we shall accomplish nothing. The restatement with all its promise of cooperative effort will turn out, they say, to be a one-man job like the one-man opinions which we hear of in appellate courts. The bar and the bench will resent as an intrusion the entry upon the scene of a new force which pretends to a composite wisdom. I have even been assured that such plans are alien to the spirit of a democratic form of government. They suggest a monopoly or at least an aristocracy of learning. Better the path of ignorance, blazed by individual initiative, than this imperial highway with signposts so commanding. But the final thrust is worst of all, its poison most corrosive. Your great highway, if you build it, will be already obsolete when it is finished. Your restatement will be no sooner made than it will have to be torn down, and made over. You are the Sisyphus of the century. It is all futility and vanity.

"Let us see whether there is anything in these criticisms to make us pause upon our course. I recur to the image of the statue, pitiless and changeless. I have loved the living law too well, I have followed and studied too long her changing moods and phases, the lines of her growth, the vital processes of her being, to be willing to give her up for any marble simulacrum. The trouble with criticism of this order is that it is founded in misconception of the whole project of restatement. . . . The judicial process . . . is a technique that is founded upon the experience of judges and not a technique that is founded upon the interpretation of authoritative texts. They fancy that we shall impose shackles, when we seek to loose and free. They fancy that we are building a new labyrinth in which justice will be imprisoned, when we are seeking to give a key to the ancient labyrinth from which she has long cried to us for outlet and escape. This will be no code to be fought over and dissected as if its every line were invested with authority, a deliverance from on high with every word inspired. This will be merely considered counsel and advice, fallible doubtless, and at times we may assume erroneous, but conceived, nonetheless, in the high and scientific spirit of a disinterested quest for truth—considered counsel and advice of experts from all the groups, universities and bench and bar, that have a hand and a voice today in the making of our law."

In the next few passages of his address Cardozo dwelt on the forward-looking contributions of great American jurists of the past, great teachers of the present. "Did Kent in his day congeal the flowing waters of jurisprudence? . . .

Did Story prove a repressive or a liberating force? . . .
These reverberating echoes refuse to be silenced by derision.
. . .

"I am not moved or deterred, therefore," Cardozo went on, "by those who say that our work, when it is finished, will be still unfinished, that when made it must be remade, that the flux is inevitable and endless. I should despair of the work of our hands if I thought that we meant to prostrate ourselves before it as before something closed and perfect. I spoke in jest, at the beginning, of the coming of the good time when lawyers and judges might cease to think and study. Better that they should stray as they are straying in the wilderness of precedents with all the snares and entanglements and underbrush of dicta, than that they should lose the divine impulse to move onward and upward in the slow and toilsome process of renewing the foundations and the structure of justice upon earth."

The address—here given only in part—came to an end. The Chief Justice arose. His ponderous body, almost three hundred pounds of Taft, contrasted with the slender form of Cardozo. His broad smile was engaging, though its appeal was of another kind than that of Cardozo's ever-diffident smile. "I am sure," said the Chief Justice, "that everyone who has had the privilege of hearing and following the distinguished jurist in this beautiful, powerful, analytical address, in which he gives us the reasons for the faith that is in him in this great work, rejoices that he has been here."

Taft, in thanking the preceding speakers of the evening, had expressed appreciation for the "inspiring address" by Secretary of State Hughes and "great pleasure" at having heard Judge Faville's words. When the Chief Justice thanked Cardozo he introduced the warmer personal note, the note of rejoicing at the man's presence. It is easy to understand this. It is how so many persons felt whenever the semirecluse joined their company. There was an other-

[104]

worldly quality about Cardozo. For all the sorrow of his life, there was "something afar from the sphere of our sorrow." People felt finer, or at least felt the desire to become finer, when he was among them. We all felt it.

Cardozo's faith in the possibilities of the American Law Institute has been justified by the years. If Elihu Root was the greatest leader in the work, which has so thrived under the direction of Dr. Lewis, if distinguished teachers of law have contributed quite as valuable service to the Institute as did Cardozo, his address at that dinner in Washington still remains the clarion call in an undertaking of immeasurable worth to American justice.

Throughout his years in Albany the Judge kept in touch with the needs of instruction in the leading law schools of America. His correspondence of 1923 refers, in a letter to Nicholas Murray Butler, to his satisfaction with the progress being made in the Columbia Law School under the deanship of Harlan F. Stone.

"I read your annual reports," he writes, "with never failing delight. Presidents of all kinds, whether heads of universities or heads of States, should take them for a model. If that were done, official messages would cease to be a synonym for prosy platitudes. I would not write, however, merely to tell you this. What moves me to trouble you now is that in your last report you make some observations upon the study of the law which have interested me a good deal. I have had occasion of recent years, partly through my work on the bench and partly through contact with professors in the law schools, to gain some pretty definite impressions about the tendencies of the universities, including Columbia, in the development of legal thought. I have felt that I might be pardoned in putting my impressions before you for whatever they may be worth. I am quite convinced that within the last fifteen or twenty years the study of the law has been filled with a new spirit, that this spirit is animating more and more the work of bench and bar, that it is based upon a new conception not wholly articulate as yet but gradually gaining form and definiteness, and that the universities have been the place of its origin, the home of its nurture.

"Of course, there is much that remains to be done. I have no doubt that this is what you meant to emphasize by your report, though perhaps a careless reader might fancy that you did not appreciate the work that has been done already. To appreciate is, after all, less important than to stimulate and arouse. I have tried in a small way myself to bring home to bench and bar an understanding of the truth that our progress must be irregular and stumbling until we arrive at some agreement about fundamentals, until a sound legal philosophy shall rationalize the judicial process. I feel, however, that I owe a large debt for the little that I have learned and done to the men in the universities, who, far from shirking these problems, have brought them into the foreground where they can no longer be ignored. I am proud and happy that in this work the law school of Alma Mater takes rank among the best."

The year 1924 marked the close of Cardozo's first decade on the bench. In Europe, the Ruhr Valley had been occupied by the French, against the protest of Russia, who saw in the occupation the threat of future wars. The German Republic was carrying on a struggle against the hard conditions of the Versailles Treaty. Lenin died and the dictatorship of the Soviets passed into the hands of Stalin. By 1924, the last of the American Expeditionary Force had left the Rhine, and the United States was attending to business as usual. Woodrow Wilson was dead, and with him died, in great part, all popular effort to further American participation in the League of Nations. Harding was dead, fortunately for him thus to escape the corrupt revelations of those associates who had betrayed his confidence. Calvin

Coolidge had, at early dawn in his father's Vermont farm-house, taken the presidential oath. There had been strikes, one involving over 125,000 railroad shopmen. Labor unions were increasing in power. The struggle between capital and labor, the difficulties of farmers, did not, how-ever, greatly interfere with the general prosperity of postwar days. Before 1924 had ended, a bull market saw over 11,000,000 shares change hands on the New York Stock Exchange within one week.

Cardozo did not join his fellow countrymen in the mad carnival which later reached frenzied heights before the col-lapse in 1929, with its 16,000,000 shares in a single day. When the pillars of finance crumbled into humiliating dust he remained largely unscathed. The Judge never gambled or even bought common shares. His earnings and savings were invested mainly in bonds and in real estate first mortgages. Watching the ways of high finance, he was intent, in so far as his decisions could avail, to prevent vultures of capitalism from finding meshes through which to escape the law's restraining net, while at the same time he did not wish to make "a scarecrow of the law":

> Setting it up to fear the birds of prey,
> And let it keep one shape till custom make it
> Their perch and not their terror.

Cardozo's business was justice. While, in the closing months of 1924, the tide of speculation was rising, the Judge returned to the college of his youth and delivered one of his most illuminating addresses at the installation of Dean Hugh W. Jervey, Harlan Stone's successor as the head of Columbia's Law School.

"I entered the Columbia Law School," he told his listeners, "in the days when the Dwight system prevailed. I left it in 1891 as a startled and bewildered class was trying to thread its way through the mazes of a new system which descended upon it overnight . . . with my going went, too, the old business college of my day and of the days before me. The business college stage was succeeded by a new one, which, for lack of a better name, I may call the stage of legal science. Dean Stone in a recent address styled it, more happily perhaps, the Period of Survey . . . No longer did the student learn by rote out of a textbook some hasty and imperfect generalization, swallowed whole as it was given him. He was put to work at the sources. With the cases themselves before him, he analyzed the facts, dissected the reasoning, criticized the conclusion. . . .

"A decision of the Supreme Court, a fortiori or, I suppose, more reasonably a decision of the Court of Appeals, is no longer a postulate to be accepted. It is a thesis to be debated. It is no longer a starting point, a premise for new deductions. It is food for criticism and discussion. If there is anything evil in this tendency, it is overborne by the good . . . The great scholars of the universities with their organ of expression in the university law reviews have given us for the first time a body of critics as sleepless as they are alert. There are now watchmen upon the towers . . . I often ask myself disconsolately what is the origin, the secret, of their power, what subtle emanation issues forth from the halls of universities to fill them with its essence. I think the answer must be that they never dull the edge of learning by the rust of inaction and indifference. Judges follow often, and properly enough, the line of least resistance. If they see a clear basis for giving judgment for one party or the other, they put off the evil day when some other question, more difficult or doubtful, may drive them to the unpleasant duty of making up their minds. Not so the teacher of law. He runs out to meet the difficulty which the court has timorously shunned. He is not oppressed by that sense of responsibility which comes to judges who know that the opinions they are rendering will make law not only for the parties, but for

[108]

others to come later. Our teacher has no such fear. He does what so few of us do, he thinks his problems through. . . .

"Law is no longer thought of as something cabined and confined in a narrow compartment of its own to be opened only by the specialist. We are looking at it more and more as a means to an end; and in thus looking at it, the conviction is gaining ground that there can be no adaptation of means to ends without knowledge of many things that lawyers have at times neglected, without scrutiny of many forces, social, economic, ethical, as well as legalistic. The university has fulfilled a part, and a part only, of its task when it has gathered a company of scholars steeped in knowledge of the history and content of the legal precepts of the past. The task remains to discover and formulate a principle of growth that will give sanity and justice to the law of the present and the future. The school of legal science becomes a school of philosophy, a school of jurisprudence . . . In the cathedral of law, as in the cathedrals of a living faith, the consecrated labors, the hopes and prayers and yearnings and aspirings of multitudes that have gone before us, some of them remembered, many more of them forgotten, have been built into the walls, and speak their message yet to the ears of the devout. Other things, indeed, have been built there too—errors and superstitions and cruelties and hatreds. The blight of decay is on them, and they crumble with the years. The walls stand firm withal. Spire and minaret and dome still struggle toward the skies."

The address had come to an end. In summoning up the picture of the cathedral of law Cardozo had fittingly drawn on a symbol of religion for the metaphors of his faith. Justice was not only Cardozo's business. It was his religion.

VIII

THE summer of 1922 was drawing to its close—months during which Cardozo had labored assiduously in tilling the field whose harvests were to be the illuminating publications of the American Law Institute. It had already become known that Justice William R. Day was soon to retire from the United States Supreme Court. President Harding was considering his successor. He had previously appointed former President Taft and Senator Sutherland, leaving only two Democrats on the tribunal at Washington. Charles Evans Hughes had resigned from the Court in 1916, to run against Woodrow Wilson. In 1922 the present Chief Justice was the Secretary of State. No New Yorker sat in the Supreme Court.

President Harding desired to name Nathan L. Miller, the Republican Governor of New York, who, however, was unwilling to accept. He was then asked by Mr. Harding's representative to suggest names of other New Yorkers. The Governor suggested three: Chief Judge Frank H. Hiscock of the Court of Appeals, the famous lawyer William D. Guthrie, and Benjamin N. Cardozo. Justice McKenna was then seventy-nine years old. Justice Holmes was eighty-one.

There was a feeling that no old man should be appointed. Judge Hiscock perhaps shared this feeling. In any event, he told the Governor that he was sixty-five years old and that the change would not be agreeable to him. Mr. Guthrie, with his enormous law practice and his important duties in the New York Bar Association, was likewise unwilling to go to Washington. Cardozo, however, would at that time have welcomed the appointment.

On September 9 the *Syracuse Post-Standard* published an editorial whose concluding paragraph stated that if the President intended to consider a New Yorker, and that New Yorker a Democrat, Cardozo was the man. This was the first time his name was editorially recommended for the Supreme Court.

Immediately a movement developed in behalf of Cardozo. Among those who started it was Morris J. Hirsch, Cardozo's lifelong friend to whom the Judge wrote: "You're a brick and true as gold but no gold brick either." Governor Miller had informed Mr. Hirsch that "he would exert himself in the interest of Judge Cardozo" and had given permission to have his promise of support relayed to William D. Guthrie. That leader of the bar proceeded to show his enthusiasm through active collaboration. As Chief Judge Hiscock was known to be interested in the *Syracuse Post-Standard*, which had editorially advocated Cardozo's nomination, two of the three men suggested by the Governor —Hiscock and Guthrie—could now be reported as in favor of the Governor's third choice.

Within another two weeks a large number of distinguished lawyers signed the proposed endorsement. However, the terms in which the endorsement had been phrased led to various criticisms from some of the signers. One of them wrote: "It is like the candidate—too modest. As I had occasion to tell Mr. Cardozo himself, he'll find that his chief supporters are not only those who have been associated with him at the bar, but especially those who have been opposed to him in the legal arena. He possesses the rare quality of being able to,make not only friends but admirers of his very opponents." Said another: "My criticism of it is that it is too colorless and without sufficient ginger. I think, in his case, there is occasion for the use of superlatives, and that the statement that he is the best qualified nominee for the position in years by common consent is not a whit too strong."

Cardozo, however, would not agree to any superlative phrase. He was much gratified at the outset when friends sent him the editorial from the upstate Republican paper, but, taking it somewhat lightly, wrote that he would have two copies of the editorial framed with his golf records. He took his golf—he played an awful game—equally lightly. As the movement gained headway, the Judge became increasingly interested. When early in October the rumor spread about that Martin T. Manton, of the United States Circuit Court of Appeals, was scheduled for appointment to the Supreme Court, Cardozo, showing astonishment, doubted its verity. Other New York jurists were being mentioned, one of them an associate of Cardozo's. In this situation he was being urged by his supporters to have a talk with the Governor. With his invariable sense of dignity he wrote: "I don't want to see Miller. I feel I ought not to take the position of an active candidate. That is especially so with another aspirant for the place in my own court." The campaign in his behalf went on, the Judge following with close interest the activities of George Wickersham, and particularly of Mr. Guthrie who was already discussing the subject with the New York senators. However, the person of greatest influence with President Harding was his intimate friend, Attorney General Daugherty. Mr. Daugherty was not in favor of Cardozo, and other Republicans of influence in Washington also were opposed to the appointment of a man who was both a Democrat and a Jew.

Cardozo had written to Mr. Hirsch: "If the bar wishes me, that is their affair. I shan't be a bit disappointed if the prize goes elsewhere." Certainly he made no personal effort to obtain the nomination, but equally certainly he would have been delighted to receive it.

Among his associates at Albany Cardozo's reputation, already firmly established, gathered much weight that same year, despite various of the opinions in which he dissented from the decisions of the Chief Judge. His preparatory work and his great background of knowledge often led him to know more about the details of a case than the lawyers themselves. "I used to tell him," said Judge Hand, "that he was unfair to the bar. He anticipated it all. 'Who is this man,' the lawyers would say, 'who knows it all beforehand?' He would sometimes interrupt at the commencement of an argument, his question indicating that he knew what the lawyers were going to say much further on."

But Cardozo's reputation extended beyond American law circles. Gradually his opinions were becoming known as far away as Australia, where, according to H. V. Evatt, the decisions of the Albany court, "although only of persuasive authority in Australia, came to be cited to and used by some of the judges of the courts of appeal. On one occasion, the High Court adopted the reasoning of the New York court on an important question of principle affecting the interpretation of workmen's compensation legislation, and rejected a contrary ruling of the English Court of Appeal."

Cases coming before the court at Albany frequently brought in the individual human note as contrasted with the more general constitutional questions of the later years at Washington. Frequently, also, Cardozo's human approach led him to the less formalistic interpretation of the law. An instance in point was that of a suit of Arthur Wagner against the International Railway Company. He and his cousin Herbert were standing on the platform of a car that

[113]

ran between Niagara Falls and Buffalo. The car was so crowded that they had no choice. At a curve in the road approaching the bridge Herbert was thrown off. His cousin jumped out to go to his aid. The jury in the lower court had relieved the Company of responsibility for the consequent injuries to Arthur, inasmuch as he had of his own accord walked on the trestle.

In his opinion Cardozo wrote: "Danger invites rescue. The cry of distress is a summons to relief. . . . The law does not discriminate between the rescuer oblivious of peril and the one who counts the cost. It is enough that the act, whether impulsive or deliberate, is a child of the occasion."

When Cardozo said that Arthur Wagner had not gone on the bridge "to view the landscape," we should like to have read the thoughts, to have seen the face, of the counsel for the International Railway at this touch of irony. Should the normal act of a relative's solicitude result in the deprivation of normal rights by reason of a far-fetched legal technicality? Not so, thought Cardozo, and not so his associates who doubtless enjoyed the seldom indulged-in scorching touch of Cardozo's irony. The verdict was directed against the railroad.

That same year Cardozo wrote the dissenting opinion in a case where the *New York Times* was being sued for libel. While obtaining a divorce Mrs. Abigail Bishop saw her reputation smirched by her husband who accused her of drunkenness and taking drugs to such an extent that she was virtually insane. Her little girl was affected by these charges. They led the child to such a dislike for her mother that she wanted to leave her. Though there was no doubt of the pain and unhappiness suffered by Mrs. Bishop, and though the jury in the first instance had believed that the newspaper accounts were libelous, the Court of Appeals, in its majority opinion, decided that the jury had been prejudiced by the woman's grief and that the recital of the little girl's reaction should carry no weight as to the awarding of damages. In Cardozo's eyes it was bad enough to be even slightly discourteous to any woman; but to defame a woman to an extent that her child should turn against her was revolting. His feelings thus affected, he instinctively sought legal arguments to protect the rights of Mrs. Bishop and he characterized the majority opinion as resulting in "a restriction of liability for the consequences of defamatory writings to which I am unable to assent."

Two other decisions of that year one would not willingly forego. Both had to do with writings, but writings very different in nature. Both were handed down on the twelfth of July. One of these publications was the "Left Wing Manifesto" issued and distributed by Benjamin Gitlow, a violent Socialist who was attempting to foment strikes throughout the United States. He was undoubtedly an enemy of the government which he was hoping to overthrow. He was seeking the collapse of the entire capitalistic system. He might well be regarded as an enemy of the commonwealth. Yet, as no violence had resulted from his fulminations, Cardozo, together with Judge Cuthbert Pound, agreed that he was protected by the Constitution in his use of free speech. When the case reached the Supreme Court, Holmes and Brandeis took the same point of view in their dissenting opinions. Gitlow went to prison, but Cardozo had once again shown his profound attachment to the Bill of Rights, despite his abhorrence of the doctrines held by the man he defended.

The other case of a publication brings us to those days when now comparatively innocent sex novels were attacked by the New York Society for the Suppression of Vice. It is almost funny to recall that the beautifully written novel by Théophile Gautier was considered obscene. Books permitted to go through the mails during the past ten or fifteen years would make *Mademoiselle de Maupin* read, in comparison, like a Sunday-school tract. In deciding that the book-store clerk who had sold this novel had violated no law, Cardozo agreed with Judge Andrews and their other associates in regarding Gautier's novel as a work of art whose passages concerning passion did not interfere with its permanent value as literature. The decision was important in opening the way to the publication of a flood of books where sex relations are discussed with a frankness that often shocked Cardozo's sense of delicacy. Yet the Court of Appeals is not a court of censorship, but of law interpretation. As long as writings were not manifestly salacious, with salaciousness as the predominant motivation, the principle of liberty of expression must prevail.

Cardozo's appreciation of style, his love of literature, of course affected his decision that it would be absurd to make a French masterpiece unavailable to the American reading public. In agreeing with his fellow judges in the case of Arthur Wagner, and in dissenting from them where Abigail Bishop was concerned, his human feelings had manifested themselves in characteristic manner. In none of these cases did he fail to find legal arguments to sustain his contentions.

Subtle interpretations, Cardozo remained aware, should, however, not be attempted when the law itself was clear. Here emotions of sympathy must give way. If, in 1922, Cardozo ruled in favor of Arthur Wagner against a railway corporation, in 1923 he wrote, with no more hesitation, an opinion in favor of the Cunard Steamship Corporation. He was humanly sorry for Luke J. Murray, a second-cabin passenger who had suffered a severe accident on the *Mauretania*. But the steamship ticket contained in its contract a clause to the effect that, in case of injuries, the Company must receive written notice within forty days after the passenger had left the ship. Murray's lawyer pleaded that his client had not read the terms, and offered as further excuse for delay in notification that Murray had been for many weeks in a hospital in Ireland.

Cardozo wrote: "Even if we were to assume in his favor that there was incapacity for a time, with a resulting extension of the period for notice, he did not make a move within forty days thereafter. Limitations of this kind have their justification in the need of some safeguard to protect the carrier against fraud. Passengers on steamships scatter in all directions when the voyage is at an end. If claims may be presented at any time within a term of years permitted by the statute of limitations, the opportunity for investigation will often be lost beyond recall."

The law was clear. The poor chap who had been injured received no damages. His had been an unfortunate act of omission. There was nothing to be done about it. The wealthy corporation had its just rights. They must be protected.

One case of the year 1924 shows in marked manner Cardozo's insistence on the sacredness of family life. Is it going too far to suggest that his attitude was affected by those traditions which always carried much weight with the people of his own race? The Jews, thrown back upon themselves in centuries of ghetto existence, have observed the ties of family with especial devotion. A poor woman, Mrs. Matejka by name, was the wife of a workman in a New York factory. Among their many children was little two-year-old Ellen. The child was taken to Buffalo, in 1920, by her aunt Mary, housekeeper to a wealthy family that lived in the outskirts of the upstate city. These people—Bistany was their name—became attached to the child and kept her in their home for two years, taking the first legal steps toward adoption. They then claimed that the mother had abandoned the child, having left her so long in their keeping. Mrs. Matejka contended that, what with so many other children to take care of, and with subsequent childbirths, she had been willing to have Ellen benefit by her stay with the Bistanys, but they should not have refused her request for the little girl's return home.

Cardozo, in reversing the decision of the trial judge, admitted that Ellen might possibly be better taken care of by the wealthy people who wished to become her foster parents than in the crowded home on the East Side of New York, but he did not admit that she had been abandoned. He insisted that the actual parents had not lost their rights. There was dissenting opinion among his associates, yet not sufficient to override Cardozo's contention that the family circle should not be broken into.

Another case of the same year shows Cardozo and his associates passing on a constitutional question directly affecting the amusement-loving public of New York. Did the statute enacted two years earlier destroy any private rights when it stipulated that theater tickets must not be sold at an advance of more than fifty cents over the regular price? The Albany court decided that the business of selling theater tickets was a business of public interest and that the statute, accordingly, was constitutional. Cardozo was not dissuaded from this point of view despite the eloquent argument of Louis Marshall, a personal acquaintance. However, as Mr. Pollard has pointed out, Marshall was later to argue a similar case successfully before the conservative justices in the Supreme Court during President Harding's administration. The earlier case remains an interesting illustration of that social point of view which led Cardozo to interpret the Constitution as a living organism whose main motive is the benefit of the general public.

In another case during 1924 we see the Judge, despite his distrust of Socialism, and his repugnance toward Communism, deciding in favor of a Russian citizen as against one of the most powerful of New York's financial institutions. The Soviet Republic had seized the deposits in the Petro-

Cardozo at the age of twelve

(Facing page 118)

grad branch of the National City Bank. Thereupon the Bank disclaimed responsibility in connection with $30,000 deposited by Sokoloff. But the American government had not yet recognized the Soviet government, and the action of the Communist leaders could thus not be regarded as the act of a sovereign state and could not therefore legally affect, in American eyes, the corporate life, and with it the corporate obligations, of the Bank. International and local law were clear in the matter, and the opinion written by Cardozo was the unanimous opinion of the Court of Appeals. The curious individual point in this case has to do with the necessity faced by Morris Hillquit as lawyer for the plaintiff. The Socialist leader was in favor of the Russian Revolution, but in order to achieve a decision for his client, Hillquit had to argue that the decrees of the Soviet were, in this instance, to be considered void.

In the same year—1924—Irving Lehman, another Columbia jurist, joined the Court of Appeals. Cardozo and he had long been friends. The closer association of Albany led to the intensification of a friendship that found its culmination when, during Cardozo's final days, Lehman's home was made his. The two men were sympathetic in many ways—both of them modest, generous, and gentle. Apart from the bench, they had many intellectual interests in common. On the bench they sometimes, though not often, disagreed. The younger judge was on one occasion the sole dissenter. The case was that of Robert Dean against his wife Amelia, a decidedly interesting case involving laws of Canada and the United States.

Dean had left his wife and children in Ontario. Claiming she had refused to follow him to Pennsylvania, he then obtained a divorce on the ground of desertion. She did not oppose the suit, because she did not know it was pending. Five years after her marriage she moved to Buffalo where she learned what had happened. She sued for divorce.

Could the Court of Appeals at Albany negate the action of the Pennsylvania court even though it had been misled by the charges made by her husband, charges that did not at the time come to her knowledge? Judge Lehman thought not. It seemed to him that New York State, with no jurisdiction over the marriage of Robert and Amelia Dean, might be acting against public policy in upsetting the decree of a sister state. Yet the conflict of laws did not prevent the decision in the wife's favor. "An abandoned and defrauded wife," wrote Cardozo, "asks us to maintain her status as it was fixed by the law of her domicile at the date of the fraudulent decree. We cannot say that conceptions of public policy and justice require us to change it."

The Dean case belongs to 1925. And other cases of that year and the next greatly tempt discussion. Cardozo's inherited respect for religious sentiment is beautifully brought out in the opinion forbidding the removal of Yome's body from Brooklyn's Holy Cross Cemetery. "A benevolent discretion, giving heed to all those promptings and emotions that men and women hold for sacred in the disposition of their dead, must render judgment as it appraises the worth of the competing forces . . . Only some rare emergency could move a court of equity to take a body from its grave in consecrated ground."

In the Yome case the conflict to be resolved was between the perhaps temporary sentiment of a wife and the permanent sentiment and the centuried customs of the Roman Catholic Church. Cardozo pondered both, paid honor to both. The latter weighed more in his scales of equity. Doubtless less difficult of decision was another case of that year. There we meet the Judge and his associates far removed from the quiet resting places of the dead. We are again in the world of business, of subterfuges for the purpose of profit. A brokerage firm is acting in the sale of some New York City real estate. Unknown to the seller, the purchaser, using a corporation controlled by him as the ostensible buyer, is a member of the real estate firm that consummates the sale. "As broker for the seller," said Cardozo, "the duty of this fiduciary was to make the terms as favorable to his employer and the price as high as possible. As president and manager of the buyer corporation, its sole representative in the transaction, his duty was just the opposite . . . If dual interests are to be served, the disclosure to be effective must lay bare the truth, without ambiguity or reservation, in all its stark significance." Cardozo, strictly emphasizing the implications of business honor, allowed the claim of the property's original owner.

IX

A man of letters amongst men of the world.

MACAULAY

BENJAMIN CARDOZO was always an indefatigable worker, putting in twelve to fourteen hours a day at his desk. But while he gave unstintingly of his energy to his work on the bench, other activities required at least a share of his time. More and more he was in demand as an orator, after his first lectures in book form had attracted wide attention to him as stylist and philosopher as well as man of law.

From the days when that earnest young tutor, Horatio Alger, had shared with him his literary enthusiasms, Cardozo had been a confirmed lover of books. Reading both the classical authors and the significant moderns, his style developed. The oratory of Cicero, the younger Pliny, Epictetus on the "Power of Speaking," were familiar to him before his instructors recommended them. Edmund Burke, Thomas Hobbes, John Locke were among the young lawyer's evening companions. In the pages of Jebb he walked with the orators of Athens whose words he knew in their original Greek. From fellow Americans, preeminently William James and John Dewey, he gained a clearer view into the philosophy of pragmatism which, mingling with his own idealism, was to bring forth so much of near and far value in Cardozo's pronouncements as a judge. With undeviating vision he pursued his quest, learning, to use his own words, "that the quest is greater than what is sought."

At the age of thirty-three Cardozo had his first book published. *The Jurisdiction of the Court of Appeals of the State of New York* remains the authoritative work on its subject. As a factual handbook it covers the field. In addition, there will be found in it characteristic touches of style as, for instance: "The wrongs of aggrieved suitors are only the algebraic symbols from which the court is to work out the formula of justice." The court, Cardozo maintained, "exists not for the individual litigant." The wide-reaching principle, the profounder equity, the more general advantage—these must be the basis for the structure of justice, when in the interpretation of law, conflict arises between private and public rights and benefits.

In 1921, after the conclusion of the Storrs Lectures at Yale, they were collected and issued by the Yale University Press, with the title *The Nature of the Judicial Process*. When Judge Cardozo was informed by Professor Corbin that they wanted his manuscript for publication, he demurred, relates Professor Corbin, "showing real doubt and hesitation, with some half-humorous remarks that the publication of his lectures might destroy his usefulness as a judge or even lead to impeachment. I was told that within a short period some 3,000 copies had been sold to the bar of New York alone. Anyone who reads the book can see why so many bought it and also why it did not result in impeachment. Instead, along with his opinions and subsequent lectures, it eventually translated him to the Supreme Court of the United States. It was an electric flash from the high heavens, clearing away the murk, illuminating the purpose and methods of the law, and spreading broadcast the stimulating ozone of Cardozo's style, thought, and personality."

The book was an astounding success. It went through edition after edition, to become one of the most widely read publications from the pen of an American jurist.

In 1924 the Yale University Press published a second book of lectures which Cardozo had delivered the previous December before an intent and enthusiastic audience at New Haven. Quiet talks, wise talks, of literary grace but with no flamboyance. When these lectures were issued in book form Cardozo, in an Introductory Note, stated that they were to be regarded as a supplement to the lectures given at Yale in 1921. He added that "some thoughts, imperfectly developed in the first series, seemed to call for fuller and more explicit statement in the second, even at some risk of repetition." The book, under the title *The Growth of the Law*, discussed in critical manner the need of scientific restatement, of constructive legal philosophy, of methods of judging, and the functions and the ends of law. The lectures were complementary in that the earlier addresses, *The Nature of the Judicial Process*, were given over primarily to exposition, while the latter group were in the main critical. It is tempting to give a synopsis, or at least to review at length, these illuminating talks of 1924 which evoked such high praise throughout the American law world. Let us, however, limit ourselves to the selection of passages illustrating personal qualities of Cardozo and, very especially, his literary style.

First, then, a sense of humor. The Judge had one or two impoverished relatives, to whose support he contributed as far as possible without their knowledge. Neither to them nor to anyone else could Ben Cardozo be condescending. Yet, in discussing the relationship of various approaches to judging, he wrote: "We might recognize the kinship if we chose, but always in the spirit of condescension that is due to poor relations." Again, while problems of philosophy were ever in his mind, he quoted the remark addressed by

[124]

the Duchess of Marlborough to Voltaire. "I thought the man had sense," said the Duchess, "but I find him at bottom either a fool or a philosopher."

Cardozo's overmodesty shows itself frequently in these lectures; for instance, where he writes: "The passing years have not brought to me the gift of wisdom, but they have at least opened my eyes to the perception that distinctions which in those early days seemed sharp and obvious are in truth shadowy and blurred." The sense of justice which was his passion is made evident in one quotable phrase after another. "Justice remains to some extent, when all is said and done, the synonym of an aspiration, a mood of exaltation, a yearning for what is fine and high."

Cardozo displays, in the footnotes, his indebtedness to many contemporary writers on the law, and in the body of his addresses he draws on illuminating phrases from the pens or the lips of Holmes and Brandeis and Pound, of Bergson and Dewey and Keynes and Frankfurter, and of many others. French, Russian, and German writers are quoted, and even one Chinese—Dr. John C. H. Wu, who revered Justice Holmes and profoundly admired Justice Cardozo. When Dr. Wu published his notable volume of legal essays, Cardozo's was among the first of the names of various jurists inscribed on the dedication page. Because of his own felicity of phrase, it was unnecessary to draw upon others as frequently as he did. That he chose to do so, to give credit to others where their thoughts coincided, was part of the man's essential courtesy.

For us the main interest in these addresses rests less in their evidence of the growth of the law than in the growth of the author's literary style. In his decisions from the bench there are comparatively few metaphors and similes. Early public addresses, including the 1921 lectures at Yale, disclose a fair number of apposite and delightful figures of speech. But Cardozo became more and more the man of letters as his first decade on the bench drew to a close. The addresses published in 1924 contain literally scores of phrases enriched by metaphors. In discussing the fecundity of case laws, and in indicating the confusion involved in the multiplication of decisions, the Judge, still recognizing the value of adherence to precedents, wrote: "We did not sacrifice any of the brood and now the spawning progeny, forgetful of our mercy, are rending those who spared them." A little further on he leaves behind him the Malthusian theory and resorts to natural history in the insect field for another metaphor where he says that "we shall be caught in the tentacles of the web, unless some superintending mind imparts the secret of the structure, lifting us to a height where the unity of the circle will be visible as it lies below. The perplexity of the judge becomes the scholar's opportunity."

Pursuing the thought that a "spurious consistency" is sometimes "preserved by artificial and unreal distinctions," Cardozo goes to religious rites. "The idol is discredited but he is honored with lip service, the rubrics of the ancient ritual." Then, as the first of these lectures reaches its conclusion, a verse from Omar Khayyám may have led the Judge to suggest to his hearers that "the inn that shelters for the night is not the journey's end. The law, like the traveler, must be ready for the morrow. It must have a principle of growth."

In the second of these lectures Cardozo has, near the outset, recourse both to military movements and to mythology. "Neither lawyer nor judge, pressing forward along one line or retreating along another, is conscious at all times that it is philosophy which is impelling him to the front or driving him to the rear. None the less, the goad is there. If we cannot escape the Furies, we shall do well to understand them."

"There have been two paths ever open," Cardozo wrote

of the difficulty of choice, "though leading to different goals. The fork in the road has not been neutralized for the traveler by a barrier across one of the prongs with the label of 'no thoroughfare.' He must gather his wits, pluck up his courage, go forward one way or the other, and pray that he may be walking, not into ambush, morass, and darkness, but into safety, the open spaces and the light." Cardozo admits his own doubts, his own difficulties in a choice where regularity according to ancient precedents comes into conflict with the promptings of what may be a wider justice. "Judges march at times to pitiless conclusions under the prod of a remorseless logic which is supposed to leave them no alternative. They deplore the sacrificial rite. They perform it none the less with averted gaze, convinced as they plunge the knife that they obey the bidding of their office. The victim is offered up to the gods of jurisprudence on the altar of regularity."

The lover of Homer, the lover of Greek literature, knew the cruelty and the futility of those ancient sacrifices from which he took his illustration. In his next metaphor he leaves the altar for the harvest field, suggesting how "the field of private law always will yield one crop or another with the method which the husbandman applies."

But no method is perfect: "We shall say to ourselves that it is vain to seek a sovereign talisman; that the treasure box does not spring open at the magic of a whispered word; that there is no one method of judging, supreme over its competitors, but only a choice of methods changing with the changing problem."

Cardozo's figures of speech give evidence of the wideness of his culture, his intimacy with writings old and new in many fields. In discussing the decision in the case of *Wyoming v. Colorado*, irrigation, mining, and manufacturing—the economic use of water—entered into the argument. In showing where the argument led, "Here," writes Cardozo, "we

[127]

have the conscious departure from the known rule and the deliberate adoption of a new one in obedience to the promptings of a social need so obvious and so insistent as to overrun the ancient channel and cut a new one for itself." Where could one find a more apposite metaphor?

More winning, perhaps, is the one where, a little further along, Cardozo evokes a picture. "Justice," he says, "is not to be taken by storm. She is to be wooed by slow advances." . . . "We shall see," he writes in one of his closing sentences, "that our little parish has its vistas that lie open to the infinite."

The magic of words never lost its potency for Cardozo. Whenever possible, he was surrounded by books. In writing to his cousin Annie he described how he missed the sight of books in a house which he had rented for the summer. "You must be happy in Professor Conklin's house with its bookish atmosphere," he said. "Last summer I occupied a house where there was hardly a single shelf of books. It gave me such a strange feeling, as though one were camping out in savage islands. This summer's landlord seems to have some recognition of the fact that there are such subjects of human concern as literature and science. I breathe an ampler air."

"I haven't read as much as I expected," he wrote to her on another occasion, "though Lord knows I had plenty of time. I give a good many hours to the study of Italian which I began last summer, promptly forgot during the winter, and am now trying to regain. These forced plants of the mind—languages studied intensively in a couple of months and then laid aside—are like the forced plants of the conservatory—they wither pretty quickly. Some seeds are left over, none the less, and perhaps they can be induced to sprout.

"I have been gathering together a half dozen or more essays and addresses which I have written in the last five or six years, and Harcourt, Brace & Co. will bring them out as a volume, but the publication will probably be delayed until the beginning of next year. Some of them are hardly worth preserving, but there are one or two that I would not willingly let die. Publication in a magazine is equivalent to burial after a few years have gone by."

Paradoxes of Legal Science, a collection of lectures delivered at Columbia, was published in 1928 by the Columbia University Press. "Stability and Progress," "The Meaning of Justice," "The Science of Values," "The Individual and Society," "Liberty and Government"—these were some of the subjects discussed in the suggestive and illuminating manner of the earlier addresses at Yale. "I heard the first lecture with great satisfaction and shall be delighted to study the entire volume," President Butler wrote to Cardozo. The Judge replied: "I have a wretched, sinking feeling as I survey the bound volume. How did I ever bring myself to believe that the lectures were worth publishing? That is always my feeling at the beginning. I can only hope that time will soften it."

The last of Cardozo's books was *Law and Literature*, issued by Harcourt, Brace & Co. Dedicated to "the sacred memory" of his sister Ellen—Ben's beloved Nell—it is one of the most distinguished volumes in the record of American letters. Seven addresses make up its contents. From these eloquent pages it would be easily possible to educe the mind and character of the author.

"I am told at times by friends," the book begins, "that the judicial opinion has no business to be literary. The idol must be ugly or he may be taken for a common man." Aware that "philosophers have been trying for some hundreds of years to draw the distinction between substance and mere appearance in the world of matter," Cardozo doubts "whether they succeed better when they attempt a like distinction in the world of thought. Form is not something added to substance as a mere protuberant adornment. The two are fused into a unity."

In the foregoing quotation we have Cardozo's avowal of faith in the essential value of literary style. He recognizes that "the sovereign virtue for the Judge is clearness," but it is not the only quality to be sought. "The opinion will need persuasive force, or the impressive virtue of sincerity and fire or the mnemonic power of illustration and antithesis or the terseness and tang of the proverb and the maxim. Neglect the help of these allies and it may never win its way." Then going on with the metaphor drawn from the game of golf which Cardozo played so poorly: "Traps and obstacles and hazards confronted us on every hand. Only blindness or indifference will fail to turn, in all humility, for guidance or for warning to the study of examples." Cardozo's humor soon becomes manifest where, in discussing various types of writing, he paraphrases the famous speech of Falstaff: "There is a type magisterial or imperative; a type laconic or sententious; a type conversational or homely; a type refined or artificial; smelling of the lamp, verging at times on preciosity or euphuism; a type demonstrative or persuasive; and finally a type tonsorial or agglutenative, so called from the shears and the paste pot which are its implements and emblem."

There are a few qualified critics who consider some of Cardozo's opinions as falling into the class of what he himself termed the refined or artificial, smelling a little of the lamp. Cardozo was well aware of the literary style which "had its dangers, for unless well kept in hand, it verges at times upon preciosity and euphuism." But with "due restraint it lends itself admirably to cases where there is need of delicate decision . . . Occasionally it shades into a faint and gentle sarcasm which is sometimes the refuge of a spokesman of a minority expressing his dissent . . . Such a method has its charm and its attraction, though one feels at times the yearning for another, more robust and virile."

Let us admit that here and there in his choice of words Cardozo is somewhat of a purist. Now and then, also, perhaps not without a sense of subtle humor, he selects recherché words so unfamiliar to the common run of men as to leave them, if not critical, at least slightly embarrassed. Yet it is not the shadow of purism, but rather the flame of purity that is impressive. In the second of the papers in *Law and Literature*, originally printed in the *Harvard Law Review* and entitled "A Ministry of Justice," Cardozo's inspiring morality is shown in an exposition very simply set forth and with few graces of style. There he suggests that "some agency must be found to mediate" between "judges left to fight against anachronism and injustice by the methods of judge-made law" and the enactments of legislatures "informed only casually and intermittently of the needs and problems of the courts." Cardozo dwells on how judges are often "distracted by the conflicting promptings of justice and logic, of consistency and mercy" and how "the output of their labors bears the tokens of the strain." He suggests the creation of a committee that should be organized as a ministry of justice. Its members should include representatives "of the faculties of law and political science in institutes of learning, together with representatives of the bench and of the bar." Such a board of law "would enlighten itself consistently through all available sources of guidance and instruction; through consultation with scholars, through study of law reviews, the journals of social science, the publications of the learned generally; and through investigation of remedies and methods in other jurisdictions, foreign and domestic."

Cardozo gives credit to many other thinkers in his field— Professors Moore and Borchard and Chafee and Lorenzen

[131]

and others of like scholarship—in connection with the plan he is proposing. It is a plan that, of course, has as its basis recognition of the necessity of attaining to a higher plane of justice than any yet available to the profession of the law.

Felicities of turn of phrase are less important than what Cardozo calls the "architectonics of opinions—the groupings of fact and argument and illustration so as to produce the cumulative and mass effect." In indicating the technique to achieve this result, in his happy illustrations of such accomplishment, Cardozo shows himself a foremost teacher, not only for lawyers but for writers, of the power and the inspiration of words born of deep thought. Cardozo's style has in it pragmatic implications, is related to attending circumstances, has to do with the expected reactions of his hearers or readers. This is the realist in him. But its chief claim to permanent value as literature lies in beauty of expression flowing from the culture of a student of past greatness in literature, in the culture of a philosopher, a wit, and, essentially, a poet.

"What Medicine Can Do for the Law"—is the subject of one of the papers in *Law and Literature*. Given as an address before the New York Academy of Medicine, it was heard with astonishment as well as admiration by a large group of physicians. Here was a judge who had studied hygiene, who knew the theories of the effect of glands on personality, was familiar with the writings of Jung and Freud, was familiar with special writings on behaviorism, and who could apply studies of all this material to his own decisions as a judge.

"Only the other day," Cardozo told his hearers, "my court had to deal with the propriety of the tubercular test as applied to herds of cattle, the unfortunates who responded to the test being marked for quarantine or slaughter. A question of scientific fact is at the core of other problems juridical, and yet intense, or so I hear, is their emotional appeal. What is a beverage, and when is it intoxicating? Let me not open ancient wounds by a reminder of the answer."

After this light reference to Prohibition, Cardozo became serious in his discussion of the new sociolegal attitude toward crime. Various reforms, suggested by Governor Smith, by Judge Victor P. Arnold, are brought into the picture, in which Cardozo suggests that the present system of punishment for crime is, in many instances, too punitive. "Punishment is necessary, indeed, not only to deter the man who is a criminal at heart, who has felt the criminal impulse, who is on the brink of indecision, but also to deter others . . . The discoverers of the new theory that virtue and vice are synonyms for spontaneous secretions may have overshot the mark." Yet "the present system is stern often when it should be mild and mild often when it should be stern . . . Students of mind and body are insisting as never before, that in much of our criminology there is futility and waste . . . Adjustment of some sort there must be if we are to fill the measure of our duty to our defective fellow beings. Run your eye over the life history of a man sentenced to the chair. There, spread before you in all its inevitable sequence, is the story of the Rake's Progress more implacable than any that was ever painted by Hogarth. The Correctional School, the Reformatory, Sing Sing or Danemorra, and then at last the chair. The heavy hand of doom was on his head from the beginning. The sin, in truth, is ours—the sin of a penal system that leaves the victim to his fate when the course that he is going is written down so plainly in the files of the courts and the stigmata of mind and body."

During the past quarter century there has been progress in the preventive detention of youth and in ways of redeeming the elder criminal. Cardozo looked forward to "the combined labors of men in many callings and most of all of your own" when he called attention to various possibilities of immediate cooperation of physicians in connection with crime and punishment. He showed them how necessary it is for the psychiatrist or the alienist to help judges and juries in deciding between murder and manslaughter. After a fight in which the defendant had stabbed a man who had trespassed upon his property, was his action in killing the victim with an ax a premeditated deed? If so, it was murder in the first degree. Or, "blinded by pain or rage," did the man almost automatically or spontaneously do the killing? Was it a conditioned reflex, as students of behaviorism might say?

Upon the basis of such a fine distinction, "with its obscure and mystifying psychology, scores of men have gone to their death." "I think," Cardozo told the physicians, "it is time for us to speak with authority as to the life of the mind, to say whether the distinction has such substance and soundness that it should be permitted to survive." Some committee there should be "in the Bar Associations, on the one hand, and in this Academy on the other (if none already exists), whereby the resources of the two professions can be pooled in matters such as these where society has so much to gain from cooperative endeavor."

The Judge gave them instances of cases where men or women killed because of the thought that it was a moral duty. There was the case of a priest who slew his paramour, claiming that "he had heard the voice of God calling upon him by day and night to sacrifice and slay." He yielded to the call of "moral duty." The trial judge held that this belief was no defense if he knew the nature of the act and knew it to be wrong in the sense of being prohibited by law. But did not the word "wrong" in that statutory definition refer to the moral quality of the act? Did Mary Lamb, sister of the beloved Charles Lamb, commit a "wrong" when, in a fit of delirium, she killed their mother?

"I am not unmindful," Cardozo told his audience, "of the difficulty of framing a definition of insanity that will not be so broad as to open wide the door to evasion and imposture . . . I am reluctant to concede that science is so impotent . . . Of this at least I am persuaded: the medical profession is at stake, the students of the life of the mind in health and in disease should combine with students of the law in a scientific and deliberate effort to frame a definition and a system of administration that will combine efficiency with truth . . . If Insanity is not to be a defense, let us say so frankly and even brutally, but let us not mock ourselves with a definition that palters with reality."

The next problem discussed is that of euthanasia. Should physicians be privileged to end painlessly the lives of tortured sufferers from incurable disease? Should a man be indicted for murder if he has taken the life of one or more of his fellows for the sole purpose of saving the lives of a greater number? There was the case of the ship *William Brown* which, on its journey from Liverpool to Philadelphia, sank after striking an iceberg. One of the lifeboats was so overweighted by its forty-two occupants—nine of them members of the crew—that, when the boat was in danger of foundering, Holmes, the first mate in charge, gave orders to throw overboard a number of the men. This action saved the remnant when, the following morning, a rescuing boat hove in sight. The grand jury refused to indict for murder but it did indict for manslaughter. Holmes was imprisoned for an act of good faith, though the sentence was for only six months. Similarly when two men, made desperate by hunger, killed and devoured a lad who for days had been adrift with them in a little boat, an imprisonment for months was substituted for the death sentence. "The law," said Cardozo, "falters and averts her face and sheathes her sword when pronouncing judgment on creatures of flesh and blood thus goaded by the Furies."

Another of the addresses in this volume had been delivered to the Third Annual meeting of the American Law Institute, to whose progress Cardozo devoted so much of his mind and heart. His associates and he, in their restatement of the law, have, Cardozo admits, not overcome all obstacles, have not always found "definiteness and assurance and finality in fields where definiteness and assurance and finality must be left to the agency of time." But he believes that they have helped to solve "the age-long problem of uniting flexibility to certainty."

"It is but a human impulse," the Judge tells his associates of bench and bar, "if the framers of a restatement are tempted to declare the law not only as the past has shaped it in judgments already rendered, but as the future ought to shape it in cases yet to come. Those of us whose lives have been spent on the bench or at the bar have learned caution and reticence perhaps even in excess. We know the value of the vague phrase, the blurred edge, the uncertain line. Well, I am strong for them even now, at least in their proper places."

Law and Literature was received with unanimous praise by the critics of the press. Here was a series of essays and addresses of a professional nature, and yet full of interest and inspiration for the wider public. Of course, Cardozo received praise from many judges and lawyers. That of Judge Clearwater may serve as an example. It begins: "Permit me, on my own behalf, and that of the larger element in our American life that is appreciative but inarticulate, to convey my own and their thanks for the trouble you have taken to correct and reprint your essays. As you well suggest, unless ephemera is presented in a form permitting permanent preservation, it disappears into the limbo of forgotten things, and this, in your case, would be a misfortune to humanity. Also, your contributions are characterized by wisdom, breadth of view, charity, charm and clarity." Judge Clearwater had recently been discussing with Lord Haldane "the great flexibility of the English Constitution predicated upon customs of judicial decision and acts of Parliament." He writes to Cardozo: "You will have been an archangel many centuries before our Constitution will be equally pliable."

Cardozo's reply proves in a nutshell his own attitude. "I think," he said, "a written constitution must be construed in a spirit of liberality; if read in any other spirit, there is danger that the strain upon its principles will be too great, with the result that destruction rather than conservation will be the final outcome.

"Of course, the whole question in the end is a question of degree. We must be liberal, but not too liberal. Probably you and I would not differ very often when we had to judge as to the rule for a concrete situation, even if we might formulate the guiding principle a little differently while the problem was merely abstract.

"But the older I grow and the more cases I decide, the less certain I become that I am right about anything. In this flux and uncertainty, it is a comfort to know that I can count upon your friendship as an assured and unchanging good."

This lover of books and lover of music was not really a lover of art, although he enjoyed the company of artists. A. Vincent Tack painted the portrait of the Judge which now hangs in the courthouse at Albany. Cardozo, in judicial robes, is standing behind a table on which his left hand rests. He holds his eyeglasses in his right hand. The pose is natural enough, yet the ascetic and spiritual qualities of the Judge are so accentuated that the picture has an almost unearthly feeling.

"I get a shock every time I look at it," Cardozo wrote to his cousin Annie, "but I think it is interesting none the less and I'm satisfied to have it stand for me in the years to come when I shall be gone as well as those who knew me in the life."

To the artist himself, he said: "You know, when you started this portrait you made me look like the devil. Now you've made me look like a saint."

"He *is* a saint," said Kate Tracy.

Later, when Cardozo was asked whether he would be willing to pose for a talented but impoverished artist, he replied: "After having two portraits painted, and one bust molded, I feel that I must separate myself from the artists for a time. I don't like to say no, but requests for sittings multiply so rapidly that there seems to be no alternative."

Incidentally, the bust referred to was made by a Russian sculptor, Serge Konenkov, an artist whose drawings and wood carvings are notably fine. Copies of the bust were sent to law schools throughout the country. Very interesting it is to compare Konenkov's bronze of Cardozo with the canvas portraiture by Tack. The painter had evoked the poetical, the mystical. The sculptor, on the other hand, felt and brought out the strength of character. The very physique is, perhaps symbolically, that of a strong man. Both the portrait and bust show the profound intellectualist. Studied together they give a completer picture than either can do alone.

Cardozo seldom went to galleries or museums. Sometimes he would see an exhibition at the National Arts Club in New York, going on the invitation of his cousin Annie, or would look at pictures at the Town Hall Club in company with his cousin Maud. But he pretended neither to knowledge of painting and sculpture nor to enthusiasm for them. Even the beauty of nature stirred him less aesthetically than intellectually. But when it came to the art of literature he was, both in appreciation and in creative effort, a devotee. Conversant with French, Latin, and Greek, and not unfamiliar with the Italian language,

[138]

Cardozo was at home with the masterpieces of European literature. Great writings of European countries—England especially—had been known to him since his boyhood days. Of course, there was nothing important in the literature of the law that ever escaped him. The philosophers and the historians were his companions. He pondered their thoughts and he studied their style. The technique of authorship fascinated him.

One day when we were having luncheon at the Columbia University Club, he said, "Tell me, how do you go about writing a book?" At the reply that the beginning was made at the end, the Judge asked, "Why?"

"Something worth while to arrive at. If the ending is good, one is the more encouraged to do all the work leading up to it."

"Don't you plan your chapters in a novel, for instance?"

"No. The characters once created, are left to take care of themselves. I never know beforehand what they are going to do in any chapter, except the last."

The Judge shook his head, no doubt partially in surprise, but perhaps in inadvertent and unconscious deprecation of such a lazy, unworkmanlike approach.

"And when it comes to the actual writing itself," he asked, "do you use longhand or the typewriter?"

"I walk up and down the room smoking a cigarette, and dictating to my secretary who takes the words in shorthand. Next morning the typewritten sheets are corrected."

The Judge sighed. "How I envy you," he said. "I sweat blood over every page."

Of course, this was an exaggeration—one of his characteristic self-deprecating remarks. But it is true that Cardozo —also walking up and down his study, but without a cigarette—wrote and rewrote sentences on sheets of paper. Then, after the phrasing had been developed to his satisfaction, he would sit down to the composition in longhand. The subsequent typewritten sheets needed little correction, so intense had been the search for just the right word, so happy the discovery of the appropriate metaphor. "Revision," Cardozo wrote to his cousin Annie, "is for me a difficult and unpleasant task. When the molds are once fixed, I find it next to impossible to break them up and make a new distribution of their contents." Cardozo hailed his friends among writers—John Erskine, Melville Cane, his cousin Robert Nathan, and a few others—as artists, and called himself "a pedestrian artisan." Well, if he was a "pedestrian," there are many of us who wish we could walk his paths of literary beauty.

It happened that, in spite of his devotion to books, the Judge had never seen the treasures gathered by the elder J. Pierpont Morgan, the greatest collector of modern times. He was easily persuaded to take a few hours off from work. We strolled down Fifth Avenue from his office in Forty-fourth Street—the Judge never walked rapidly—and after crossing Madison Avenue at Thirty-sixth Street, entered the little marble palace of wonder where Miss Greene awaited us. In those days Belle da Costa Greene was the presiding genius of Mr. Morgan's library—a very private library—where now she is the director of an institution open to the public.

The first quarter of an hour was spent in the great room at the east. Bookcases on all four sides reaching almost to the decorated Renaissance ceiling. From the shelves with series of Bibles of many centuries, Miss Greene drew forth the Gutenberg Bible, the monument of early printing with movable type. Block books were then shown to us, and volumes, French, German, Italian, and Spanish, in silver and gold covers, some of them ornamented with ivory reliefs, and others resplendent with jewels—rubies, pearls, emeralds, and other precious or semiprecious stones.

There were manuscripts of the four Gospels with illumina-
tions or fascinating miniatures. In some manuscripts the
letters themselves were written in burnished gold. Hours
of the Virgin, psalters, chronicles, manuscripts portraying
animals—many of these on vellum and beautified by the
loving hands of artists of many centuries. Judge Cardozo,
to whom such treasures were a revelation, listened fascinated to Miss Greene's comments on the provenance of
items gathered for Mr. Morgan from all parts of the world.
He held with reverence the first Folio of Shakespeare's
plays and other great books of English literature—first
editions of *Paradise Lost*, of Bacon's Essays, of Montaigne,
and other famous volumes whose contents had been his
familiars, were, in a measure, a part of his being. But there
was so much more to be seen, and reluctantly he left the
great room.

Passing through the entrance hall with its marbles and
bronzes, we went to the western end of the building. There
it was that Pierpont Morgan received the dealers, the
experts and scholars, who came to offer him their finds
and to report their researches. One can still see the great
financier seated at his table, playing the solitaire that
was Napoleon's favorite game, listening attentively, every
now and then asking a searching question, and flashing his
piercing dark eyes at his visitor. Miss Greene and I told
the Judge various anecdotes having to do with Mr. Morgan's ways as a collector. His passion for amassing treasures
in every field, but always with taste, with increasing knowledge, and with that vision which led him to purchase
generously, confident that the prices he paid would in
future years be considered modest.

Miss Greene remembered the day when a shaft of green
flame darted forth from the fireplace and Mr. Morgan
remarked, "I shot an arrow into the air." Having that
very moment entered the room, "Here, Mr. Morgan," I

[141]

said, "is the manuscript," and I drew Longfellow's verses from my pocket.

For the most part Cardozo's conversation was in the form of questions. He was constantly eliciting information from Miss Greene concerning the enamels and bronzes and the other art objects decorating the room, admiring its paintings—the Ghirlandaio, the Fra Angelico, the Filippo Lippi—pausing to comment on the lovely Virgin and Child by Donatello. Some of these paintings are no longer there, while nowadays the walls are covered with a far greater number of masterpieces. The entire room, though still livable in its aspects, has more of a museum appearance than in the calm days when Mr. Morgan played solitaire there, or the exciting night when the heads of New York's great banking institutions met during panic times to have their leader save the financial day.

Yet not in the room itself did Cardozo show his greatest enthusiasm, his greatest surprise. A door led from its southeast corner into a fireproof vault, housing the literary manuscripts. Row upon row they stood there—the original manuscripts of *Vanity Fair*, *The Virginians*, and others of Thackeray's writings, works of Charles Dickens, the manuscript of *Paradise Lost*, series of volumes of the manuscripts of Burns and of Byron, famous books of French literature, and the greatest collection in all the world of American literary manuscripts.

"Which would you like to see first, Judge?" asked Miss Greene.

"May I not leave it to you?" Cardozo answered.

"No, please, Judge—you say," replied Miss Greene.

"Well, then, if I may, could it be some of Shelley's poems?"

So Cardozo was shown manuscripts of Shelley, and then of Keats—poems he loved. He turned the pages of *Childe Harold* in Byron's difficult handwriting; read "Auld Lang

[142]

Syne" in the flowing script of Robert Burns, marveled at the beautiful handwriting of Thackeray in *The Rose and the Ring*, whose pages were decorated with illustrations Thackeray himself had drawn and colored. It was a feast such as the Judge never had known before. His delight was unbounded. As for Miss Greene, she had never more greatly enjoyed showing Mr. Morgan's treasures. Indeed, she had never been more delighted in meeting any man for the first time.

X

Wearing all that weight of learning lightly
like a flower.   TENNYSON

TOWARD the end of 1926 it became necessary to appoint a successor to Judge Hiscock, Chief Judge of the New York Court of Appeals, who had recently retired. Among the enthusiastic advocates of Cardozo as Hiscock's successor was Judge Elkus, who subsequent to being the American ambassador to Turkey was Cardozo's associate on the Court of Appeals. The former ambassador was, of course, only one of many distinguished lawyers to urge the appointment. But his influence was considerable. His correspondence with Governor Smith brought forth the statement: "I am strong with you for Judge Cardozo." Judge Seabury wrote that there could be no difference of opinion between them as to the great advantage to the court and to New York State of having Cardozo selected, and he proceeded to aid toward the result which eventuated in 1926.

William D. Guthrie gave wise advice in regard to consulting the leaders of both Republican and Democratic parties. Adolph S. Ochs, publisher of the *New York Times*, offered to favor Cardozo's promotion. Charles E. Hughes, now Chief Justice of the Supreme Court of the United

[144]

States, wrote that no one could esteem Cardozo more highly than he did. Yet of all the many missives received by Judge Elkus, the letter from the Vice-chancellor of the University of the State of New York, Adelbert Moot, sets forth most clearly why no other choice could so appropriately have been made.

"Judge Cardozo is a jurist," he wrote. "I use the word 'jurist' with proper consideration, for there are many judges, but only a few of them are jurists. Judge Cardozo has a national reputation, because of his keen, clear-cut opinions, his abundant learning, his discriminating application of his learning, his instructive lectures at Yale, his work in the Law Institute, and other things that might be mentioned, were that necessary. I hope the State Bar Association will have the courage to come right out and endorse him on a nonpartisan basis, as the proper man to succeed Chief Judge Hiscock. I am sorry we must lose Judge Hiscock December 31, 1926, but I shall be reconciled as much as one can be if he is to be succeeded by Judge Cardozo. Could we have such a chief judge as Judge Cardozo for fourteen years, he would certainly add to the high standing of our Court of Appeals in every state in this Union."

Elkus sent Cardozo a copy of the Vice-chancellor's letter. "Many thanks," answered Ben. "Your friend brings a blush of modesty to my youthful cheek."

To Cardozo, 1927 was probably the red-letter year of his life. True, 1932 brought the supreme honor of the Supreme Court, but it brought it to a reluctant candidate. Not so the election to the chief judgeship of the Court of Appeals. It was then that he became the titular leader of the loving and admiring associates of whom in so many ways he had long been the informal leader. In later years he wrote to George R. Farnum, former Attorney General of the United States: "Again and again, in moments of revery, the thought of my association with the justices of

[145]

the Court of Appeals in Albany through many busy and happy years, has brought the mingled joy and sadness with which time sanctifies the past."

Let us pause in this study of a personality to devote a few pages to the review of some of Cardozo's opinions during a single year. The choice falls on 1927 not because his decisions were more valuable then than in some preceding or later period, but because that was the initial period of his chief judgeship.

The foremost interest of surveying the work of a single twelvemonth arises from the condensed picture it gives of the manifold contacts of a judge of the Court of Appeals with questions involving the life of society in its personal as well as its general aspects. Crime of many kinds, labor troubles, civil rights, business ethics, marital disturbances, as well as international affairs, and technical constitutional problems figure in the panorama unfolding itself before the eyes of justice. As we have already said, the human note is sounded in the courthouse, the intimate human interest emphasized far more frequently at Albany than at Washington. However private in his personal life, Cardozo at Albany entered upon the vast stage of business competition, into the arena of sordid crime, and, with sympathy and understanding, into touching little scenes of domestic life.

The month of February offers a group of illuminating cases. That, for instance, of Leon and Elsie Hoadley. They had been married for ten years. They had two children. Then the husband sued for annulment of the marriage as his wife was pronounced insane. She had not been in her right mind at the time of their marriage, though the husband was not aware of it.

The constitutional point leading Cardozo to refuse the annulment was this: the statute was for the protection of the insane party, and had conferred no privilege on the sane partner. What if a man should marry an insane woman, to enjoy her physically, and then, if he so desired, later to cast her aside? Cardozo, with his protective feeling toward all women, shrank with repugnance from the very possibility. He saw, however, that in the case before the court his decision involved the husband in unmerited hardship. It was not fair that a man should be bound to a wife in an insane asylum. Very well, then, let the New York State legislature amend the statute so that the sane partner in marriage might be treated with due justice. Cardozo's suggestion was acted upon without delay. In this case, as in many others, the lawmakers at Albany followed the counsel of the great judge.

In the Hoadley case the decision went against the husband, because the statute as it then stood seemed clear to Cardozo and his associates. For the same reason, the Court of Appeals handed down a decision in favor of a husband who had, in a moment of fury, caused the arrest of his innocent wife. Judge Andrews and Judge Cuthbert Pound dissented. Not so Cardozo. He recognized that the statutes had not yet granted women legal rights in cases such as this. Remedy must lie in legislative action. If Cardozo could have found a way to interpret the law so as to punish the husband's malice, he would eagerly have done so. Not finding it, he adhered to his theory of the judge's function. Precedents established, laws enacted, still were bridges that must not be emotionally swept away. Faulty bridges should be reconstructed by the legislators. *Festina lente*— make haste slowly—was a favorite adage of the Emperor Augustus. Cardozo knew its value.

Opinions made public the same day the Hoadley decision was announced included several of more general interest. We find Cardozo ruling against a taxpayer who had sued New York City in connection with its payment of wages to laborers in public projects. We find him deciding in favor of a man who had sued the *New York American* for libel.

Hearst's publication had printed the man's portrait to illustrate the account of a case of seduction charged against another man. Similarity in names had led to the error. The same day Cardozo agreed in the opinion written by Judge Crane that the court could not interfere with the statute providing for life imprisonment after a criminal had been convicted a fourth time. Too cruel a punishment, undoubtedly, in some instances; but a statute susceptible of only one interpretation and not in conflict with the Constitution remained the law.

The following month—March—brings us to an unusual picture in the Court of Appeals. A Russian refugee has sued the New York Life Insurance Company for 20,000 rubles in connection with a policy which had been issued some quarter of a century earlier during the days of the Czars. A New York statute rendered payment nonobligatory until after American recognition of the Soviet government. Was this statute, in conflicting with contracted rights, unconstitutional? Yes, it was, the court unanimously agreed. No state legislature had power to favor a wealthy corporation and in this manner cancel rights safeguarded by the Constitution. No emergency existed, no international situation, to justify the statute.

The main interest of this case is in its legal actors. Cardozo, the Chief Judge, saw before him two famous men, both friends of his, arguing for the Insurance Company. Charles E. Hughes, previously Secretary of State, and later Chief Justice of the United States, was one. The other was John W. Davis, formerly ambassador to the Court of St. James, and at that time a presidential possibility. Among the opposing counsel were Louis Marshall, one of the foremost lawyers of his day, and Walter Pollak. A constellation of legal stars lighted the Albany courtroom.

Cardozo did not retain for himself the writing of the court's opinion in this case involving constitutional and international considerations. This possibly because distinguished associates of his years as a lawyer—some of them close personal friends—were pleading on each side. The opinion came from the pen of Judge Henry T. Kellogg.

"Our beloved chief," is the way that Judge Kellogg still speaks of Cardozo. "He was one of the most gentle of chiefs, I dare say, the Court of Appeals has ever had, never losing his temper or hurting anyone's feelings in any way. He never criticized an opinion in a sharp way but made suggestions and corrections in so kindly a manner that our feelings could not possibly be hurt. Needless to say, he was always right in his criticisms of our work."

The gentleness stressed by Judge Kellogg is exemplified in an episode related by another member of Cardozo's court. At a luncheon given in honor of Chief Judge Crane, I asked the late Judge O'Brien whether he had ever seen Cardozo angry.

"Well," answered the jurist, "on one occasion we were listening to the arguments of opposing counsel. One of the two lawyers had interrupted Judge Cardozo two or three times while he was giving them his opinion on a point of law. Whereupon Judge Cardozo took the little blotter lying in front of him, and with it tapped gently on the desk. 'When the court and counsel wish to speak at the same time,' he said, 'it *does* seem to me that the court should have precedence.' That," added Judge O'Brien, "is as angry as I ever saw him."

Judge John F. O'Brien became a member of the Court of Appeals the same year—1927—during which Cardozo arrived at the chief judgeship. Governor Smith was not personally acquainted with O'Brien at the time he decided to appoint him. In later weeks the Judge asked the Governor how he had come to name him. With characteristic candor, Al Smith answered, "Cardozo told me to." "Cardozo told me to" was a wholly sufficient recommendation for any appointment to judicial office, however high.

His advice was sought by men in high places as it was by young, aspiring lawyers and writers on law. To one of them, H. H. Nordlinger, the Judge wrote, in regard to a paper on "The Price of Justice": "I am not prepared yet to advocate costs that would compensate for the expenses of a lawsuit. I have seen enough of the judicial process to know its imperfections. I would not lay too heavy a burden upon the unsuccessful litigant. Some of the losses that are incidental to the establishment of rights and the redress of wrongs through the processes of courts should be allowed, as a matter of social engineering, to lie where they fall. Very likely, heavier burdens should be imposed where there is evidence of bad faith or mere dogged perversity."

During proceedings in 1927 at the Albany court there were two decidedly interesting cases in the not always merry month of May. Certainly it was an anxious period for the Waiters' Union affiliated with the American Federation of Labor, and for four waitresses who had picketed a bakery. The girls had joined the union after they had been taken on by the restaurant's proprietor who had informed them that he employed only nonunion workers. Their low wages —about half of that received by waiters and waitresses in the union—led to their joining the union without the knowledge of the proprietor. The subsequent calling of the strike thus had elements of unfairness to their employer.

Judge Crane and two of his associates, therefore, regarded the picketing as unjustifiable, and approved the lower court's order granting an injunction. Cardozo saw no violation of law in the peaceful picketing. The methods by which the strike was brought about did not appeal to him; but he resented more strongly the starvation wages of $8 a week that the waitresses had no longer been willing to accept. By a vote of four to three the Court of Appeals decided in favor of the union.

Aside from the humanitarian angle of the decision, wider

First voyage to Europe

Cardozo at Venice

importance arises from consideration of that chain of judicial pronouncements wherein it is one of the significant links. Prior to the first presidential term of Woodrow Wilson, the Federal courts had been very generous in granting injunctions that nowadays would be regarded as crass violations of the Bill of Rights. Oliver Wendell Holmes and Louis D. Brandeis were magnificent pioneers in the Supreme Court to protect the workingmen of America from what they regarded as unfair interference with free speech and nonviolent acts aimed at improving the conditions of the laboring classes. Cardozo at Albany had for years followed in the liberal footsteps of the greatest two justices among his contemporary predecessors at Washington. When his leadership and his single vote turned the scales in the bakery decision he was continuing to walk true to form in the march of social progress.

Social progress, national or international, as well as relationships among individuals, has in the past hundred years been intimately affected by the march of science. Illustrations of this truism are too obvious and too manifold for detailed recital, yet the radio may be instanced as one of the outstanding influences in "the complexities of modern life"—the phrase is Cardozo's—wherein "one does not know where the ordinary ends and the extraordinary begins." The radio brought to his court the problem whether a steamship company was entitled to damages of thousands of dollars for the nondelivery of a message in cipher. Through inadvertence the translation of the telegram did not reach its destination in the Philippine Islands. As a result, one of the marine company's ships failed to receive a cargo and lost its potential freight profits. Should the Radio Company of America be held liable beyond the price paid for the message? Should the Company have recognized that, because the message was in cipher, it was of importance financially?

[151]

In his opinion, unanimously concurred in by his associates, Cardozo showed his keen understanding of business transactions. Precedents based on "the doctrine that notice is essential" determined his decision, though he saw much in the plaintiff's argument. "The truth seems to be that neither the clerk who receives the message over the counter nor the operator who transmits it nor any other employee gives or is expected to give any thought to the sense of what he is receiving or transmitting. This imparts to the whole doctrine as to the need for notice an air of unreality. The doctrine, however, has prevailed for years, so many that it is tantamount to a rule of property. The companies have regulated their rates upon the basis of its continuance. They have omitted precautions that they might have thought it necessary to adopt if the hazard of the business was to be indefinitely increased. Nor is the doctrine without other foundation in utility and justice. Much may be said in favor of the social policy of a rule whereby the companies have been relieved of liabilities that might otherwise be crushing. The sender can protect himself by insurance in one form or another if the risk of nondelivery or error appears to be too great." Then Cardozo, as ever intent on the clarification and improvement of law, writes in conclusion: "Telegraph companies in interstate and foreign commerce are subject to the power of Congress. If the rule of damages long recognized by state and Federal decision is to give way to another, the change should come through legislation."

The kind of legislation which Cardozo decidedly did not approve was that obtained through lobbyists in special favor whether of individuals or of corporations. When the American Express Company sought to collect from New York City payments no longer due because of the statute of limitations, a bill enacted at Albany did not help the Company. Cardozo framed the argument pronouncing the

[152]

later statute unconstitutional. It was an act of obviously local application and, as such, a violation of the Home Rule Amendment. There was irony in the words Cardozo used in characterizing the purpose and effect of the legislation. So, too, when a police officer attempted, through a special bill, to reach the rank of captain over the heads of other lieutenants. Cardozo saw no reason why through legislative act this officer should escape the usual civil service regulations. Heroism or genius might justify exceptions, but not merely the "plodding virtues" which were, incidentally, the only virtues Cardozo claimed as his own. When the constitutionality of the Soldiers' Bonus came up for decision before the Court, Cardozo, we remember was one of the two judges who argued that the soldiers had the right to be thus favored. Heroism and sacrifice called for special gratitude on the part of the State.

In conferring benefits, or in withholding them, a judge must be "equally solicitous toward the well-intentioned and the evil-minded." Cardozo loathed crime but, like all his associates at Albany, he would not let the criminal be unfairly treated. "However shocking the crime," he must not lose life or liberty "till tried and convicted in conformity with law." So when Thomas Moran was convicted of first-degree murder, on the theory that he was committing a felony in attempting to escape before shooting two police officers, Cardozo's court, deciding that the trial judge had made a mistaken charge to the jury, ordered a new trial. "The judgment is reversed because of basic error . . . There was ample evidence," said Cardozo, "to justify a verdict of deliberate and premeditated murder if that had been submitted." At the next trial it was submitted. The murderer was executed. This case was, of course, somewhat technical. It involved the judicial interpretation of felony, under those circumstances. Cardozo and his associates were, however, reasonably certain that the murderer would get his deserts, without any infraction upon correct or unbiased procedure in the courts.

Conviction for murder was reversed, and a lighter charge substituted in a second trial, in a case unusually pathetic. A poor Italian laborer was waiting at the bedside of his dangerously ill little boy—waiting for the doctor who did not come until after the child had died. The father mistook a twitching in the doctor's face for a heartless smile. The father had told the physician of his son's death—and the man had smiled! There was a knife near by. The father, maddened by grief, in a spasm of enraged resentment killed the doctor.

Walter Pollak, who tried the case before the Court of Appeals, has told us how Cardozo stopped him, so greatly were all the judges affected by the pathos of the poor ignorant Italian's emotional deed. The lawyer was asked not to go on with the reading of the record. "We'll read every word of it ourselves," said Cardozo.

What New Yorker, or for that matter what American, has forgotten the most sensational of all murder cases during the year 1927? Two lovers had acted together in killing the woman's husband. They were tried together. Against this, Ruth Snyder had protested. Because of this, she claimed violation of her legal rights. The case went to the Court of Appeals. Judd had confessed, had given a full account of the ghastly killing. He had made clear how his mistress had inveigled him into becoming her accomplice in the crime. Cardozo saw no unfairness in the trial. No statute made the joint indictment illegal. Ruth Snyder went to the chair.

Two months after that murder the American public was even more avidly reading accounts of an achievement that thrilled the heart of the nation not with horror but with pride. On May 20, Charles A. Lindbergh flew from Long Island. The next day the young captain arrived in

Paris. The poetry of the flight, all that it implied for the spirit of man, stirred Cardozo's imagination. Here, indeed, was a reality, but one that outsoared the crass realities of everyday life.

Quietly going his way, Cardozo followed events with keen observation. He liked to discuss both foreign and domestic affairs with George Engelhard and others of his few intimates. His main interest continued to lie in developments of social significance and legal advance. In those days he was still warmed by the vision of international justice. "Perhaps you do not realize," Nicholas Murray Butler wrote to him, "what a source of strength and pride you are to those of us who have faith unweakened by any happenings in our American democracy, in its opportunities and in its conquests."

Thick and fast the honors were falling on Cardozo during this year of 1927. He was offered a seat in the Permanent Court of Arbitration and for a while pondered over his answer to the invitation of President Coolidge. On receiving a letter of congratulation from his cousin Maud upon the invitation, he wrote to her:

"I am anxious to accept the invitation, but am still debating the question whether I ought to do so while retaining my present office. I shall have to make up my mind soon. . . . If the lady at The Hague is as nice as you— but then, of course, she isn't!"

Reflection that his best service to the public called for nonacceptance of Mr. Coolidge's nomination, led him, a few days later, to explain his refusal.

"An enthusiastic friend," he wrote to his cousin Maud, "has just written a letter to me placing me in nomination for the presidency, with the understanding, of course, that I am to spurn the office as incompatible with my present duties.

"Won't you second the nomination and give me the éclat of renouncing another honor?

[155]

"I am grateful for what you write. I feel sure I made the proper choice. I am often doubtful about these matters till I have decided them. After that I can generally tell by my state of mind whether I have chosen well or ill.

"In point of fact, the renunciation was not as great as it might seem. The Permanent Court of Arbitration has been substantially superseded by a later court, the Court of International Justice. Membership in the earlier court is a fine honor, but no longer a great opportunity for public service."

To his cousin Annie, Cardozo explained his attitude in greater detail. "You must not think," he said, "I am putting aside an opportunity for great service. Such is not the fact. There is a good deal of misunderstanding about the functions of the Permanent Court of Arbitration. It is only the simulacrum of a court. It is a panel of two hundred lawyers from whom arbitrators may be selected by the nations of the world if they wish that form of trial. In practice it has been substantially superseded by the Permanent Court of International Justice created by the Treaty of Versailles. The earlier court has for its chief function now the election of the members of the new court. No one submits cases to the old court, though of course they may do so if they wish and conceivably will do so someday. Even then, the chance that they will select a particular judge out of two hundred is slight. Mr. Root, for example, has been a member many years and has never been called upon to act. Appointment is a fine honor like an LL.D. It is not very important in other ways.

"The post of chief judge of the Court of Appeals is in my opinion one of the great official positions in the land. It is too fine for the proprieties of the conduct of its incumbent to be made a subject for debate. You will see from my letter to Judge Hughes how my acceptance of the new appointment might be the occasion for criticism which I think I should avoid."

He accounts for the grounds of criticism in his letter to Judge Stone: "I felt constrained to decline the appointment to the Permanent Court of Arbitration, though I did so with deep regret. As you know, the constitution of the state provides that no judge of the Court of Appeals or justice of the Supreme Court shall hold any other office or public trust. I am satisfied in my own mind that membership in the Hague Tribunal is not within that prohibition. At the same time there is need of a good deal of explanation and analysis to make this plain. Many might feel in the end that I was violating the spirit of the law if not the letter. So I had to say 'no.' After all, the office I now hold is too high to justify me in putting myself in a position where the propriety of my conduct might become a subject for debate. There was not even the opportunity for great public service to be offset against that possibility. The Court of Arbitration has been pretty nearly superseded by the Court of International Justice."

The Judge's particular sense of honor had directed his decision as it did, in 1928, in a case in which he had no parallel precedent to guide him. The lawsuit of *Meinhard v. Salmon* is the case in point. There Cardozo underlined with unprecedented strokes the responsibilities of partnership. The two men had leased for twenty years the Bristol, a hotel on Forty-second Street and Fifth Avenue, New York, and had made various alterations for business purposes. The property belonged to Commodore Elbridge T. Gerry when the lease neared its end. Without informing his partner, Mr. Salmon entered into an agreement with Mr. Gerry to erect a large office building on the site of the hotel. In deciding whether Mr. Meinhard was justified in his action against Mr. Salmon, Cardozo said: "We have no thought to hold that Salmon was guilty of a conscious purpose to defraud. Very likely he assumed in all good faith that, with the approaching end of the adventure, he might ignore his coadventurer and take the extension for himself. He had given to the enterprise time and labor as well as money. He had made it a success. Meinhard, who had given money, but neither time nor labor, had already been richly paid. There might be something grasping in his insistence upon more. Such recriminations are not unusual when coadventurers fall out. They are not without their force if conduct is to be judged by the common standards of competitors. That is not to say they have pertinency here. Salmon had put himself into the position in which thought of self was to be renounced however hard the abnegation. He was much more than the coadventurer. He was a managing coadventurer. For him and for those like him, the rule of undivided loyalty is relentless and supreme."

Strong arguments were possible in opposition to Cardozo's view or Justices Andrews and Kellogg and O'Brien would not have dissented. Justices Pound and Crane and Lehman concurred with Cardozo. In so close a vote the Chief Justice of New York State had raised the standards of business honor and had shown how imponderable values still have the greatest weight.

Many lawyers have expressed their belief that the New York State Court of Appeals was, in all its history, at its very height under the chief judgeship of Benjamin Cardozo. Its influence spread throughout the courts of the land. There are those who say that it outranked the contemporary United States Supreme Court in importance—certainly in its wide-visioned development of American law. But not to Cardozo alone is the credit due. Far from it. He was the "gentle philosopher and friend" of his associates. Yet, though his charm and his wisdom counted for much in their counsels, Judge Pound was a great figure, and the present Chief Judge, Irving Lehman, and the others were men of high legal talent—independent men not subserviently following anyone. Time and time again, at the end of Cardozo's decisions during his closing years at Albany, after the words "ordered accordingly," we find "Pound, Crane, Lehman, Kellogg, O'Brien and Hubbs, JJ concur." Yet often there are dissenting or separate opinions by Cardozo's associates. In illustration both of unanimity and of disagreement, a few interesting cases are offered.

In 1929 Judge Kellogg dissented when the Court of Appeals sustained the verdict of a lower court in allowing compensation to the widow of a taxicab driver. The man had obeyed the order of a police officer in pursuing another car. A collision followed, and the man was killed. Were his employers liable under the Workmen's Compensation Act?

In following Cardozo's argument, what interests us especially is the evidence of his familiarity with precedents of centuries ago. How many other judges would take us into the picturesque and exciting days of England in the thirteenth century to illustrate public duties of the present day? In the time of Edward I, a statute was enacted providing that any man who was worth as much as fifteen pounds should have in his house, in order to keep the peace, "a hauberk of iron, a Sword, a Knife and an horse." Cardozo was sure that "the man who failed to use his horse" in pursuit of a robber "would have to answer to the king." The Judge then goes on to state that a man is called upon to aid in preserving the peace "with whatever implements and facilities are convenient and at hand." In obeying the officer, the taxicab driver was bound to assume the risk of the pursuit, and the corporation which employed him must or should have known that in sending the driver on the highway he would rightly be subject to the kind of request which might end in fatality.

Judge Kellogg maintained that the driver was acting as a temporary member of the Police Department rather than as an employee of the Yellow Taxi Corporation; but he was the only dissenter from Cardozo's opinion.

From opinions of the following year—1930—we choose one which illustrates how absurd statutes and customs may be when there is an ulterior object. Granted that the reputation of women should be carefully guarded, that a husband should be protected from undeserved horns of cuckoldry, old English laws carried the matter to an extent which Cardozo no doubt enjoyed ridiculing in the opinion he wrote. The case was that of a woman, Anne Brooks by name, who some seventy-five years ago deserted her husband and three children in England and ran away with her lover, James Findlay. She bore him three sons, the youngest in the United States. One of her legitimate children died in 1926 in Long Island. He left no will. One of the illegitimate sons, William, thereupon claimed the estate, asserting that he was really the child of Anne's deserted husband. To establish his claim, it was necessary to advance the theory that Anne and her husband had had intercourse after she had run away from him and was living with another man.

It was doubtful that Anne was still in England at the time of William's birth. It was certain that William had previously admitted he was the son of her lover. Cardozo, with full knowledge of the precedents, where the presumption of legitimacy overrode many reasonable doubts, decided in this instance that the presumption "would not bear so great a strain." He knew that, in times past, "if a husband not physically incapable was in the four seas of England during the period of gestation, the court would not listen to evidence casting doubt on his paternity. The presumption in such circumstances was said to be conclusive 'on account of its absolute nonsense.' " He remembered Lord Campbell's dictum "that a mulatto child born of a white mother must be ascribed to the white husband and not to the black paramour if the husband had access to his wife during the period of gestation." But he would have no absolute nonsense in his court and dismissed all statements, arguments, and theories that might have established William's claim with the final phrase: "This is the presumption of legitimacy gone mad."

The two cases drawn upon have, like many others in the preceding pages, been selected largely on account of their human interest. The importance of Cardozo's opinions in cases having to do with business in general, with public policy, with international law, was, as the world knows, very decided. During his last year in Albany, a case came up of such significance for the business world that we give it at the risk of boring our readers and ourselves.

A firm of public accountants, Touche, Nevin & Co., had gone over the books of a corporation—Fred Stern & Co.—which dealt in rubber. The books had been dishonestly written up. As a result, the accountants had reported the condition so favorably that the Stern Company was able to obtain a large loan from the Ultra-Mares Corporation. Were the accountants liable for damages when the rubber company went bankrupt?

In one of the longest of his opinions, Cardozo argues that, though there may have been some negligence in the audit, as long as there was no fraud on the part of the firm of accountants, the question to be decided was whether they owed a duty "to creditors and investors to whom the employer exhibited the certificate, to make it without negligence." He maintained that "if liability for negligence exists, a thoughtless slip or blunder, the failure to detect a theft or forgery beneath the cover of deceptive entries, may expose accountants to a liability in an indeterminate amount for an indeterminate time to an indeterminate class. The hazards of a business conducted on these terms are so extreme as to enkindle doubt whether a flaw may not exist in the implication of a duty that exposed to these consequences." After pages of argument, Cardozo writes:

[161]

"Liability for negligence as adjudged in this case would extend to many callings other than an auditor's. Lawyers who certify their opinion as to the validity of municipal or corporate bonds, with knowledge that the opinion will be brought to the notice of the public, will become liable to the investors if they have overlooked a statute or a decision to the same extent as if the controversy were one between client and adviser. Title companies insuring titles to a tract of land, with knowledge that at the approaching auction the fact that they have insured will be stated to the bidders, will become liable to purchasers who may wish the benefit of a policy without payment of a premium. These ills may seem to be extreme, but they go little, if any, further than we are invited to go now."

The importance of Cardozo's opinion in the case of the *Ultra-Mares Corporation v. Touche, Nevin & Co.* becomes obvious when one considers the ramifications of its application. It established a precedent protecting business relations, commerce, finance, in many directions. Without it the entire profession of public accountants would thenceforth have stood shivering on dangerous ground, ever subject to the chicanery of firms requesting their services. Cardozo's opinion, in this case unanimously concurred in by his associates, is widely regarded as one of his most valuable.

XI

The spirit of man is divine.   BYRON

ON CARDOZO's sixty-first birthday, May 24, 1931, he
delivered the noblest of all his speeches. When the
time comes to publish all his public addresses, this
one, "Values," might well give the title to such a volume. It
was delivered at the Sixth Annual Commencement Exercises
of the Jewish Institute of Religion.

Cardozo had long ago given up attendance at synagogue
services, although he had retained his membership in the
Spanish-Portuguese congregation, and his inherited right
of voting concerning its affairs. The orthodox teachings had
had a part in molding the character of young Benjamin
Cardozo. But after, at the age of thirteen, he had been
confirmed in the faith of his fathers, the outreachings of
his mind led him away from conviction in the absolute
value of such commandments as "marry not with those
not of thy faith" and "defile not thy soul by the eating of
forbidden food." True, that in his own home of later years
filial or fraternal sentiment led him to abstain from serving
food forbidden by the ancient precepts, yet ritualism in
itself was alien to his philosophy. It is possible that his
father's devotion to the tenets of his faith and his lack of
devotion to his public duties were an evidence of depart-

mentalizing minds and ethics which had great influence on Cardozo in weakening his ties with orthodoxy.

Only once, as a young man in his twenties, had he forcefully defended the traditional religious customs of his forebears. When, in 1897, the Spanish-Portuguese congregation moved from its Nineteenth Street synagogue to its present location on Central Park West, there was considerable discussion among its members as to giving up some of the orthodox customs. Was there to be a continuation of the services in Hebrew? Of hats and praying shawls to be worn by the men? The women to be allowed only in the gallery? No boy to be permitted in the gallery even with his mother?

Members of the same family were divided on these questions. Many wished to have family pews where both sexes could sit together. This was already the custom in the Temple Emanu-El where worshiped the majority of the most prominent and wealthy Jewish families of the day. With the Spanish-Portuguese synagogue as the outstanding exception, social prestige was represented by Reformed Judaism.

When those of the congregation qualified to vote were about to pass on the test question of whether men and women might sit together, it was—in the words of Dr. David de Sola Pool, the distinguished clergyman—"a crucial moment for Shearith Israel." Young Benjamin Cardozo asked if he might speak before the vote was taken. The request was granted—indeed, he had the hereditary right to be heard. He was the only speaker. He talked for an hour or more, pleading for continuance along the old lines which had been followed for centuries. He was appealing to sentiment; and then he left sentiment behind. He denied the right of the congregation to go against the stipulation of its own constitution. Then the man who throughout his years used persuasion resorted to a threat. A storm was raging without—rain and wind and thunder. His voice rose above them as he said, "We have the law very clearly on our side, and if you outvote us there are laws outside."

At that moment there was a great flash of lightning and a terrific thunderbolt. It seemed almost as if Jehovah himself were sending a warning from on high.

The vote was taken. To this day the ancient customs of Shearith Israel remain unchanged. For the student of Cardozo's mind and nature this, the most dramatic episode of his undramatic life, offers fascinating problems. Was his speech motivated foremost by a juristic sense of right—by the conviction that a constitution which unmistakably set forth the obligations of the congregation must not be violated? Was Cardozo's main motive—for all his personal relinquishment of orthodoxy—the sense of tradition, the poet's loyalty, profounder than all intellectualism, to the poetry of ancient ways? Here only a seeming paradox—and none at all in the young lawyer's defense of the synagogue's constitution? In later days his country's Constitution was for Cardozo a living thing, to be interpreted with progressive vision according to the changing needs of the nation—but only where such interpretation would not conflict with definite and clear provisions. The constitution of the synagogue was definite and clear. All were free to leave the congregation. Remaining within it, obedience was, maintained Cardozo, obligatory.

A further question suggests itself. How far, if at all, did family sentiment, family pride, if you will, enter into that speech which so swayed Cardozo's hearers? For generations men of his family had been the rabbis and the presidents of Shearith Israel. Should their revered and deeply beloved place of worship depart from its traditions?

These questions we leave unanswered. Yet their very propounding throws light on the mind and nature of Cardozo. His mentality was opposed to formalism, and during his later life Cardozo never attended religious exercises at the synagogue. He shared, however, in the activities of the Jewish Educational Association, a coordinating body for stimulating interest in Jewish culture. He became a trustee of the Hebrew University in Jerusalem. Although in its early stages Cardozo held aloof from Zionism, he consented, after the ending of the Great War, to preside at a dinner meeting to raise money for Palestine. "Growth or experience," he said on that occasion to an enthusiastic Zionist, Mr. Abraham Tulin, "nearly always produced a deepening of understanding." Palestine, he felt, might serve admirably as a center of Jewish culture, but he was too American to enjoy the thought of an exclusively Jewish nation. Events in Europe after 1932 led him to see the value of Palestine as a haven for the oppressed of his race who had been barred from their own countries.

When his friend Stephen Wise asked him to be the chief speaker at the Commencement exercises, Cardozo questioned his own fitness to address a graduating class of young rabbis. Dr. Wise, aware that Cardozo, however indifferent he might be to the forms of religious services, was yet inspiringly endowed with spiritual qualities, persuaded him to accept the invitation. The address is one of such beauty that we give it in full.

"Defying the ancient canon of the rhetoricians," said the Judge, "I begin with an apology. I do not know whether I have the right to talk to you today. I have felt that to earn that right I should be able to say to you that your beliefs are wholly mine, that the devastating years have not obliterated youthful faiths, and that in the darkness of the universe I can see with clearness and certainty a consoling shaft of light. Unable to say this, I have wondered whether my message could be of worth to you—to you who are going forth to spread the teachings of religion—

[166]

wondered whether with good cause you might not even resent it as an impertinence; at the very least whether fitness and good taste might not exact another spokesman for the lesson of the hour.

"The great spiritual leader who has given to this Institute the dignity and glory of his leadership has talked with me about these things, and has brought me to believe that my troubles are unreal. He has said that a message would be welcome from anyone who has been able, however black the depths of nescience, to hold fast to certain values transcending the physical and temporal. He has assured me that what such a one would say would be listened to without resentment, and even indeed with gladness by those of greater faith, with the gladness born of the perception that what is noble and high and sacred reveals itself in many forms and is discerned in many aspects by the faltering sons of men.

"Sixty years and more ago Huxley published to the world a memorable volume which is known by the title *Lay Sermons and Addresses*. A lay sermon by one whose beliefs are not so very far removed from Huxley's is what you will hear from me today. And to hold fast to what your leader said to me, to shelter myself squarely behind the shield of his authority, I am going to talk to you of 'values.'

"A theme is here, not for a brief fragment of an hour, but for a lecture, a series of lectures, a volume, almost, one might say, a library. What values shall we choose—those of today, or of tomorrow, or of a future that is close at hand, or of the unplumbed future, trackless as the sea? Every one of them is a good. Let us not make the blunder of decrying any of them. Asceticism has made that blunder at times, and has suffered for its partial view of the shifting aspects of reality. The values of today are good, and those of tomorrow are good, and those of a future that is not remote, and those of an unplumbed future, trackless as the

[167]

sea. If we could have them all, it would be well, but seldom can we have them all. There is need to make a choice. How shall it be guided? Not all of us will make the same choice, not all of us ought to make the same. What choice is it worth while to make if one feels the mystery of the universe more deeply than one's fellows? What choice will be made by you? Before that question is answered, let me tell you an anecdote. Let me tell you of the choice that about four centuries ago was made by someone else. Let me tell you of the choice that was made by Tycho Brahe.

"Tycho Brahe was born in Denmark of goodly lineage, and educated in youth at the University of Copenhagen. He thought in his boyhood that he would like to study law, but he became diverted from law to the study of astronomy. While yet a young man he discovered a new star, and the discovery brought him fame at home and in many distant lands. Denmark had a king who was a patron of learning, and the king built an observatory for Tycho at the center of a little island, and Tycho called the place Uraniborg, the City of the Heavens. Here for years and years Tycho worked day and night, watching the heavens by night, and figuring his observations by day, till star after star with exquisite precision had been set down upon his chart. But Frederick, the king, died, and young Prince Christian came upon the throne with a host of flippant courtiers, who grudged the treasure that had been lavished upon the upkeep of the observatory and this feckless charting of the stars. They could not see the value of it all, and so at last messengers went forward in the name of the new king, who were to visit Tycho Brahe, to learn, if they could, the use of all his labor, to quiz him about it, and to pit their values against his.

"You will find the tale set forth with moving eloquence and beauty in a poem by Alfred Noyes, the noble and inspiring poem which he calls 'The Watchers of the Skies.'

[168]

The messengers asked what Tycho had been doing these five and twenty years. He showed them tables of the stars, seven hundred set down, each in its proper place. "And is this all?" they asked. "Not all, I hope," said Tycho, "for I think before I die I shall have marked a thousand." You can almost hear their laughter, can you not? All the prophets and the years have listened to the like. Einstein has heard it in our day, and every lover of truth and beauty, every man who has seen visions and tried to live them in his life, has heard the same sardonic mirth. To what end, said the messengers, to what end the travail and the waste? Show its uses to us now, show them now before we go. Resounding through the centuries I hear familiar echoes. Never a philosopher has lived, nor a saint nor a scientist nor an artist, but has been summoned to a like proof—to show the value for today—not the value for the unplumbed future, but the value for today. I will read you Tycho Brahe's answer as I find it in the poem:

'In the time to come,'
Said Tycho Brahe, 'perhaps a hundred years,
Perhaps a thousand, when our own poor names
Are quite forgotten, and our Kingdom's dust,
On one sure certain day, the torchbearers
Will, at some point of contact, see a light
Moving upon this chaos. Though our eyes
Be shut forever in an iron sleep,
Their eyes shall see the Kingdom of the law,
Our undiscovered cosmos. They shall see it—
A new creation rising from the deep,
Beautiful, whole.
We are like men that hear
Disjointed notes of some supernal choir.
Year after year we patiently record
All we can gather. In that far off time
A people that we have not known shall hear them
Moving like music to a single end.'

[169]

"They could not understand—the messengers who had come to appraise the values and report. They went back to the king, their master, and they said that Tycho Brahe's dreams were fruitless, and worse than fruitless, perilous, since 'any fruit they bore would fall in distant years to alien hands.' Tycho went forth to exile, and Uraniborg, City of the Heavens, went down into the dust.

'Yes, I still hope,' he said,
'Yes, I still hope in some more generous land
To make my thousand up before I die.
Little enough, I know—a midget's work.
The men that follow me with more delicate art
May add their tens of thousands; yet my sum
Will save them just that five and twenty years
Of patience, bring them sooner to their goal,
That Kingdom of the law I shall not see.
We are on the verge of great discoveries.
I feel them as a dreamer feels the dawn
Before his eyes are opened. Many of you
Will see them. In that day you will recall
This, our last meeting at Uraniborg,
And how I told you that this work of ours
Would lead to victories for the coming age.
The victors may forget us. What of that?
Theirs be the palms, the shouting and the praise,
Ours be the fathers' glory in the sons.'

"That, gentlemen of the Institute, was Tycho Brahe's choice of values. If you are true to your mission as sons of this Institute of Religion, summoned from this day forth to live its deepest verities, your choice will be the same. The submergence of self in the pursuit of an ideal, the readiness to spend oneself without measure, prodigally, almost ecstatically, for something intuitively apprehended as great and noble, spend oneself one knows not why—some of us like to believe that this is what religion means. True, I am

sure, it is that values such as these will be found to have
survived when creeds are shattered and schisms healed and
sects forgotten and the things of brass and stone are one
with Nineveh and Tyre.

"I have spoken of a man who was one of the famous of the
earth, whose name has reechoed through the corridors of
time. Let us not make the blunder of supposing that to live
in communion with these ineffable values of the spirit, to
spend oneself utterly in sacrifice and devotion, is a lot
reserved for a chosen few, for an aristocracy of genius, for
those that will be ranked in history among the mighty or the
great. Not so, friends and brothers. To the glory of our
humanity, the lowly equally with the mighty may be par-
takers in this bliss. I have seen it in my own life, and so I
am sure have many within the compass of my voice. Along
the common ways I have walked with men and women who
have made the choice of Tycho Brahe. They had made it in
humbler forms, by love, by gentleness, by sweetness, by
devotion, by sacrifice of self within the narrow circle of the
home; but be it said to their undying glory, they had made
it, none the less. We know it when death takes them if
in hours of pride and darkness we have been blind to it
before. The life seemed simple while it lasted. We may not
always have been conscious of its beauty. The end comes,
and behold it is illuminated with the white and piercing
light of the divinity within it. We have walked with angels
unawares.

"This is the summons that I give to you today. These
are the values—the values of the spirit—that by your witness
shall prevail. I have been reminded by Felix Frankfurter
of the noble words of Huxley in celebrating the opening of
Johns Hopkins University. 'I cannot say' (said Huxley) 'that
I am in the slightest degree impressed by your bigness (i.e.,
the bigness of America), or your material resources as such.
Size is not grandeur, and territory does not make a nation.

[171]

The great issue about which hangs a true sublimity, and the terror of overhanging fate, is what are you going to do with all these things? What is to be the end to which these are to be the means?' So it is, my friends, with all the teachings of universities and schools. The learning and the wisdom stored in many books have been taught to the youth, the rabbis of the future, who have come together in these halls. All the study has been wasted except in proportion as it strengthens them to make a choice hereafter between competing and conflicting values. It is wasted unless it strengthens them to the choice of Tycho Brahe.

"One life I have singled out as the subject of my parable. I could have chosen many others, the lives of men and women of our race, the lives of prophets and saints and heroes and martyrs, who were kinsmen in spirit of that watcher of the skies. In persecution and contumely they knew that there were values of the spirit greater than any others, values for whose fruits they would have to wait, 'perhaps a hundred years, perhaps a thousand,' values whose fruits might elude them altogether, yet values to be chosen, unfalteringly, uncomplainingly, with cheer and even joy. What does a ministry of religion mean if it does not mean the preaching and living of that truth? For what have we come together this morning, in the springtime of the year, unless to say to this little band of eager men, still in the springtime of their lives: You are going forth today as preachers of the eternal values. You will find mockery and temptation on the highways, and for the values that you hold to be eternal many a tinsel token will be offered in exchange. Sycophants and timeservers and courtiers and all the lovers of the fleshpots will assail you with warnings that you are squandering the happy days under the sun, and will ask you to tell them to what use, just as in the Danish city of Uraniborg, City of the Heavens, the messengers of the Danish king taunted and challenged and drove at last into exile, that other watcher of

[172]

the skies. Then will be the time when you will need to gird yourselves with the strength that this Institute of Religion, this Institute of the better life, has striven with all her might to bestow upon her sons. Then will be the time when you will need to bethink yourselves of the values that were chosen by the prophets and saints of Israel, and by the goodly and noble of every race and clime. You will remember in that hour the choice of Tycho Brahe.

"When the course is finished, when the task is ended, when the books are closed, may the last appraisal of all values reveal his choice as yours."

This address seems to us the finest of all Cardozo's speeches. Here the man who was so usefully the pragmatist, in the Jamesian sense, shines forth most poetically as the idealist. And yet, as one ponders the title, there is a wave of pity that Cardozo himself, having to choose between the values of life, spent himself, to use his own phrase, "in sacrifice and devotion." The "lot reserved for a chosen few, for an aristocracy of genius, for those that will be ranked in history among the mighty or the great." Cardozo would have been unwilling to place himself in this category of the "great," although, in the opinion of America, he already deserves that place. He might also have been unwilling to admit that he had lost some of the finest experiences of life through sacrifice and devotion—sacrifice through his years of toil to accomplish the restoration of the family name to honor, and that devotion to his sister Nell which, through love and loyalty and gratitude, deflected him from many paths of happiness and enjoyment. He never deviated from his search for the eternal values, but, alas, at what cost!

This quest for values is brought out again in another example of his proffering advice to the young. There was a young fellow—Harold Roland Shapiro his name—whose early ambition was to become a rabbi. As he went on with his studies doubts began to assail him. Religious by nature,

[173]

still he commenced to question his own convictions concerning some of the old laws and rituals of his faith. This was during the *Sturm und Drang* period of youth when the mind is in ferment. Cardozo had gone through the same experience. To Cardozo he would turn for advice.

The Judge, deeply sympathetic, did not urge the young man to give up an ambition which had so long been dear. This would be assuming too great a responsibility. Human beings must make their own decisions. Yet what the ends of different roads are might advisedly be suggested. Cardozo, adopting the Socratic method, addressed questions to the young man who had come to him for advice. His exact words are forgotten, but the gist of them remains.

"If you are puzzled now," said the Judge, "and are still wishing to continue your studies for the rabbinate, why not project yourself into the future years? How will you feel in the face of your congregation if you still have any doubts left in regard to the rituals which you will then yourself be conducting?"

Cardozo indulged in no moralizing. His sense of ethics was not set forth in any grandiose phrases, yet devotion to intellectual integrity was apparant. His pragmatism—the sense of reality—was sufficiently evident in his suggestive questioning; and with it the poet's quality for visualizing the future.

Shapiro turned to his secondary love, the law.

For Cardozo's friends, aware of his life of self-abnegation in its loyalty to his sense of values, there is some compensation in recalling that occasional gatherings of comradeship brightened the days of this lonely scholar. In 1931, Cardozo enjoyed various public luncheons and dinners, these in addition, of course, to frequent evenings at hospitable homes of friends in New York and Albany, and during the summer months. Certainly the dinner given by the Jewish Welfare Board in honor of Judge Lehman was one that gave Cardozo

[174]

immense personal satisfaction. When he was invited by Congressman Siegel, father of one of Cardozo's law secretaries, to be the chief speaker of the occasion, the Judge at first replied: "My admiration and affection for Judge Lehman are unbounded, and I am always ready to proclaim to the world my deep appreciation of his wonderful qualities and my gratitude for the privilege of his friendship. I cannot quite satisfy myself, however, that I ought to speak on this occasion. The relations between us are so close that praise of him at this time from one of his brethren in the court will give to the affair the aspect of a mutual admiration society. I really believe it would be pleasanter to him to be eulogized by someone not quite so close to him. If he were about to retire from the court and sever our official relations, the situation would, of course, be different. I should seem to be praising the court itself were I to eulogize him at this time. I am giving you with candor my reaction to your invitation. Perhaps when you think it over you will agree with me."

The Congressman did not agree and entered into an argument wherein he suggested that, as Cardozo "had not been drafted during the World War," he should submit to being drafted now. So finally Cardozo went to the dinner and delivered a speech of tribute to a judge to whom he was devoted and in whose home he was to die.

A few weeks later Cardozo himself was guest of honor at a dinner, given by the New York County Lawyers' Association, at which the chief speech of tribute was made by Dr. Nicholas Murray Butler. "My part this evening," said Dr. Butler, "is less lugubrious than that of the late Mark Antony, for I come not to bury our Caesar but to praise him."

In that period of black depression when the year 1931 was drawing to its close, Dr. Butler devoted many portions of his address to the necessity of "labors to restore this broken world of ours." "Our program tomorrow," he said, "is to unite in counsel with our like-minded fellow men in every land and address ourselves to a world-wide effort to relieve world-wide conditions." The great service of such men as Holmes and Cardozo, said Butler, was not alone to their courts, but as "captains of the armies of defense of ideas and ideals, to the nation at large and to all mankind."

The slender, white-haired, ascetic-looking man, the favorite of the American bar, rose to speak. Before him was a sea of legal talent, a sea whose waves of affection touched him greatly. The Judge began with evidence of self-examination. "When one looks back and tries to estimate it impartially," he said, "one has hours of disillusionment, hours filled with wonder whether one has been traveling on the right track or the wrong one, or on any track at all. Should one have been more liberal or more conservative, or should one have tried more constantly to follow a line along the middle of the road? The very work that one thought was one's best and wisest when one did it may seem to a great many others, quite as sensible and able, to be a pattern of egregious error, and the work that one most distrusted may win the approval of the years, the wise and discerning years, so much juster than the passing hour."

Pushed by this "divine unrest," Cardozo spoke of the "heartbreaking sort of game" that judges "play from day to day"; yet this man who had suffered so much in life recorded his belief that "no game that is quite without heartbreak was ever worth the playing . . . Down through the centuries we are given glimpses of endeavor—intermittent but persistent to make the processes of justice more faithful in their response to the cause which they are meant to further . . . Out of the new ferment there will come a new philosophy that will guide the thought of our successors when those of us in place today shall have vanished from the scene."

[176]

Dr. Butler had discussed contemporary problems in his preceding speech, and had suggested how international counsel and collaboration must be the way of progress. Cardozo did not take up the appalling questions confronting America and other countries. His theme concerned itself with values eternal in their aspect. The lover of justice and the philosopher were manifest in his words, but even more the poet. It is the poet who stresses "the power and significance of myths." To his audience of lawyers—practitioners in the field of facts—Cardozo says: "You will find every now and again that the myths are really the main thing and that the efforts and institutions to which they are supposed to be secondary would have little meaning today, and little value—whatever meaning and value they may have had once upon a time—if it were not for the encrustations of myth and fable." The Magna Charta is an example. "What lives in the Charter today is the myth that is gathered around it—the things that it has come to stand for in the thought of successive generations—not the pristine core within but the encrustations that have formed without."

So, too, with the Constitution of the United States. "The Bill of Rights is much more important for the spirit it enshrines than for this or the other privilege or immunity which it professes to secure. Some of them have a vital meaning even to this day, others are reminiscent of battles long ago. The myth that has enveloped them has become greater than the reality, or rather, in a sense, the genuine reality."

The Judge then discussed the myth which had developed concerning the profession of the law, "a fable, a tradition, not always the truth as seen and realized in conduct, but none the less the chief thing about the profession, the thing that ennobles it, the thing that it really is in its best and truest moments." This myth, this tradition, "is a bond between its members in one of the great concerns of man, the

[177]

cause of justice upon earth . . . We may tell judges until Doomsday that they are to love logic more than justice; as in affairs of the heart generally it is easier to give the command than to cause it to be heeded." The imperious command of Cardozo's soul was this passion for justice. The "myth" that it finely animated the entire profession of the law, judges and lawyers alike, remained the essential faith without which the profession of the law "would wither and die."

"We are fallen," the Judge added, "upon days that are spoken of by many as cynical and sordid. The profession is given over, we are told, to the pursuit of power and pelf. Let us beware of underrating the springs of altruism and energy that lie ready to be realized at the call of a great example, the summons of an urgent method . . . It has been given to you and to me to prove in our own lives that the truth is in the myth and not in the sordid appearances."

In an editorial commenting on his speech, the *New York Times* referred to Cardozo's power of persuasive reasoning. He had, said the editorial, made the law a living thing. "These," to use his own words, "are the values—the values of the spirit—that by your witness shall prevail."

XII

I sit beside my lonely fire
And pray for wisdom yet:
For calmness to remember
Or courage to forget.   F. H. AÏDE

IT IS paradoxical that a man as deeply loved by his friends as Cardozo ever was should have been preeminently a lonely man. The loneliness may be accounted for in various ways—by the unselfish devotion to his sister Nell, which excluded him, voluntarily, it is true, from a normal social life; by the early determination to clear his family's name of dishonor, which drove him like a goad through his early life; by his essential shyness and diffidence.

"Your letter charms but does not comfort me," he wrote on one occasion to his cousin Annie. "I sit upon my little handful of thorns and look with sad eyes upon the glories of creation. Dante reserved a special place for those who sulked under the sunshine, and doubtless the hot corner is held for my use. . . . I suppose the difference is just what you point out, that you don't know the meaning of the word loneliness. To me it is a very vivid thing. The sense of being an atom in all this vast universe without any other atom traveling the same daily orbit is annihilating. . . . It doesn't help me much to know that atoms more or less akin are traveling orbits not very distant with feelings of atomic friendship."

"He never quite wanted anybody to penetrate into his inner life," Judge Hand said of him. It is from his own self-accusations rather than from the testimony of those who knew him that one can learn of his weaknesses. A touch of vanity, a shy liking for flattery, an overgenerous tendency to praise, a magnanimous unselfishness toward Nellie—weaknesses, if you will, yet ingratiating weaknesses. To a friend, Aline Goldstone, he wrote, accusing himself of being egocentric. In her reply his friend discussed his self-arraignment. The Judge took up the subject further in his next letter.

"You tried to console me," he writes, "for being egocentric by saying that the most seemingly detached and speculative thought is always tied to some ego more important than itself. Of course, we can't free ourselves from our physical integument, and it conditions all our thinking. Even so, there are some rare beings who seem to transcend these limitations, or at least make one forget them. Perhaps to achieve that goal one must be a saint or at all events a poet, which is something more interesting than sainthood.

"I have been reading Dante in Italian with the aid of a translation; from him I went over to Milton, whom I reread with delight, and then to Bryant's translation of the *Odyssey*, which you must read, if you haven't. Such swiftness of narrative, such absorbing variety of plot! I could hardly put the book down for interest in the story."

Egocentric he might term himself, but it was not a term applied to him by others. In his devotion to Nell he was, as has been suggested, guilty of the weakness of overmagnanimity. Her name runs like a colored thread through his letters, never overlooked. In 1919 she began to experience heart attacks and from then until her death in 1929 she became more and more of an invalid. To Mrs. Seligman, at her camp in the Adirondacks, Cardozo wrote in 1919: "I am grateful to you for your most fine and thoughtful invitation.

I haven't the slightest doubt that I should have a splendid time. But none the less I shall have to say 'no.' I don't feel that I can go away from my sister this summer. She has had some bad heart attacks recently and I must be with her as much as possible. But it was fine of you to ask me."

In 1922 Nellie and Ben underwent the greatest sorrow of their middle years. That April the youngest, the gayest, and the dearest of their sisters had died. When, four years earlier, Lizzie's life came to an end, there was at least the consolation that to a sufferer of incessant illness the shadowy hand of Death had now offered the gift of peace. How different with Emily, of bright and resilient nature, and the only one of these Cardozos who had experienced the sustaining warmth of companionship in marriage! And how great was Cardozo's devotion to her and his admiration for her!

He asked Stephen Wise to officiate at the funeral. He could not ask the rabbi of the Spanish-Portuguese synagogue to which he belonged, as Emily had left the synagogue and had married Frank Bent, a Christian. To Dr. Wise, whose wife, Louise, had known Emily since girlhood, he knew he could turn in his hour of sorrow. Dr. Wise did not know Emily at all intimately, and so her brother thought it well to give a brief picture of her for the purposes of the funeral address. There is nothing in the writings of Benjamin Cardozo making a profounder appeal to human sentiments than the paper he then wrote:

"Emily C. Bent was my twin sister.

"I am going to ask you to believe, on the faith of my word, that she had traits of character which were very distinctive and very beautiful.

"First, perhaps, I would place a warmth and cheerfulness and cordiality of disposition which made her love everyone, and which in turn made everyone love her. I do not know anyone else who was able to elicit such friendships almost overnight. You will see it at her funeral. Her friends *loved* her—not in the loose sense in which we often use that word, but truly and deeply. Of course, she did not receive without giving. She loved her friends in return. They were all precious to her. People who seemed tiresome or flat or commonplace or even a bit vulgar to Nellie and me were all dear to her. She saw the essential human traits, and what we often thought her blindness was truer than our wisdom.

"But, dear Doctor, there is another trait which I must mention and which moves me very deeply—that is her generosity, her unselfishness. She did not have many wordly goods. She saw others about her—her brother and sister— who had much more. Never in all her life did I note even a passing shadow of jealousy or envy, never did she seem to wish that they might have a little less and she a little more, never was there anything but happiness and joy in every success and blessing that came to them, and gratitude far beyond their deserts, for every little kindness that they bestowed and every trifling help that they might offer.

"She loved her husband with the utmost devotion. She often said she did not wish to survive him. She said the same, indeed, of Nellie and me. Her last illness was greatly soothed by his loving care, and by that of his brother who made his home with them, and who tended her with a devotion which has won my gratitude and affection.

"I have spoken of her traits as distinctive, but I suppose that this is wrong. After all, they are the fundamental traits which redeem and transfigure our weak humanity, the fundamental traits which place saints and angels in every home, the great and eternal virtues of gentleness and charity which shine for each of us in the faces and the conduct of those we love and cherish."

The day after the funeral Cardozo sent Stephen Wise the following letter:

"As I look back on the ceremonies of yesterday afternoon, and think of them in the more tranquil hours of today, they

Cardozo's sisters, Elizabeth and Emily

seem to me to be the most beautiful that I ever heard. You said the right thing with such grace and delicacy and charm. It was a prose poem. I knew it would be, or at least I thought I knew, and I was right."

Brother and sister were now very much alone in the world. The life in the home in Seventy-fifth Street went on more quietly than ever; and so, too, the summer days at Allenhurst. During the winter the Judge came down from Albany more frequently to be with Nellie in New York. Now and then a few close friends or relatives, among them Judge and Mrs. Bijur, would spend the evening. Perhaps once a week Cardozo left his work to dine out in Albany; less frequently during his New York nights. For the most part Ben and Nellie stayed at home, reading together, or playing the piano, until it was time for the sister to go to bed and for the brother to continue the work of the day.

By 1926 Nell's condition had begun to be an incessant worry, and Ben's anxiety crept into his correspondence. Writing from Allenhurst, during the summer to his cousin Maud Nathan, he said: "I had Dr. Keating come down from New York to see her. The regular doctor here—Dr. Woolley—is a good man, but Keating knows the case. He consoled me somewhat—didn't think the symptoms as bad as I did; but irrespective of anything that doctors may tell me, I know that things are not as well as they should be. She has lost strength visibly since we came here and is pitifully inert and quiet. So I am having a sad summer. But let me lay my dolorous tale aside and talk of other things. . . .

"I have tried to do some writing, but I am not sure whether anything will come of it. With so much illness and the house so quiet, there is need of occupying one's thoughts in some way. So I waste paper and ink in precious vaporings that give amusement to me if they profit no one else.

"Aline sent me Sandburg's *Lincoln*, which moved me greatly. I thought the early years of Lincoln's life might be

[183]

wearisome, but Sandburg makes the record of them a noble prelude to the majestic end.

"I suppose you have visited the Lincoln Memorial in Washington. I saw it this spring for the first time, and it almost took my breath away. French, the sculptor, has put into the figure and face of Lincoln more than one could suppose that sculpture would express, and the statue is housed in a temple that is worthy of it.

"After all, Lincoln atones for a good many weaknesses and faults in the great Republic. . . . As I read this over, it looks as if I had been employed to boom Lincoln. But it isn't so. The gentleman was well known before I discovered him."

That same summer he wrote to Aline Goldstone: "My chronicle begins and ends with Nell, whose condition is recorded daily and hourly in the 'log' . . . Her appetite was greatly quickened by the change of air, and for a day or so I thought her much improved. Today and yesterday she seems not quite so well, but I am still hopeful that the summer when it is over will tell a tale of progress.

"I have pretty nearly finished my work on the cases, and am brooding mighty plans which will never be fulfilled. I'm lucky if I succeed in writing a short article. I have come here free from entangling commitments, so if I write, it will be for the love of the thing, and not under the galling pressure of an implacable promise, insisting that it be redeemed. I know how it will end. My indolence will get the better of me, and nothing will be done. . . .

"Our rides along Ocean Avenue have lost the point and tang they had in former years. Seabright has lost its brightness and its villas crumble and decay. I recall that in one villa in particular the decaying process had set in some time ago, but now the blight is general. . . .

"I suppose Maud will do something worth while during her summer—institute a reform to provide the birds and the other wild things of the woods with suitable accommodations and hygienic nests and coverts."

Early in 1928 Nell suffered a second stroke. Her illness became grave. Cardozo stayed in Albany as little as possible. Every day he was there Kate Tracy faithfully telephoned him at length concerning the patient's condition. Back and forth, while the court was in session, he traveled the weary miles between Albany and New York. When in New York he gave up all social enjoyment. "Except for necessity," he wrote to Nicholas Murray Butler, "I do not leave her side."

That summer they returned again to Allenhurst. "We came here about the end of June," Cardozo wrote to Maud Nathan, "making the journey in a private ambulance. Nell stood the trip well, and the change of air seems to have helped her a little, though in truth I hardly know. It is hard to note the differences when one is with the patient all the time. I think, however, take it all in all, that she has improved a little, but, of course, not a great deal. My own work is now over except for some addresses that I must prepare, for we had our final session in Albany last week. I fear time will hang heavy on my hands during the weeks of vacation that are ahead." And a few weeks later: "I am firmly rooted here. Nell has so many ups and downs that I am nervous as soon as I am out of her sight. With all the enforced absences of the court year, I feel that I must keep close to the home in the weeks of vacation . . . My days are pretty monotonous. I have done a good deal of miscellaneous reading, a little— a very little—miscellaneous writing, and have played one game of golf, which will enable me to face my friends with a bold front when vacation days are over."

To Mrs. Stephen Wise he wrote that summer of Nell: "I think the change of air has helped her to some extent. At all events I am sure she would have found the summer hard in town. One day I think her better, and another not so well, yet perhaps on the whole there has been some improvement, but nothing great enough to bring with it much happiness or cheer. I try to console myself with the thought that I have kept her at all, knowing how deep for me would be the void without her."

As the summer drew to a close, he wrote to Aline Goldstone: "I have been worried again about Nell. She hasn't been so well for the last week—a slight temperature in the afternoon, a quicker pulse at times, and speech more incoherent. Dr. Woolley has visited her daily, and I am going to have Dr. Keating come here from New York. So the summer creeps its weary length along. I'll be glad to be home. One feels safer in the great city. For all the good the country has done me, I might as well have stayed away. Only one game of golf this year. With that exception and the exception of a visit to Judge Elkus, I have hardly left the house. Don't think this is worthy of pity. I am so grateful my dear patient has been spared to me at all that I feel quite ashamed when I read a letter over and find that I seem to be complaining of my lot."

Then, a little better: "There has been no recurrence of the alarming seizure of a fortnight ago, but I cannot tell when one may come.

"Your vivid description of the chaos of moving stirs my sense of pity even as a Greek tragedy. The remorseless Furies sitting upon those mounting barrels lacerate the heart of the compassionate beholder. I have always looked upon a change of home as one of the major crises of a lifetime, though like many other crises the result is very often a cleansing and purifying and life-giving regeneration, spiritual as well as physical. . . .

"I am sending you some snapshots of Nell that were taken a few weeks ago while she was sitting on the porch. I think she looks sweet, and remarkably well, all things considered . . . All happiness to you and yours!"

For Cardozo himself, all happiness went out of life when, in November, 1929, Nellie died. There is nothing in the record of American families quite comparable to the relationship between this brother and sister. True, she had taken much, had in younger days been jealously fearful that Ben might marry. Hers was a possessive nature, and he was her cherished possession. She had mothered him when he was a little lad. With advice and with inspiration she had furthered the career which was to redeem the family name. She was so proud of him, and he so loyal to her, and so grateful. Noble pride and a sublimated love held them together in very private and very pure affection.

If the Judge was held in reverence by the world at large as well as by those who saw him often, there was one old lady to whom he ever remained the young cousin not without weaknesses. Sarah Lyons was the strong-minded daughter of the rabbi of the Spanish-Portuguese synagogue in whose home Cardozo's uncle had spent his last evening before the murder that brought such sorrow to Cardozo's mother. In her old age, the family affluence a thing of the past, Sarah Lyons lived in a somewhat disheveled apartment not far away from the New York house where Cardozo dwelt alone after Nell's death. A woman who did not compromise and whose sharpness of tongue must be forgiven because of the firmness of principle underlying her utterances. Shortly after Nellie Cardozo's death the Judge went to see the old lady. Some reference was made to Nellie and Cardozo's eyes became moist. Aunt Sally wanted no sentimentality, no sign of weakness in any of her clan.

"Now, Ben Cardozo," she said sternly, "you're not to cry."

The Chief Judge of New York State answered with the voice of a schoolboy who has been reprimanded, "I'm not crying, Aunt Sally." And for the rest of the afternoon there was no further show of emotion.

The man who felt such deep concern over his sister's ill-ness disregarded as far as possible ill-health of his own. Before Nellie's stroke, Cardozo suffered a bone infection of the face so serious that it could easily have affected the brain. Statistics were against a successful operation, but Dr. Martin decided that it should be done. He was deeply impressed by Cardozo's courage. "There was a kind of serenity about his courage," he commented, "the courage of a man who does not exaggerate the importance of his own life, knows that all men must die, and takes things with serene philosophy." Cardozo referred to the illness in a letter which he wrote to Justice Stone on March 6, 1925.

"About the middle of January," he said, "I suffered a dangerous infection of the face which has caused me to be viewed as something of a prodigy for being alive. I went back to my court on February 23, thinking that I had fully recovered, only to be sent home the next day and to the hospital again. Some of the invading germs had lodged in the kidney, where they set up a disturbance that caused the most excruciating pain. I think the invaders have been routed again; and unless they surprise me anew, I expect to be as well as ever, though the doctors are anxious that I should avoid unnecessary exertion.

"In these circumstances, I do not dare to promise a trip to Washington at present, tempted though I am by the bait which your letter holds before me. If all goes well, however, I expect to make the trip when the American Law Institute meets about the first of May, and then, if not before, I hope that I may be able to see you and perhaps get a glimpse of Judge Holmes, whom I have so long admired and rever-enced from afar." A month later: " . . . for the next few months I am warned by my doctors to confine my activities to my regular judicial work, though so far as I can discover I am now as well as ever."

The period of recuperation was given over to the enjoyment of fiction, for which his labors as a judge had previously left him little leisure. With especial delight he followed the adventures of Helen of Troy as narrated by John Erskine.

In those preceding New York days of critical illness his friends had feared for his life. Their fears arose again when in 1930, on the street in Albany, Cardozo suffered the first of his heart attacks. In the years that followed they occurred from time to time, the pains coming on suddenly. He never wanted to tell anybody about them. Frequently he tried to fight them off without taking any medicine. In his last years nitroglycerin tablets were usually in his pocket. Nevertheless, he continued to do a prodigious amount of work, writing in longhand, and frequently working twelve to fourteen hours a day, a man of fabulous energy.

"Don't overburden yourself," Justice Stone was to warn him during the coming years. If Cardozo had been more cautious, Stone believes, he might have lived many years more. He suggested that Cardozo take more care of himself and think less of service to others; but Cardozo pushed away the suggestion. "No," he said, "I have not much interest left in life now except to work."

He had never cared much for sports. He had long ago given up the tennis of early years and he didn't care much for ocean bathing. He disliked walking. He was a duffer at golf. Though sometimes, to his great surprise, Cardozo made a good shot, more frequently the course over which he had been playing "would," said the Judge, "seem to have been excavated." Drives with his sister Nellie, almost the most violent of his exercises, belonged to the past.

As with many solitary men, his favorite refuge was in books. "I do love words," he wrote to a friend, "more, probably, than a wise man should." It was to books that he turned more readily than to people. His letters are filled with references to his reading, particularly those written to

Aline Goldstone. Referring to Amy Lowell, he wrote: "I read the article about Miss Lowell with interest. I think she isn't so horrible a poetess as I fancied. But melody and simplicity still attract me more than they should. I am too lazy to dive deep or dig hard for hidden treasure. So let your lyre be tuneful when you come to serenade me—if fair ladies ever do that sort of thing for gentlemen past middle age." Later he wrote to her: "Thank you for the arch and graceful verses which will help to smooth my declining years. Ah! my child, these philosophies are all very well for those who have a buoyant heart and need no philosophies. Will they ever convert the dismal? But that is true of reasoning in every field. You should read a book called *Thobbing* which shows us forth as slaves of preconceived desires. I'll lend it to you when I am back in town, the more readily because it has some pages in praise of me. Praise in a bound volume! Think of it!"

A few weeks later, Cardozo began giving the series of lectures called *Paradoxes of Legal Science*. Meanwhile his friend had fallen ill, and Cardozo wrote gaily to her:

"I have just had a telephone talk with Lafe. He says your stern jailers allow letters to be slipped in to you without censorship of the contents, and without counting the heart-beats or blood corpuscles before and after. . . .

"The egoist in me asserts itself at once, and helpless and prostrate though you are I begin by talking about myself. I have given two out of the four lectures, and still live. I know they were pretty bad, but at least I held my audience. The whole auditorium of the McMillin Theater—even the gallery—filled—standing room only—and this for the *second* talk as well as for the first. What amazes me is that a subject so abstract should interest so many. In the days when I was a law student, the thing would have been impossible.

"I'm glad Katherine Mansfield's Journal was a happy choice. I ran over a list of books in the *New Republic*, and when I lighted on the Journal, I recalled the fact that you had mentioned it. I'm sure it would be above me—the sublimated froth—froth isn't the right word—but at any rate the fine and pure essence which poets relish, and no others . . .

"Lafe tells me your physical diet is chiefly mush, but that you are entitled to whatever literary pabulum is most agreeable to your palate.

"I had to spend all day at a meeting of the American Jewish Committee—interesting in a way, but exasperating like all committee meetings because of the waste of time. This evening I am going to my friends the Goldmans to hear some music. The gay life will be the death of me.

"It's time to stop and put on a dinner coat. I do hope you'll be well soon, and that you will be released by Friday with all allowance for good behavior. I'll hire a brass band, or if that is too exciting, I'll get an accordion or something of that sort, to greet you."

"You poets," he told her on another occasion, "have your own inner circle where the uninitiated cannot enter. Your taste is occasionally a trifle too mystical for me. Yet I find the books that strike your fancy always interesting and suggestive. That may not be a great compliment, but at least it implies a community of spirit."

The first summer after Nell's death, Cardozo preferred to remain, a lonely man, in the Seventy-fifth Street house, its rooms redolent with memories of his sister. Now and then friends visited him. "My associate, Judge Crane, dropped in to see me, and the two of us went to the Metropolitan Museum, where we looked, first of all, at the Havemeyer collection, but like the nimble style epistolary flitted lightly through the centuries, which had brought some of their finest produce and laid them at our feet. Have you been to the Museum recently? Almost as one enters, one is greeted by two gigantic effigies of the Pharaoh of the Exodus, a gift of

[191]

the Egyptian government, brought from the temple at Luxor and wrought by some Egyptian sculptor about 1250 B.C. If the effigies could see, they would probably surmise that New York was the place to which the Jews, driven forth from the land of Egypt, had been guided by the wise old Moses.

"My reading has been desultory. I have been almost as otiose as my friends at New London. . . .

"As to vacation, my plans, as the lawyers say, are still *in fieri*. I am in correspondence with the Law Institute men at North End Harbor, but if I visit them at all, which is still uncertain, it will be only for a few days.

"If your friend the palmist were to come here and look at the seams on my hand, she would find that a tendency to keep to the old familiar places, with a sense of homesickness when separated from them, was one of my distinctive traits."

Yet the home in which he now lived alone could hardly be a cheerful place. The house was comfortable enough, but one could not consider it in any way artistic. The brownstone front, the bay windows decorated with some scrollwork, were typical of their period. There were two large rooms to a floor and a good-sized sitting room in the basement. Halfway up the narrow staircase from the first floor the banisters deflected to provide for a curved seat on which the invalid Nell could rest in her ascent. The furniture, much of it from the old Madison Avenue home, was stodgy Victorian. Books, thousands of books, were the most attractive decoration.

The piano was silent. Cardozo never played after his sister's death. On some occasion he was informed by Mrs. Arthur Strasser that the Hudson Guild had no piano. Cardozo promptly offered his own. He was aware of the fine work being done by the institution headed by Dr. John Lovejoy Elliott. On his arrival home he discovered to his chagrin that his caretaker, knowing he no longer played, had sold the piano. Cardozo at once wrote, explaining the mishap, and enclosed the check which had been received for the piano.

The Judge who now lived so like a recluse had a rare gift for friendship, a quality which he displayed not only in his association with his colleagues and with men and women of his own generation, but which was especially apparent in his relations with children. The Judge always had a way with children. At home with him, they felt his sympathy and at the same time a courtesy not generally accorded to their years. When the daughters of Judge Learned Hand, still in their early teens, entered the room where Cardozo was sitting with their parents, the guest would rise to greet them, an instinctive act of deference appreciated by any woman young or old.

And he, on his part, liked the lack of awe which a child could make manifest. On one occasion, after a luncheon in the country, when a group of young men and women clustered around him, listening well-nigh reverently to the Justice's replies to their questions on matters of law and of public interest, the hostess's grandson, aged five, was constantly passing sandwiches around and frequently interrupting the honored guest with his own little boyish remarks. On leaving, Cardozo said to his hostess that the most delightful moments of his visit had come with the little lad's spontaneous approaches.

At Washington Cardozo called on a lady who was not quite ready to see him. The lady sent down her seven-year-old daughter Elizabeth to say that she would be there presently. Cardozo had a delightful time with the little girl. When the mother came down and began to express regret at keeping the Justice waiting, "Don't apologize," he said, "I've enjoyed my talk with Elizabeth and I envy her her social grace."

Once when Nellie Cohen and Hortense Hirsch, daughter-in-law of the lawyer who had greatly befriended Cardozo in his early days at the bar, took their little girls to have luncheon at the apartment in Connecticut Avenue, in Washington, the children addressed a characteristic series of intimate comments and questions to the amused host.

Caviar was being served as an hors d'oeuvre. One of the children was considerably impressed. "We don't get this at home," she informed the Judge, "but can you really afford it?" Cardozo thought he could. The little girl went on with her quest for information. Did he pay for his automobile himself or did the government foot the bill? He paid for it himself. "That," she told him sympathetically, "is too bad."

On one of his frequent visits to Judge Elkus at Red Bank, a town in New Jersey not so far from Allenhurst, he met young James Elkus, then a boy in his early teens, who was accompanied by a great St. Bernard. Cardozo pretended to be afraid of the animal, shrinking back as the dog romped up to him; the boy called, "Don't be afraid; he won't hurt you," and rushed to his protection.

Cardozo was very fond of dogs. There are many anecdotes illustrating his affection for them. At the town home of his close friend, Judge Nathan Bijur, Cardozo would often go to the end of the dining room and roll a ball way to the end of the parlor to have it retrieved by Kiki, the Airedale belonging to Judge Bijur's grandson Regan. Another favorite animal of Cardozo's was his cousin Maud's Roddy. When he learned that the animal had been run over by an automobile, he sent the following letter from Albany:

"I cannot go to bed without writing you a line of condolence on the death of poor Roddy. He had, I am sure, all the virtues appropriate to a dog and very likely many that are appropriate for men. Withal he had soulful eyes and a way of his own which must have endeared him to his fellow dogs and to humankind as well. I feel much distressed at his tragic going."

Devotion to his work and to his sister had, as we know, set

self-imposed limits beyond which Cardozo seldom found leisure to go. But his interest in science, in education, in literature, and in statesmanship remained keen, while through the Round Table in New York, during these Albany years, various friendly acquaintanceships developed.

The Round Table is the most distinguished and presumably the oldest extant of New York's dining clubs. In the more than seventy years of its existence it has had approximately only a hundred members. The list includes Presidents of the United States, Cabinet members, senators, generals, presidents of Yale and Princeton and Columbia, bishops, many editors and authors, painters and architects, geologists and astronomers, physicians, bankers and heads of great business corporations, and, notably, famous lawyers. It has had in its membership only one Justice of the Supreme Court of the United States—Cardozo.

In 1927 Brander Matthews, Columbia Professor of American Literature, wrote a privately printed history of the Round Table. He was the only official of the club, and it was he, as Honorary Secretary, who invited Cardozo to join. The Judge accepted, knowing that dinners presided over by New York's famous raconteur would be full of good talk. To President Butler, Cardozo wrote: "It did not take the charming sketch by Brander Matthews to make me grasp with eagerness the invitation to join the group of the Round Table. Somehow or other I have fancied that I could read in the honor the promptings of your friendly interest; and I thank you for this new evidence of a regard which is in itself an honor, and a precious one."

Professor Phelps, of Yale, speaking of meeting Cardozo at these dinners, said: "We had intimate conversation. I was always impressed by the clearness of his mind which seemed to illuminate every subject he discussed. But even more was I impressed by the extraordinary charm and infinite benevolence of his character."

Charm he had, which was felt by all who knew him, this gift for attracting friends. But he was able as well to feel deep friendship, never better made evident than in his eulogy on the death of Maurice J. Hirsch. His heart spoke through his lips in an address as memorable as that of Robert Ingersoll over the bier of Roscoe Conkling.

"The voice of a friend," he began, "must speak a parting word. I am sure that he would have wished it so, for in this form, while there was life, the fires of friendship burned with an irradiating warmth. You will forgive me if I speak of myself. I do so only because, to tell you what he was, I must tell you what he was to me. As I look back at our friendship through the mists of many years, I find myself wondering how it started. We came together first in the contacts of our profession, and there, if he had been like others, it would have ended. In those springtime hours, I was but a youth, and he was at the threshold of middle age, though he seemed older then to me, for gaps of that kind are longer at the beginning than they seem later near the end. I cannot tell you how or why in those distant days he took me to himself, and gave me so lavishly of his interest and his encouragement and an affection almost brotherly. I had done nothing to deserve it. I could offer nothing in return for it, not wisdom of counsel, for I was young, not the glamour of place, for I was powerless, not even the return of equal friendship, for as I measure myself with him, I know that then at least I was incapable of it. I cannot account for these things, yet they were there. These were the flowers and fruit that his nature put forth. They were mysterious and divine, like fruit and flowers everywhere. If I could tell you how they were born, I could explain the soul of a man. Not for us is such knowledge. We can only reverence and worship.

"The years went by, and our friendship deepened and strengthened. It became richer and more personal as time

[196]

lessened the disparity of years, and we grew more into mates and comrades. I think of it sometimes as a friendship very special and individual, and so indeed it was, and yet from his side less in a sense than from mine. For he had such a genius for friendship that he could distribute it widely and yet have more to spare. So I came to see in time that his friendship for me was only a fragment of a larger whole, a type or sample of the friendship that in flowerings of kindness and generosity and, if need be, even charity, he was showing to many others. His delight was to give delight. He knew as few men have known the power of little tokens of attention to cheer and strengthen. There was the handclasp and the heartening word and the gift—a trifle, if you please—that was the visible message of remembrance and encouragement. He wished so much to help . . .

"In my description of the friend, I have ignored many phases of the man, the wise counselor, the sagacious lawyer, the graceful and ready speaker at many a happy banquet, the writer of countless letters bristling with quips and repartee and all the gaieties of a nimble wit. Precious are these memories, yet they are not the memories that are surging at this hour in your hearts and in mine. We are thinking of other things, the great fundamental virtues of tenderness and gentleness and charity. These are the things that last. The life seemed simple while it lasted. We may not always have been conscious of its beauty. The end comes; and behold it is illumined with the white and piercing light of the divinity within it. Let us give thanks that it is so.

"I have spoken of the friend who has left us the things that would rejoice our hearts if anyone could say them of us. I have tried to say them simply. I know that I have said them truly. And I have said them with the voice of a friend.

"When the course is finished, when the play is ended, when the lights are out, may the voice of a friend be able to say like things of us."

XIII

None knew thee but to love thee,
Nor named thee but to praise.

FITZ GREENE HALLECK

OLIVER WENDELL HOLMES had served on the bench for nearly half a century. After twenty-nine years in the Supreme Court of Massachusetts, he was appointed by Theodore Roosevelt in 1902 to the Supreme Court of the United States. His is an unparalleled record, not only by reason of length of service as a jurist, and the value of that service, but notably because as a man of eighty, as a man of ninety, his were the great spirit and the great mind among his fellow Justices.

To Holmes fittingly belongs that title of "the Master" accorded him by Cardozo. Two generations of lawyers, teachers of law, judges, listened to him, followed in his footsteps. In the dissenting opinions—far rarer than is generally believed—of Oliver Wendell Holmes, there was invariably the fructifying seed of liberal thought. "Free thought for those who agree with us, but freedom for the thought we hate," he wrote with Voltairean courage in declaring that Rosika Schwimmer should not be barred from citizenship because she refused to bear arms. And this from the man who had fought in battle after battle of the Civil

War, and to whom patriotism was dear. His own personal feelings, or even past beliefs upon which his conduct of life had been based, did not retard the progress of his philosophy. His aristocratic background did not interfere with his early pronouncement of the right of workingmen to combine for their own interests "so long as they do no violence or threaten no violence." Here, as in others of his constitutional opinions, the pioneer.

On January 12, 1932, Holmes, then past fourscore and ten years of age, laid down the cares of high office. He had given his associates in the Supreme Court no definite information concerning the date of his resignation, though there was gossip in Washington that he intended to retire before long. According to an article in the *New York Tribune*, Holmes, on being helped into his overcoat in the cloakroom the previous evening, remarked, "I won't be down tomorrow." Those who overheard him did not know that his letter of resignation was already written and that these five words were his valedictory.

President Hoover accepted his resignation with reluctance, for Holmes, despite ill-health, still functioned with wisdom and brilliancy. His associates, headed by Chief Justice Hughes, immediately sent their revered colleague a letter of admiration and affection. "Your profound learning and philosophic outlook," it reads in part, "have found expression in opinions which have become classics, enriching the literature of the law, as well as its substance."

That same night there took place in Washington a dinner of significance in the career of Benjamin Cardozo. Five senators and fifteen or twenty members of the House of Representatives had been gathered together for the purpose of affording Bishop McConnell and Rabbi Wise the opportunity of urging these legislators to support old-age pensions. During the meal there was, of course, talk concerning the resignation of Justice Holmes, and his possible successor.

Dr. Wise was delighted to find practically everyone present speaking of his friend, the Chief Judge of New York State, "in terms of almost unlimited admiration of his learning and character." Dr. Wise thereupon suggested to Senator Brookhart that Senator Borah "might well urge the President to name Cardozo."

Three days later the influential New York clergyman received the following telegram from the progressive Idaho statesman: "Am anxious to see Judge Cardozo advanced to the Supreme Court. Can we help the cause along. Confidential." Borah had already spoken to President Hoover, who was fully aware of what the entire American bar thought of New York's Chief Judge. Hoover himself had been greatly impressed by Cardozo during a meeting at the White House. The only difficulty advanced by the President in the initial talk with Senator Borah was the matter of geographical consideration. Forty-eight states, and nine members of the Supreme Court. Hughes and Stone already represented New York. Should a third resident of the metropolis be appointed? Borah's reply was that Cardozo was a national, not a local, candidate. He belonged as much to the West as to the East, to Idaho as to New York.

The President did not immediately assent, and Senator Borah realized the necessity of having Western lawyers urge the appointment.

Newton D. Baker of Cincinnati was being considered as the successor to Holmes. Dr. Wise got President Wilson's Secretary of War on the telephone and asked him "whether he was thinking of Holmes's place." "Yes," answered Mr. Baker, "but not for myself." Wise then asked him whether he would wire and write to Mr. Hoover in favor of Cardozo. "I'll do it within an hour," the former Cabinet member said. "I'll tell the President the appointment ought to be decided by mentality and not geography."

The ball had been set rolling. Governors of various

[200]

states, presidents of bar associations throughout the nation, leading lawyers, businessmen, and just plain ordinary citizens petitioned the President to appoint Cardozo. Felix Frankfurter, one of the most eminent among professors of law, was ardently in favor of Cardozo. Nicholas Murray Butler, a leader in Republican councils, was, foremost among university heads, in his favor. In personal conversation with Mr. Hoover he urged the President to appoint Cardozo. What in these critical weeks was going on behind the scenes was withheld from the knowledge of Cardozo himself, lest he impose any restraint on his backers. Among these was Senator Wagner of New York who realized that the humanitarian point of view shown by Cardozo in opinions from the bench was similar to his own in legislative matters.

They, indeed, pulled the strings—Borah, Wagner and Wickersham, Butler and Wise and Baker, and influential newspapermen such as Mark Sullivan, and many leaders of bench and bar—but not the strings of any puppet. They were pulling the strings of a curtain. When it parted, it disclosed the leaders of law, the educators of the nation's youth, the editors of the nation's press, well-nigh unanimous in their agreement that there was only one man who should succeed Oliver Wendell Holmes.

On January 23, 1932, the New York State Bar Association held a meeting at the Hotel Astor. Samuel Seabury, on succeeding former Chief Judge Hiscock to the presidency, read to the assembled members the telegram of endorsement prepared to be sent to the President of the United States. The message concluded with these words: "In the conviction that the matter is too important to be affected by geographical considerations and that only the welfare of the nation should be considered, this association presents the name of the man recognized by the profession and the people alike as the most distinguished jurist of our age—Chief Judge

[201]

Benjamin N. Cardozo of the Court of Appeals of the State of New York." With one accord, all the eight hundred judges and lawyers present rose to their feet and voted their approval.

Cardozo, very happy, of course, at the warmth of his legal brethren, showed his quiet sense of humor at the luncheon of the judicial section. He related the answer of a high-school graduate who wrote that the "Supreme Court of the United States consists of a Chief Justice and eight sociable justices." "I am afraid," Cardozo added smilingly, "I have never been much of a success as a sociable man."

President Hoover was fully entitled to ponder his decision —to take into consideration the advisability of three Supreme Court Justices from a single state; even to give thought to the possibility of increase in anti-Semitism in adding a Cardozo to a Brandeis. Mr. Hoover was devoid of racial prejudice. The thought he gave to this angle of the advocated appointment was based solely on his unwillingness to add fuel to an incipient flame.

Mr. Hoover laid aside his list of Western possibilities, headed by Judge James of California. After the final talk with Senator Borah, the Republican Chief Executive signed the nomination of the New York judge, a Democrat. Call it, if you will, as writers in the press have called it, the arrival at high office by acclamation, comparable to the election of George Washington. Call Senator Borah the *deus ex machina* who arranged the happy ending. The fact remains that Mr. Hoover had the deciding vote. Lasting credit is his that he gave it.

For weeks Cardozo had known his name was being considered at the White House. Could he refuse if the invitation were tendered? Hardly. Would he accept? Only with hardship. He was torn this way and that. The ambition of a lifetime had been consummated on ascending the Supreme Court bench from which his father had stepped down. In

Albany he was in a circle of friends who were devoted to him and to whom he was devoted. He was the shy man whose sister was no longer alive, and for whom the wives and daughters of the Albany judges felt protective affection. How would it be at Washington, with its raucous political voices, its formal social demands, its homes devoid of the friendships formed in his native and his adopted cities? It would, Cardozo knew, be lonely beyond words.

In 1922, when his candidacy for the Supreme Court had first been suggested, Cardozo would have been delighted to receive the appointment. In 1932 he was sincerely reluctant to have the high honor awarded him. But the situation, in 1922, had been entirely different. He was not only ten years younger; he was ten years less weary of life. Nellie was still alive. She had not yet suffered the stroke which incapacitated her from building up a new home in Washington for her brother and herself. Cardozo had not yet become the idolized Chief Judge of the Court of Appeals, deeply loved in all circles of Albany. In 1922 his own health was sufficient for new and strenuous labor. Several years were still to pass before the warnings of his first heart attacks. A man still in the comparative vigor of middle life could have been appointed by President Harding, the appointment welcomed.

In 1928 Cardozo wrote to his cousin Maud: "I have no doubt I'd take a Washington appointment if it came along, though I think my present office is in many ways of greater significance for the development of the law. So I am not greatly concerned one way or the other. Things fall out in such matters as they will, and one feels oneself in the hands of destiny." There is a contrast between the tone of this letter and the one he wrote her on January 17, 1932.

"I am trying to stave off the appointment," he said. "Whatever reputation I have built up has been made as a state judge. I don't want to start all over again and build up another. But most of all I don't want to live in utter loneliness away from my present associates in the Court of Appeals to whom I am much attached and away from all my relatives and friends here whom I love even better."

In contrast to his weariness and lack of enthusiasm over the appointment, "There was," said Merrill E. Otis, United States District Judge of the Western District of Missouri, "a veritable chorus proposing Cardozo's name—acclaimed by high and low, rich and poor, conservative and liberals." Otis speaks of Cardozo's architectonics of opinions—how fact, argument, and illustration produce a cumulative mass effect. "Form and substance fused. . . . The Judge in expounding a science practices an art."

Less than a fortnight after the resignation of Justice Holmes, Cardozo answered in the following terms the lines of an enthusiastic friend, a scholar and an educator to whom he was endeared, George Kohut:

"I don't know how to answer your letter. It moves me deeply. I find that I am rapidly developing into a myth. If I were not a Jew, I should expect to be transformed pretty soon into a Greek God.

"It is hard to make people believe me, but I prefer my present office to a place on the Supreme Court, though I might find myself forced to accept promotion if it were offered me. I believe I have a greater influence on the development of law where I am than I could have at Washington. Then, from the personal viewpoint, it would be very hard to pull up stakes and break the few ties that are left me.

"The best thing about the agitation is that it gives me an insight into the devotion of my friends."

To Cardozo, himself a witty versifier, more than one poem has been addressed. Typical is the sonnet by the recipient of the foregoing letter:

> Your classic brow is exquisitely wrought
> As though another Phydias had writ
> Unerringly his autograph on it—

There dwells enthroned a sovereign of thought
Inexorably logical and true
Who speaks in language crystalline as dew;
Your words make music on the printed page
And each new dictum marks you for a sage.
Your wise decisions shall be handed down
As high tradition, and from age to age
Shall wax exceeding greater your renown.
But as for us, you need no other crown
Save only this: We love you as you are,
Dear Humanist, Kind Friend, our Guiding Star!

The sonnet's closing phrase may, to those who did not
know Cardozo, seem justifiable poetic license and a happy
way to rhyme with "are." As a matter of fact he was a guiding star to many persons. Poets, clergymen of all faiths, men
of letters, ethical philosophers, teachers in colleges and
schools are frequently the torchbearers in their days and for
later generations. But how often does a New York lawyer
enter the ranks of such dispensers of light? "My judicial
idol," Professor Beale of Harvard called him.

On February 15, just about three weeks after the telegram signed by Judge Seabury arrived at the White House,
Mr. Hoover's decision was made public. The Associated
Press informed the Judge at Albany. "That is very interesting," said Cardozo, "and I thank you for the information.
There is nothing I can appropriately say at this time, however." He added later: "It is a great honor, and I appreciate
it, but I really would not care to comment."

But from what other sources the comments poured in!
Franklin D. Roosevelt, New York's Governor, congratulated
the President and the people of the United States, saying:
"I know of no jurist more learned in the law, more liberal
in its interpretation and more insistent that simple justice
keep step with the progress of civilization and the bettering
of the lot of the average individuals who make up mankind."

[205]

Herbert Lehman, then the Lieutenant Governor, expressed his delight, and similarly congratulated the nation. Alfred E. Smith, former Governor of the State of New York, spoke of his "great delight at the elevation of Benjamin Cardozo to the Supreme Court. In ability he is second to none and he will grace that bench." Nicholas Murray Butler: "This is the best possible appointment that could be made. It brings to the service of the Supreme Court the most profound and the most scholarly legal mind among all our people."

The enthusiasm of senators, Republican and Democrat alike, was no less marked. Borah of Idaho: "It is a most fortunate appointment." Watson of Indiana: "He will grace the Supreme Bench with dignity, learning, and experience." King of Utah: "No better appointment could have been made." Couzens of Michigan: "The President has done an excellent thing in the interest of public confidence in the Court." LaFollette of Wisconsin: "The appointment will meet with the overwhelming approval of the country." Wagner of New York: "The country will receive the announcement with boundless gratification."

And so on and so on from senators, congressmen, and judges of many other states, while editors throughout the country joined in the chorus of approval. Their opinions—or rather their opinion, for there was only one opinion among all of them—may be condensed into the phrase so generously used by Judge Learned Hand, whose name had been among the names considered by the President. "Judge Cardozo," said Judge Hand, "is the only possible successor to Justice Holmes."

Let the paean close on the uncontroverted and incontrovertible words of United States Attorney George Medalie, who said: "Judge Cardozo is the most beloved and admired judge in America."

Cardozo yielded to the insistent demand for the nomination and for the acceptance of the high office. There is an anecdote of his having mulled over the wording of his refusal when the anticipated letter from the President should reach him. But the invitation came personally from Mr. Hoover over the telephone, and Cardozo, thus taken unawares, stammered his thanks and his acceptance. Perhaps it is only an anecdote not susceptible of confirmation, but of his reluctance there can be no question.

Governor Herbert H. Lehman, of New York, writes: "When the announcement was made that he had been offered his appointment to the United States Supreme Court, Mrs. Lehman and I immediately called on him at his chambers in order to congratulate him on the honor that had come to him and to express our regret that he was leaving Albany where the people had loved him for so many years. We found the Justice in a sad and very subdued mood. His comment was: 'I have never so greatly enjoyed so many years of my life as I have those which I spent in Albany as a member and as Chief Judge of the Court of Appeals. I hate the thought of leaving here where I have made so many friends. Do you however,' he continued, 'see any way in which I could refuse the appointment of the President of the United States?'

"His whole attitude was one of deep humility and modesty. He seemed to care nothing for this great honor and distinction which had been conferred on him. His only thought reflected a desire to serve the people of the country to the best of his ability."

On receiving a gift of flowers from his cousin Maud on his appointment, Cardozo wrote to her: "The flowers are lovely, and in spite of the exaggerated honors, I have felt the need of something to brighten me. Many, many thanks. I'd love to say 'yes' to your invitation, but really I don't dare to do so. You see, I must wind up my work in the Court of Appeals, and I shall be busy day and night for the next week or more getting rid of my opinions. If I make evening appointments, I shall be doomed. One or two pledges made weeks ago will have to be redeemed, but it won't do to make new ones, will it? This typewritten answer is horridly bad form, but I have hundreds of letters and telegrams and my hand is worn out."

An amusing aspect of these letters was the fact that among them were scores from women who, having read of his appointment to high office, having seen his picture, having learned that he was a bachelor, immediately wrote to him proposing marriage, sending him their photographs. Cardozo, though somewhat taken aback, was much entertained by this unexpected result of his appointment, but he did not answer the letters.

Busy were the weeks subsequent to his nomination by President Hoover on February 15, and prior to the day, March 14, when Cardozo was inducted into office in the Supreme Court. Nearly eighteen years of service on the Albany bench came to an end on February 16. The Court of Appeals was about to sit for the last day of the session. The attendants were waiting for the judges to enter. Almost the only topic of their conversation concerned the fact that they would never again see the endeared Chief Judge officiating in the courtroom.

At ten o'clock the judges entered—Cardozo and Pound and Crane, Kellogg and Hubbs and O'Brien. Irving Lehman was away from Albany. There was not much on the calendar—four cases in all. The arguments of the various attorneys were heard with attention, Cardozo, every now and then, saving time in getting to the heart of the matter or in helping out some attorney who might be a little flustered. In one instance—a tax case in which the City of New York was involved—the Chief Judge referred to a similar question which had already been decided upon and of which the lawyer had no knowledge. It was but another instance of Cardozo's phenomenal memory. The entire scene in the courtroom and the incidents of this final day have been described in the *Boston Evening Transcript*. It is a picture not easily to be forgotten—the formal judicial proceedings with their deep undertone of sentiment.

When Cardozo had left the courtroom a little after the hour of eleven, there followed a brief consultation among the judges. He was to meet his colleagues in further conferences to decide on opinions concerning cases previously heard, but this in private. The public was not again to see him in the Court of Appeals.

In his chambers that day the Judge received visitors eager to congratulate him on his appointment to the Supreme Court; and reporters, of course, full of questions.

"Yes, it is hard to leave such pleasant surroundings, but I feel honored to be nominated to the Supreme Court," he said to a reporter of the *New York Times*. "There is not anything very interesting about me," he added. "I hope I shall not lose my sense of humor over all this attention."

Asked about his hobbies, he answered that he hadn't found time for any. As to reading: "Oh, law, philosophy and history, and occasionally novels." Then, laughingly, he went on: "Please don't say detective stories. I have read detective stories but not many. I prefer other books."

The interviewer asked whether Cardozo knew President Hoover. Justice Stone had, indeed, introduced Cardozo at the White House, yet the Judge characteristically answered: "I have met him once, but he wouldn't know me if he passed me. I'd know him from his pictures."

The reporter, intent on further personal data, followed the Judge to the Ten Eyck Hotel, Cardozo's Albany home.

"He's a fine man," the elevator operator said, as the Judge entered. The bellboy pushed a sheaf of telegrams into his hand, blurting, "Congratulations, Judge." The clerk at the newsstand added his "That's mighty fine, Judge. Good luck." Cardozo, one knows, was not so certain that his appointment was good luck. His friends at Albany were being left behind.

The next day Cardozo returned to New York. In the newspapers of his native city and throughout the country, he could read editorials of praise on his appointment, articles concerning his last days at Albany—all indicating the regard in which he was so widely held. All, that is, save those articles that had to do with William H. Anderson's protest against the appointment. On February 19 the former superintendent of the New York Anti-Saloon League appeared before the Senate Judiciary subcommittee to offer testimony that Cardozo was not a fit candidate for the Supreme Court. Anderson, convicted of forgery, had been sent to prison for several years after the Court of Appeals at Albany had affirmed his conviction. Here was his chance to be revenged on Cardozo who had been among the judges to reject his appeal.

The press of America, in commending Cardozo's appointment, had, with a sportsman's good taste, made no reference to his father's resignation from the bench. Mr. Anderson felt no qualms in the matter. He did not limit himself to questioning Cardozo's "fitness as indicated by his contribution to the consummation of an infamy of injustice," this being his way of alluding to his own conviction of forgery. In dragging in the ancient scandal, he maintained that the derelictions of Albert Cardozo were referred to, because they were of significance in connection with what he termed the conspiracy to deprive him of his liberties. He went so far as to characterize the upright son as a "second generation Tammany judge."

The Senate subcommittee, headed by the Republican Senator Norris of Nebraska, listened in disgust. Then, unanimously, they recommended the confirmation of Cardozo's appointment. Four days after the action of the subcommittee, the Senate Judiciary Committee, headed by

[210]

Senator Robinson of Indiana, with like unanimity reported Cardozo's name to the Senate. When, after two days had gone by, his name was brought up to be voted upon, there was no discussion, there was no roll call. The chief clerk read the name and a moment later it had been unanimously confirmed.

Even at the threshold of the Supreme Court, the stigma of his father's name, which Cardozo had labored so heroically to eradicate, followed him. How deeply that shadow affected Cardozo throughout his life no one will ever know. While he was elected to honorary membership in the Bar Association he was never willing to become a regular member. His reluctance in this respect was due to the fact that the Bar Association had preferred charges against his father.

Twice during the Albany days, Judge Elkus says, he encountered that old ghost while with Cardozo. On one occasion he remembered, "We called one day at the Supreme Court Judges' chambers in New York to see another judge. When we were coming out of the chambers we met McInernay, familiarly known as 'Mac' to everyone in New York. He greeted us warmly and said to Judge Cardozo: 'I remember the day you were born. Your father came to the chambers of the court and he said to me, 'I have another boy. Congratulate me, I am proud of it.' "

This was presumably one of the rare times when Ben Cardozo smiled pleasantly at the mention of his father. He felt quite differently when, in 1919 or 1920, Julian T. Davies, in an address to the Bar Association, without knowing that the Judge was there, mentioned Albert Cardozo's connection with the Tweed Ring. Cardozo, Judge Elkus relates, blushed painfully, but he could not make himself conspicuous by leaving the meeting. Though Cardozo had in previous years spoken to Elkus of his desire to "work away" his father's disrepute, on this occasion, as the two judges walked home together, there was almost entire silence.

During the week which saw Cardozo's appointment to the Supreme Court confirmed, the bicentennial celebration of the birth of George Washington aroused much oratory throughout the land. At Albany the chief eulogy was delivered by Governor Roosevelt. "It is only once in many centuries that this old world of ours," the Governor said, "discovers a man who combines in himself the quality of courageous and sagacious leader, with the character of simple and unaffected unselfishness. When we think of him as Commander in Chief in the War of the Revolution, and as the first President of our Republic, let us remember him, too, as a great and simple gentleman—a gentleman unafraid."

Cardozo was likewise an orator at the Albany exercises. The deathless heritage bequeathed by Washington was, the Judge maintained, not a matter of governmental structure. It was the "faith and purpose that inspired it, the faith and purpose symbolized and made incarnate" in the person of our first President. . . . Deathless the heritage is for the values it embodies, the values of the spirit."

This was the second time within four months that Cardozo had attended ceremonies identified with a great American President. The first occasion was in the month of October, 1931, when the Roosevelt Memorial Association awarded its three medals for distinguished service, the first going to Cardozo. Hamlin Garland, the historian of the Middle West, and Dr. C. Hart Merriam, founder of the United States Biological Survey, were the other recipients.

The proceedings took place in the house in Twentieth Street where Theodore Roosevelt had been born seventy-three years before. The son of another President of the United States, James R. Garfield, in presenting the medal to Cardozo, quoted the words of Alfred E. Smith, Governor of the State of New York: "He 'embodies every qualification consonant with the highest judicial ideals; a scholar of

[212]

immeasurable attainments, a lawyer of unbounded legal erudition, the very embodiment of impartiality, fairness and justice.' At a time when some of the lower courts of his State have been under fire, his integrity, love of justice, and high-minded approach to the duties of his post have been a model and an inspiration to courts throughout the country, and a token to the public of the soundness of their judicial system. His penetrating mind and unusual literary felicity have clarified for the legal world the function of the judge in shaping and developing the law."

In acknowledging the congratulations he received, Cardozo wrote to Aline Goldstone: "You and Lafe are too good to me—taking note of my little prizes and making much of them, just as if I were still at school or in college and had been encouraged to be good and studious. I had to make a speech when I got the medal, and that spoiled the evening for me. I would have released all interest in the glittering decoration if I could have decently run away before my name was called."

To his cousin Maud he had written a few months earlier: "I am specializing in medals nowadays. I got another two months ago conferred by the Harvard law faculty. When I pay that visit to you, I am going to arrive all bespangled with decorations like a foreign potentate."

It is interesting to note, in connection with the tribute to Cardozo from Al Smith quoted above, that his admiration was reciprocated by the Judge. At the time Smith ran for the presidency Cardozo had written of him, making one of his few comments on politics. "How, my dear child," he asked, "can one with your poetic insight fail to feel the charm and the power and the inspiration of Al Smith? Everything you say against him could be said—and was said—of Lincoln. Those who said it of Lincoln were—many of them—sorry for it afterwards. If this be treason, etc." Later he added: "Read Dr. Butler's letter in the *Times* today. Not in the triumph of the Republican party as it is constituted at the present time will the seer's vision be attained and realized.

"I mustn't talk politics, however. These things are, somehow or other, matters of inward, almost indefinable, feeling rather than reasoned conviction. One rarely persuades another who is not already half convinced."

On March 4, Cardozo was again in Albany—this time to hear an address in his own honor. There were a few final matters to attend to on this, his last day as Chief Judge of the Court of Appeals. These completed, the final hour arrived. Surrounded by the associate judges, Cardozo heard with deep emotion the speech made by Judge Cuthbert W. Pound in presenting the silver loving cup on which the names of all the judges were inscribed. The loving cup remained to the end of Cardozo's days the dearest of his possessions.

"You have been a member of this court for eighteen years," said Judge Pound. "All the bright spirits who were here to welcome you in 1914 have gone. For more than five years, after serving under Chief Judges Cullen, Bartlett, and Hiscock, you have sat as our head. The bar knows with what earnestness of conviction, firmness of grasp, and force and grace of utterance you have made your power felt; with what evenness, courtesy, and calmness you have presided over the sessions of the court. Only your associates can know the tender relations which have existed among us; the industry with which you have examined and considered every case that has come before us; the diligence with which you have risen before it was yet dawn and have burned the midlight lamp to satisfy yourself that no cause was being neglected. At times your patience may have been tried by the perplexities of counsel and of your associates, but nothing has ever moved you to an unkind or hasty word. You have kept the court up with its calendar

Chief Judge of the Court of Appeals

by promoting that complete harmony of purpose which is essential to effective work. The rich storehouse of your unfailing memory has always been open to us. I shall not dwell upon your rare qualifications for the bench of that incomparable tribunal of statesmanship and law, the Supreme Court of the United States. You were appointed neither for political nor for geographical considerations, but in defiance of them and because the whole country demanded the one man who could best carry on the great Holmes tradition of philosophic approach to modern American jurisprudence. Our loss is the gain of the high court to which you go. There will be no rest for you, no relaxation in your efforts to solve by legal formulas the problems of justice in the great field of constitutional law.

'And who hath trod Olympus, from his eye
Fades not the broader outlook of the gods.'

"We shall miss not only the great Chief Judge whose wisdom and understanding have added glory to the judicial office, but also the true man who has blessed us with the light of his friendship, the sunshine of his smile. Not so much honoring you, as leaving with you some reminder of our regard, we offer you this symbol of our esteem. If you miss, as you may in your new environment, the sweet serenity of your Albany life, the admiration of your brethren of some new and unexpected stroke of your genius and the tranquillity of your personal and official relations, may this memento of those who love you serve to cheer and inspire you."

While Judge Pound's speech of farewell touched Cardozo more deeply than any other of the addresses of tribute brightening the path of his years, he had unique pleasure of another kind in a tribute received a few weeks later. It came from artists and writers, fellow members in the Century Association. They wished to give a dinner in the Judge's honor and had asked A. Vincent Tack to be the one to invite Cardozo.

"Judge Cardozo," said Mr. Tack, "we are not inviting you because you are a great jurist. We painters and writers are inviting you because you are a great artist."

Cardozo, much pleased at this compliment to his literary style rather than to his achievements as a judge, thereupon accepted.

The dinner took place on March 8. It was an informal affair attended by a dozen men. Among them were Royal Cortissoz, the art editor; Austin Strong, the dramatist; Rodman Gilder, the publisher; Albert Gallatin, the collector of Greek art. There, too, were Louis V. Ledoux, an authority on Japanese prints; Howard Giles, distinguished for his illustrations; Charles Hopkinson, the portraitist; and, of course, Mr. Tack. Cardozo thus found himself, for the first time in his life, an "artist" among a group composed solely of other artists and art lovers. He was glad to forget, for the time being, that he was a judge. When he was so addressed, he said that, as he had just resigned from his Albany post and was not yet confirmed at Washington, he was neither a judge nor a justice. He suggested that he should be addressed merely as "Citizen Cardozo." He did not claim for himself the title of artist but, looking around at the men who were his hosts at the dinner, Cardozo remarked that this was the beginning of his art education.

At dinners of men, risqué stories are permissible if wit is their justification. On this occasion, however, no one cared to venture on any anecdote even bordering on the indecent. Though Cardozo was not in the least a prude, it seemed better to omit all chances of possible offense. Yet the evening was not without its amusing anecdotes. One in especial greatly entertained the judge. There was, it seems, a young Christian who, in the days of Nero, was brought into the arena to be devoured by the lions. A fierce and hungry lion was the first to approach. The young man said something to him. The lion backed away. Another and fiercer lion then came up. Again the young man whispered something. There was the same effect on a third lion, the fiercest of all. Nero, seated in his box, had the young man brought up to him. "If you will tell me what magic you used with those beasts," said the Emperor, "I will grant you your freedom." "What I said to each lion," replied the youth, "was merely this: 'Devour me if you wish, but remember that after the repast you will have to make an after-dinner speech.'"

The dinner ended, the lion—the lion of the occasion—made no formal speech, but he did say a few gracious words expressing his happiness at having these writers and artists accept him as one of them.

The day Cardozo left the Court of Appeals at Albany it was, in the opinion of Judge Hand, at its top with such men as Andrews, Kellogg, Lehman, and Pound. While Judge Seabury thinks that Judge Cuthbert Pound's opinions did as much for the liberalization of the court in its early swing from its former reactionary nature as did the opinions of Cardozo, nevertheless, it was foremost Cardozo who "steered them safely in the course they should go."

On March 15, Cardozo was initiated into office as an Associate Justice of the Supreme Court. Briefly before noon the Judge donned his black robe in the little room where Chief Justice Hughes and his colleagues were awaiting him. Here Mr. Hughes administered the constitutional oath, with none but the other Justices and the clerk of the Court as witnesses. This simple ceremony concluded, the group went across the corridor into the semicircular courtroom which, in earlier years, had been the Senate room of the United States. The voice of the clerk cried out that the Court was opened. The Chief Justice announced to the audience in the crowded room that Judge Cardozo had been appointed by President Hoover to succeed Oliver Wendell Holmes. Among those hearing the announcement were Senator Borah and Rabbi Wise, who had so ardently advocated the nomination. Various cousins of the Judge were there. No nearer kin. Parents, brother, all four sisters were dead.

The presidential commission was read aloud; the judicial oath administered by the clerk of the Court. The marshal then conducted Cardozo to his seat. The newest member of the Court was, as is the custom, placed on the extreme left of the Chief Justice. Next to him was his friend Justice Stone, who shook Cardozo's hand heartily. The ceremony was over.

"Up he goes," began an article in the *Literary Digest*, entitled "America Judges Her New Judge:" "Up he goes to the highest post an American lawyer can win—to the United States Supreme Court . . . the entire country cheering his name."

XIV

The heights by great men reached and kept
Were not attained by sudden flight.

LONGFELLOW

WHEN Cardozo took his seat in the Supreme Court, his colleagues were Chief Justice Hughes and Associate Justices Van Devanter, appointed by President Taft; McReynolds and Brandeis, by President Wilson; Sutherland and Butler, by President Harding; Stone, by President Coolidge; Roberts, by President Hoover. In the six years of Cardozo's incumbency the only changes came about with the resignation of Van Devanter in 1937 and the retirement of Sutherland in 1938. President Roosevelt replaced them with Senator Black—amid furor—and Solicitor General Reed—amid general applause.

The first-named eight Justices formed with Cardozo the group of so-called "nine old men" who made history in the years 1932–1938. To go at length into their important decisions is beyond the scope of this book. A general survey of what the Supreme Court meant in and to those years of its own transition has been splendidly presented by Charles and Mary Beard in their volume entitled *America in Midpassage*. From 1932 to 1935 the ultraconservative group, comprising Justices Sutherland, Van Devanter,

[219]

McReynolds, and Butler, were in the ascendancy. After that the more liberal views of Justices Brandeis, Stone, and Cardozo led to many majority opinions in which the careful, yet broad-minded Chief Justice, as well as Justice Roberts, frequently concurred.

Prior to brief comment on a few of the most significant cases, the attitude of his colleagues toward Cardozo and his feelings toward them should be presented. For here we have Cardozo, away from his friends and relatives in New York and Albany, sitting from noon until four-thirty with men who, even during the half-hour recess for luncheon, were at the beginning of his first term almost his only companions in Washington. Of course, all admired him—save, perhaps, Mr. Justice McReynolds. They recognized as one of the greatest of jurists the former Chief Judge of New York's Court of Appeals. They were familiar with the Albany record, where Cardozo had dissented less than a score of times in the more than five hundred opinions from his pen. They welcomed him into their midst—all save Mr. Justice McReynolds.

"Why does Justice McReynolds dislike me so?" Cardozo asked of one of his secretaries. Never before had this man whose family traditions were interwoven with American history since colonial days experienced racial prejudice.

Cardozo regarded Sutherland and Van Devanter as decidedly pleasant gentlemen, though his opinions and theirs were frequently at variance. A man of wit himself, he delighted in the Irish wit of Justice Butler. He was friendly with Roberts and was a frequent recipient of flowers sent to him by the gracious Mrs. Roberts from their place in Pennsylvania.

Cardozo had long been known to Chief Justice Hughes. The former Secretary of State had followed Cardozo's career with continued interest. While not always agreeing

[220]

with his judicial opinions, Hughes decided with the same liberal spirit in many critical cases involving social advance. Both men, in their writings as well as their speeches, had long been exponents of justice beyond the letter of the law. Each had long held the other in high regard. Hughes first met Ben Cardozo in 1884. That year Hughes had received a three-year Fellowship carrying $500 a year in the Columbia Law School. DeWitt Seligman was in the same law class. Through DeWitt, Hughes got a summer job of tutoring DeWitt's brother-in-law, Larry Bernheimer. This was at Long Branch where the Cardozos and the Seligmans then had their country homes. Hughes lived at a boardinghouse. One day a Miss Israels came down to visit the daughter of the landlady. Hughes took the two girls to a dance at the West End Hotel. While the girls and Hughes were sitting on the veranda looking in at the dance the two Cardozo boys came up. Allie was then about twenty-three, Ben still in knickerbockers, a boy of fourteen. Hughes immediately liked young Ben, with whom he then had his first conversation.

Later, when Hughes was with Chamberlin, Carter and Hornblower, and Ben was a young lawyer—this was after 1893—Hughes ran into Allie Cardozo quite frequently and met Ben as a young man. When Cardozo became a judge in January, 1914, C. E. Hughes, Jr., became his secretary until Cardozo left New York for Albany. He spoke to his father of Cardozo as being "just about superlative." On one occasion Cardozo told the elder Hughes, while he was still a lawyer, that he had come down to hear him argue cases. "How did you come to do that?" asked Hughes. Cardozo answered, "Various young fellows who have heard you told me not to miss your arguments."

Between these two men there was mutual esteem and high regard. Cardozo once spoke of Hughes as "the ideal presiding Chief Justice," while Hughes spoke of Cardozo's style as the "outflowing of his genius." "Statements," he said, "that go out like a beam of light."

Cardozo had a high opinion also of Brandeis. No week passed by without a social visit or a conference on court matters at the home of the great jurist from Massachusetts. Presumably, too, the unostentatious atmosphere of that home—the stoic simplicity so consonant with the character of its master—appealed to him. And what Brandeis thought of Cardozo is delightfully set forth in the verses which, according to Mrs. Brandeis, her husband liked to quote in speaking of Cardozo. "The Justice," Mrs. Brandeis writes, "thinks you will find them in *Iolanthe*":

> Though the views of the house have diverged
> On every conceivable motion,
> All questions of party are merged
> In the frenzy of love and devotion.

Most devoted to Cardozo of all the Justices at Washington—though hardly the type to indulge in frenzy—was Harlan Stone. Justice Stone was born in the little town of Chesterfield, N. H., two years after the birth of Cardozo in the great city of New York. Their ancestry, their entire background, was very dissimilar. Their temperaments, their ways of life, were different. Consider the powerfully built man, a former football player, who could handle a medicine ball in later life with the utmost ease, and the frail man ever averse to all exercise. The one, hearty in all his contacts, the other reserved. Yet in mind and character Cardozo and Stone were much alike. As they grew to know each other better, affection followed in the steps of admiration. They sat next to each other in the courthouse; they discussed cases after court sessions were over; they dined at each other's homes. There was deep sympathy between them. They were at one in their interpretation of justice. When either was ill, how solicitous was the other!

Stone's first visit after recovering from serious illness was to his friend's apartment. Cardozo, standing at the window, was eagerly waiting for him. He saw Stone striding swiftly across the avenue. "See," said Cardozo jubilantly to one of his secretaries, "he walks like a young boy!" For the lonely man, Stone's friendship was the warmest note in the Washington years.

For many years the two jurists had corresponded. The letters, with the exception of the early ones, have fortunately been preserved. They constitute a series rare in American annals. Two of our greatest men of law are exchanging thoughts on matters that have become a part of the history of our times. On December 30, 1927, Cardozo wrote to Justice Stone:

"We have before us in our court the question whether the so-called Jones Act, which extends the Employers' Liability Act of Congress to persons injured aboard vessels, is to be restricted to domestic vessels or applied to foreign vessels also.

"Word has just come to me, more or less vaguely, that the same question has been argued recently in the Supreme Court of the United States, and is now *sub-judice*.

"Shall I be troubling you overmuch if I ask you to let me know whether this is so?"

The information was immediately forthcoming; whereupon Cardozo as promptly expressed his appreciation. "The rumor that came to me," he wrote, "on the subject was very vague, but I thought it advisable for our court to proceed to an intermediate decision if a ruling might be expected any day from our superiors."

Many notable opinions were issuing from Cardozo's pen in 1928, and Stone frequently voiced his admiration. There was the case where the decision was reached that the Appellate Division was empowered "to direct a general inquiry into the conduct of its own officers, the members

[223]

of the bar." Cardozo ended his opinion with the memorable words: "In the long run the power now conceded will make for the health and honor of the profession and for the protection of the public. If the house is to be cleansed, it is for those who occupy it and govern it, rather than for strangers to do the noisome work."

Was it this opinion, concurred in by all the Albany judges, that led Justice Stone to send a congratulatory missive which called forth, on March 22, the following acknowledgment?

"I am grateful to you for your letter, and for the continued evidence of your friendship, which is very precious to me.

"I follow the work of the Supreme Court in these days with a more personal and intimate kind of pleasure than ever before, and with a subconscious sense of pride that one whom I hold to be a real friend is carrying forward its great traditions."

Recalling Cardozo's previous inquiry regarding the Admiralty matter, Stone sends him the Supreme Court verdict, in an opinion written by Justice McReynolds. Cardozo's acknowledgment, on May 22, shows that his own opinion is not to be revised. "Before your case was argued," he explains, "I prepared an opinion upon the question of the application of the statute, which will now have to go forth into the world and take its chances of life or death."

On May 4, 1929, Cardozo writes about a forthcoming trip to Washington: "I am very anxious to see you, and anxious also to see the President."

Justice Stone personally introduced Cardozo to Mr. Hoover. "My recollection is," he writes, "that the President was then interested in getting Judge Cardozo to go on his Prohibition Commission. I seized the opportunity to make the President acquainted with the kind of judge he ought to appoint and prefaced the call by expatiating on that topic at some length. My recollection is that I took Justice Cardozo to the President's office, introduced them and left."

Ten days later Cardozo reports the outcome of the conversation.

"The President received me very pleasantly, and I find that talking to the Chief of State is not very different from talking to other men. I did not fail to appreciate the honor of his request that I should become a member of the Commission, but reflection has confirmed my feeling that acceptance was impossible. The task that I am doing cannot be done with any reasonable efficiency if my energies are to be diverted into other forms of public service."

One surmises that quite apart from his public duty, Cardozo did not care to go on a Prohibition Commission. No drinker of liquor himself, he was aware that some of his fellow judges at Albany would take a cocktail or a highball at private homes. Cardozo disliked all governmental attempts to interfere with the normal liberties of the individual. Although he abstained from drink himself, he yet preferred not to be officially associated with any phase of the Prohibition question. Such, at least, seems one explanation not given to the President for the nonacceptance of the invitation to become a member of the Commission.

A letter of August, 1931, calls for somewhat extensive comment. The Doyle case there mentioned is one wherein Cardozo, in an oft-quoted opinion, showed that in his conscientious and often harassed search for justice he was ever willing to risk public disapproval. Judge Seabury, as chief counsel of the Hofstadter Legislative Committee, was conducting an investigation into corrupt political practices in New York. William F. Doyle, a horse doctor involved in the scandal, had refused to answer questions, claiming his constitutional rights in regard to immunity. Could the legislative resolution, which was not yet an act of legislature, restrain these rights? Cardozo did not think so. But after Doyle had accordingly been released from jail for contempt of court, Cardozo solved the difficulty by suggesting the passage of a law which, while sufficiently guarding any witness, would at the same time remove the kind of obstacle that in this case threatened to frustrate justice. The opinion which pointed out to the legislature the way to meet the problem—a way the lawmakers at Albany voted for in a special session called at once by the Governor—included the firm phrases: "We are not unmindful of the public interest, of the insistent hope and need that the ways of bribers and corruptionists shall be exposed to an indignant world. Commanding as those interests are, they do not supply us with a license to palter with the truth or to twist what has been written in the statutes into something else that we should like to see. Historic liberties and privileges are not to bend from day to day." Here he was willing to disappoint Judge Seabury and the great public naturally eager to have Doyle forced to speak. But his brilliant mind brought forth a remedy for the situation, and a valuable precedent had been established by his Court of Appeals.

Cardozo has referred to his decision in letters to his cousin Maud: "It is the kind of case that frets one till it is out of one's system. I suppose a different ruling as to some of the points would have been popular, but a judge has to school himself not to let such considerations count." And later: "I felt quite sure that I was right in the Doyle case, but, none the less, I looked for criticism—criticism from some of the newspapers eager for the man hunt and impatient of the restraints of law, and criticism by good citizens unable to follow the distinctions of the opinion and knowing only that the law had baffled them again. Your letters show me that the opinion is clear enough to be understood by clearheaded men and women who take the trouble to read it. The response by the press has been gratifying too. Many of the best papers have praised, and all, so far as I know, have readily acquiesced."

The other case to which Cardozo refers in his letter to Justice Stone—the Interborough case—was one of the most momentous cases in the field of labor conflict ever to come before Cardozo's court. New Yorkers will remember the strike which in 1926 so greatly interfered with subway transit for almost a month. The Interborough Company, fighting the Workers' Union, had allowed its employees to form a company union that was practically, if not theoretically, under the control of the Interborough. The subway officials took legal action to prevent the Workers' Union from getting members of the Company's brotherhood to join the national organization. The injunction sought was granted. The order was approved by the Appellate Division. Then came the appeal to Cardozo's court at Albany.

Four nationally famous judges—one of them later a senator—figure in important manner in the decision arrived at. In the background Justice Brandeis. He it was who in a similar case before the Supreme Court had written the forcible dissent in favor of the rights of labor. In the foreground Robert F. Wagner, ably and eloquently pleading the cause of the Workers' Union. Cardozo presiding over the court that unanimously followed his liberal leadership. Judge Irving Lehman writing the opinion, pointing out that "the union may argue the greater effectiveness of its own method, the validity of its own principles." The lower courts were overruled by the Court of Appeals, the injunction vacated.

In the years since 1931 the pendulum may have swung too far in the other direction, yet with Senator Wagner's success in the Interborough case capitalistic employers in New York State were given notice that the day of inequitable domination over employees was coming to an end.

And now, Cardozo's letter to his friend at Washington.

"I was troubled by the Doyle case. If I had given him a stay he could have gone across the river into New Jersey and laughed at an adverse decision, which would have brought the whole administration of justice into contempt.

"The appeal has now been heard and disposed of, and I am glad to have it off my hands. I fret about decisions while they are in the process of gestation, but not so much when they have been born.

"The Interborough case has had a long and troublesome history. What you tell me of your own views is full of interest. If someone could write a history of the narrow escapes of lawsuits, there would be an illuminating chapter in the history of the judicial process."

Early the following year a letter from New York City (January 20, 1932) shows the two jurists similarly minded in regard to two cases in which Justice Oliver Wendell Holmes had written the opinion. The Brett case against the United Zinc and Chemical Company has, in the succinct language of Mr. Eustace Seligman, been explained to us as follows: "Defendant owned some land on which was a pool of water, clear in appearance but dangerously poisoned with chemicals. A traveled way passed within 120 feet of the pool, and paths crossed the property. Children came upon the land, entered the water, were poisoned and died. Held, that the defendant was not liable, that a landowner owes no duty to keep his land safe for children of tender years if he has not by implication invited them on it, and that a road is not an invitation to leave it elsewhere than at its end."

In the Goodman case against the Baltimore & Ohio Railroad Company, Holmes had held "that a person who drives upon a railroad track relying upon not having heard a train, does so at his own risk and that if he cannot otherwise be sure whether a train is approaching, he must stop and get out of his vehicle and look before attempting to cross."

In the case of the children who had been poisoned, it was inevitable that Cardozo should have felt that their protection took precedence over the usual property rights and that they had not been adequately protected. Similarly as regards the Goodman case. It was, in Cardozo's view, the duty of the railroad to afford such protection as not to necessitate excessive precautions on the part of the public. Even while Holmes was alive, Cardozo did not refrain from opposing his views to those of the grand old jurist who was well-nigh his idol. Two years later, in the case of *Pokora v. the Wabash Railway Company*, Cardozo's opinion from the Supreme Court bench practically reversed the opinion of Justice Holmes. Cardozo maintained that "It was not necessarily negligent for a driver not to get out of his truck and look up the tracks before crossing."

"I am happy," he wrote to Judge Stone, "that you didn't disagree with my criticism of the Brett and Goodman cases. When I read over my address in cold type and found that I was setting up my judgment against that of Holmes, I felt inclined to buy up all the outstanding copies.

"I have little thought that the Washington appointment will come my way. Indeed, I don't believe I ought to take it. I have brought myself over to the belief that I can accomplish more for the development of the law in the office that I hold than I could in the Supreme Court. This feeling is reinforced by considerations more personal in their nature. I have suffered, as you know, a great upheaval in my home life, and it would be hard to pull up stakes and break the ties that are left. Even so, it is gratifying to be even 'mentioned' for so great an honor and with general approval."

We meet again with the correspondence in 1935 when Justice and Mrs. Stone were abroad.

"Your picture of motor rides in England," Cardozo writes on June 27, 1935, "fills me with a spirit of roving and a desire to be along with you. As ill luck will have it, I haven't been altogether well. The doctors looked me over on my reaching Rye, and found me much in need of rest and quiet. They have installed a day nurse and a night one to restrain me of my rightful liberties. I am assured, however, that rest and quiet will do the trick and that by obeying their commandments I shall be able at the end of the summer to work harder than ever before—to which one of the doctors was prudent enough to add 'if such a thing is possible.'"

A month later he writes: "At first I had two nurses; then I had one nurse and yesterday afternoon the one nurse departed. I feel much as the French must have felt on the fall of the Bastille.

"So far as I can tell I am getting along famously. I sit up a large part of the day, and am hoping pretty soon to be allowed out of doors. No one would guess from my appearance that there was anything wrong with me. For the present I am to be careful about exerting myself. The theory is that I am storing up energy. If storage continues at the present rate, I'll be a high-power live wire by the Fall."

The following summer Cardozo is again writing to his friend, this time in reference to court decisions and to the aid which Stone gave him in a year of unusual difficulties for the Washington Justices.

"I think we should be more than human," Cardozo writes on June 9, 1936, "if we failed to sit back in our chairs with a broad grin upon our faces as we watch the response to the minimum-wage decision. Is it possible that both political parties hold the view that legislation condemned by the majority of our brethren as an arbitrary and capricious assault upon liberty is so necessary and beneficent that we cannot get along without it? Perish the thought!"

On July 2, he says: "We did indeed have a hard year in the court. Next year may be bad, but certainly can't be worse. I don't need to tell you how much I leaned upon you through all the contests of the term. It would have been almost intolerable without you."

In his message of February 5, 1937, President Roosevelt surprised the country with a revolutionary proposal in regard to the Supreme Court. His triumphant reelection the previous year led him to believe that the time had come for the success of a plan whereby the liberal constructionists of the Constitution might definitely be made a majority to support the liberal policies of the nation's Chief Magistrate. Federal judges were to resign from office shortly after reaching the age of seventy. New appointees, as many as six, could be named by the President to the Supreme Court, as vacancies might arise. Such, in brief, was Mr. Roosevelt's proposal.

Many thousands of his admirers thought that the President had gone too far. Neither directly nor in roundabout manner should the Supreme Court be made the handmaiden of the President, or even remotely ancillary. Whatever the immediate benefits from such a short cut, here was a dangerous departure from the traditional path. On the road of America the Constitution had sought to erect foursquare, each with its own duties and dignity, the Capitol, the Supreme Court, and the White House. In June the Senate committee voted its opposition to Mr. Roosevelt's plan. Justice Cardozo, as the following letter makes very plain, was among those friends of the President who felt satisfaction at the defeat of the Court bill.

"I fancy," he wrote to Stone on July 2, 1937, "you have returned from Mexico and are living the primitive life that befits a fisherman. May it bring you strength to tackle the problems of the October term.

"I was in the city the other day at a little dinner given

by Augustus Hand to Wyzanski, who, to my great regret, is leaving the Department of Justice. The gossip around the table was that the compromise bill suggested by Senator Walsh was likely to pass the Senate. It is better than the bill proposed by the President, but bad enough. I am still hopeful that the whole subject will be put asleep and an indefinite postponement or a motion to recommit. *Nous verrons.*

"Except for the interruption of certioraris and applications for the stay of mandate, I live a life of idleness. In the words of Iolanthe, 'I do nothing in particular and do it very well.' Well, I'll be eligible for retirement in five years, and then the question will be squarely put to me whether I like work or idleness best. *Curia vult advisari.*"

On June 14, 1938, three weeks before his death, Cardozo sent his last letter to Justice Stone. "The doctors pronounce me better," he wrote with great difficulty, "but the am much the same and as helpless as ever." There is pathos in the slip in the word "arm," eloquent of the trouble in writing.

It is fitting that Harlan Stone was chosen to write the introductory paper for the memorial publication, in January, 1939, dedicated to Cardozo by the *Harvard Law Review*, the *Yale Law Journal*, and the *Columbia Law Review*. Famous jurists of the English-speaking world—of America, of England, of Australia—contributed laudatory articles on Cardozo the lawyer, the judge, the author. It fell to Harlan Stone to write of Cardozo's character and personality. "Few men," said Justice Stone, "have so fully realized the spiritual values of life or have been so aware of its realities. His every thought and action were mellowed by gentleness and humility of spirit and purity of soul. Nobility of character exalted and ruled the order of his life."

Greatly though Cardozo loved and admired Harlan Stone and Nathan Bijur, Learned Hand and Irving Leh-

[232]

man, there was still another judge for whom he had deeper veneration than for any other—the man whom he had succeeded on the bench. "What's the use of talking about the rest of us?" he once said to Judge Hand. "Holmes is a mountain. All we others flatten out."

Emanuel Hertz recounts an amusing anecdote concerning Holmes before he knew Cardozo well. Justice Holmes had remarked to Hertz that he never read the papers.

"Then," said Mr. Hertz, "you missed a splendid address by Judge Benjamin N. Cardozo at the graduation exercises of the Institute of Religion."

"What was the subject of his address?" asked Justice Holmes.

"Values," said Mr. Hertz.

"I should like very much to see it. How old is Judge Cardozo?"

"Sixty-two," replied Mr. Hertz, somewhat surprised.

"Oh, then he's merely a lambkin. Wait until he grows up."

In 1930, Cardozo wrote to Aline Goldstone: "I went to see Judge Holmes at Beverly Farms . . . lunched with my idol, and was back in New York Tuesday night. I had to be there the next day to talk to the Governor about some condemned man.

"Holmes is a genius and a saint, enough of the mischievous devil in him not to make the sainthood burdensome, but still, I think, a saint, and surely a genius. I wish I could talk freely like you. I'm fairly paralyzed when I meet strangers whom I admire and revere. But the old man sent word to me that he entreated me to visit him, so what could I do? My friend, Felix Frankfurter, who knows him well, drove me there from Boston, and back later to my hotel."

"I know I would love him," Holmes said of Cardozo, "if I knew him better."

In 1881, while Holmes was a professor at Harvard, he

published a work wherein law was visualized as essentially associated with the practical advancement of society. Changing conditions necessitated fresh interpretation of legal codes. *The Common Law* thrust aside the clammy weight of ancient decisions where they seemed no longer applicable to present problems. The approach was realistic, yet in it was the imaginative spirit of a poet's son and a descendant of poets.

If Holmes was "the Master," Justice Brandeis was "the Crusader." His was, during his earlier years as a lawyer, and the later period in the Supreme Court, the passionate devotion to the American ideal of individualism. Seeing that ideal observed in theory, but frustrated in practice by monopolistic capitalism, he fought for social and economic reform. He it was who most effectively led the war against predatory wealth, against bankers of undue influence in public policy. Valuing "liberty both as an end and as a means," Brandeis, ever practical, effected reforms protecting the savings of the people, assuring the rights of the laborers, bringing to book their oppressors. His theory of individualism connoted full opportunity for individual effort while rejecting such governmental paternalism as might interfere with the development of personality and the strengthening of character. In a machine age Brandeis fought for Man.

Now that labor organizations have become a power in the land, it is a bit difficult to realize the indignant opposition met by Wendell Phillips when, some seventy years ago, in demanding rights for the workingman, he advocated an eight-hour day. "The world gropes its way onward to a better civilization," the orator said to his audience in Boston. "They may lock it in; they may deride it; they may endeavor to smother it, but it is a tendency of the times and it will certainly conquer. How soon it will conquer rests with you."

If one would read the whole address, let him go to the files of old newspapers, turn to the *New York Times* for May 24, 1870—by happy coincidence the day that Benjamin Cardozo was born. For he and Brandeis and Holmes rendered their decisions in the spirit of Wendell Phillips, who said in his oration: "Yards of cotton, tons of coal, ingots of metal are not the measure of civilization. Man and woman are." They might well have paraphrased these words to read: "Yards of decisions, tons of old codes, are not the measure of justice. Man and woman are."

Cardozo, in celebration of Holmes's ninetieth birthday in 1931, wrote a paper which was published in the *Harvard Law Review*, and later used in an introduction to the volume entitled *Mr. Justice Holmes*. It opened with two lines, translated by Arthur S. Way, from the Greek of Euripides, *Iphigenia at Aulis*.

> How can I praise thee, and not overpraise
> And yet not mar the grace by stint thereof?

"To the lips of eager youth," Cardozo said, "comes at times the halting doubt whether law in its profession can fill the need for what is highest in the yearnings of the human spirit. Thus challenged, I do not argue, I point the challenger to Holmes."

Both men were skeptics, yet Cardozo's words regarding Holmes are true of both. "He may be groping for things vanished. He gives us glimpses of the things eternal." Both men were pragmatists in the finer sense. Holmes's phrases, "The life of the law has not been logic: it has been experience" and "The Constitution is an experiment, as all life is an experiment," might as well have come from the pen of Cardozo. To both these philosophers, so familiar with their Spinoza, the words of the great pantheist apply with equal truth: "I have labored carefully not to mock, lament and execrate the actions of men; I have labored to understand them."

Both Holmes and his successor in the Supreme Court deprecated the use of the Fourteenth Amendment, "beyond," wrote Holmes, "the absolute compulsion of its words to prevent the making of social experiments—though the experiment may seem futile or even noxious to me and to those whose judgment I most respect."

"No one," wrote Cardozo, "has labored more incessantly to demonstrate the truth that rights are never absolute." The right of "due process of law" granted by the Fourteenth Amendment must not be construed to place the rights of the individual above the rights of other individuals or of the community, as all rights take on different aspects by reason of economic change and social advance.

"Many an appeal to freedom," Cardozo wrote in his tribute to Holmes, "is a masquerade of privilege or inequality seeking to intrench itself behind the catchword of a principle . . . There must be give and take at many points . . . Only in one field is compromise to be excluded, or kept within the narrowest limits. There shall be no compromise of the freedom to think one's thoughts and speak them, except at those extreme borders where thought merges into action."

This uncompromising attitude toward freedom in the expression of thought was fundamental with these two skeptical idealists, these two aristocrats. In the approach to the enjoyments of life, Holmes and Cardozo walked widely separated ways. For Holmes was the gusto of life, the lustiness of it. Not so for Cardozo. They met in the appreciation of life's essential values. They met also as artists. "Law in his hands has been philosophy, but it has been literature too."

And yet it is not here that we find the most interesting resemblance, nor even in Cardozo's calm, majestic spiritual phrase concerning "the benignancy of a soul that has fashioned its own scale of virtues." It is rather where we come to unconscious autobiography peculiarly revealing. "I do not mean," wrote Cardozo of Holmes, "that he is without the pride of mind inseparable from gifts so rare. No one favored so superbly by the gods and the Muses could be lacking altogether in a sense of his own powers. The knowledge has not saved him from something like a shy distrust, a questioning and a doubting, as if he felt the need to reassure himself that in looking into his own soul he was viewing something more than a gleam of a mirage. Sceptic of many things, of many boasted certainties, he is sceptic even of himself."

When, after Holmes's death, Cardozo received some articles in the London press concerning his great predecessor, he wrote: "I was glad to have the clippings about Holmes. He was great beyond comparison. His lifework has been done, but he remained a magnificent symbol. Of course, I am not in his class at all, but even so, it gives me a thrill of pride to be spoken of as a fit successor to him by journals across the seas."

A letter which Holmes wrote to Cardozo was a continuing inspiration to him. His cousin Annie has told us "he often read and reread it. One day shortly after Holmes's death, Ben took me into his bedroom and took down the framed letter so that I could the more easily read it. It was one of the most beautiful letters it was ever my privilege to read. I can think of none comparable to it, unless perhaps that written by Whistler on the death of his wife, a letter which Mr. Freer permitted me to read while the tears ran down my cheeks. Knowing full well my cousin's modesty, I know it was not the evidence of the high esteem in which his predecessor had held him which made the letter so precious to him, nor was it alone the personal affection for him that it breathed, but with his own worship of perfection it was the beauty of the thoughts expressed so exquisitely, and the admirable quality of its philosophy of life."

Apart from its philosophy, there was a personal touch to the letter, making it all the more dearly poignant for Cardozo. The lone survivor in his family, he was still sorrowing for Nell. Holmes was sorrowing at the recent death of his wife. "There was in the letter," writes Cardozo's cousin, "a remarkably beautiful expression of grief and of all that his wife had meant to him, while there emanated from the pages an exquisite realization of the fugitiveness of all Life. With the full appreciation that he had already lived a longer span than is granted to most, nevertheless there was a quiet regret at the little it was possible to accomplish in even a long life."

"I have always thought," Holmes said to Cardozo in this letter, "that not place or power or popularity makes the success that one desires, but the trembling hope that one has come near to an ideal. The only ground that warrants a man for thinking that he is not living the fool's paradise if he ventures such a hope is the voice of a few masters."

Cardozo, Holmes made clear, was one of the few masters whose voice of approval he hoped to have.

XV

*The best-conditioned and unwearied spirit
in doing courtesies.*   SHAKESPEARE

IN THE volume of *Reports of the American Bar Association for
1938* will be found the Memorial prepared by Irving
Lehman, whose estimate of Benjamin Cardozo deserves
to be read in full. As it has appeared elsewhere between
covers, and has, moreover, been privately printed, here
shall be given just a few excerpts.

"In truth he was the master who was bringing new
methods and new ideas into Judicial decisions . . . He
wielded an influence which made the Court great . . .
He sought to know his own mind; to trace the influence
which led him to choose one course rather than another;
to appraise the value of conflicting considerations of logic
and of history, of custom and of morality, of certainty and
of flexibility, of form and of substance . . . Small wonder
then that when in the conference of the Court he discussed
legal problems with the mental quality or the great learning
which were at his command, his words often swayed the
decision of the Judges. . . .

"It was a source of abiding satisfaction to Cardozo that
Holmes had long hoped that he would succeed him . . .
Justice Cardozo arrived at his own conclusionsw ith anguish

[239]

of the soul . . . [He] felt profoundly that America is great, not because of its wealth and power, but because embodied in its Constitution are the ideas of liberty and democracy which have become part of the spirit of America. The Constitution, he believed, if properly interpreted, would conserve these ideals without blocking the road to progress. As a Justice of the Supreme Court he consecrated himself to the task of finding the right interpretation . . . He loved his country with a surpassing love."

Cardozo's faith in the Constitution as a generous conservator of American ideals underlay all the difficult decisions of the Washington years. At Albany less momentous questions came frequently before his court. The panorama of everyday life had there been continuously unfolded. If only vicariously, the judges could enter into the countless ramifications of the human maze. The man in the street gives little thought to the fascinating number of questions on which justice must seek to decide. He has presumably little idea of their extent. To instruct ourselves, similarly ignorant, we turned recently to the pages of the *General Digest of Decisions of American Courts*. Selecting some of the classifications contained therein, we jot down the following:

Admiralty, Aliens, Adoption, Adultery, Attorney and Client, Automobiles, Bankruptcy, Banks and Banking, Boundaries, Carriers, Commerce, Constitutional Law, Corporations, Criminal Law, Danger, Divorce, Elections, Eminent Domain, Equity, Evidence, Executors and Administrators, False Imprisonment, Food, Fornication, Frauds, Game.

Here we pause to explain that "Game" has nothing to do with "Frauds," though one might associate them with roulette wheels. "Game" as referred to in the *General Digest of Decisions*, relates to the laws of hunting and shooting out of season. And now to proceed.

Guardian and Ward, Homestead, Homicide, Husband

[240]

and Wife, Injunction, Insurance, Internal Revenue, Intoxicating Liquor, Landlord and Tenant, Libel and Slander, Licenses, Master and Servant, Monopolies, Mortgages, Navigable Waters, Negligence, New Trial, Nuisance, Pardon, Partnership, Patents, Physicians and Surgeons, Public Service Commission, Railroads, Rape, Robbery, Sales, Schools, Seamen, States, Statutes, Taxation, Trade-marks, Treason, Treaties, Trespass, Trial, Trusts, United States, Usury, Vendor and Purchaser, War, Waters and Water Courses, Wills, Witnesses, Workmen's Compensation.

The list has been recorded largely for the purpose of indicating the variety of the cases presented before the Albany Court of Appeals. Many belonging to the same categories find their way to Washington, but fewer of individual dramatic interest. Cardozo had in some measure to readjust himself for major considerations of constitutional questions affecting the country as a whole.

"The light of his genius continues after him to illumine the way for his own and future generations to the end of time." Such are the concluding words of Senator Wagner's preface to the volume of Cardozo's opinions edited by Mr. A. L. Sainer.

Cardozo's first participation in a question before the Supreme Court led him to dissent from the majority in a California business case of no special interest or public importance. As the "youngster," he was, indeed, not given, at the outset, the task of writing the opinion of the Court in any case of national significance. The order of seniority prevailed.

The presiding Justice presents cases so that there will be a minimum of discussion on immaterial things. After the Chief Justice states a case, the other Justices, in order of seniority, give their opinions. After that comes the vote, the junior Justice voting first and the Chief Justice last. According to Chief Justice Hughes, many people think that the junior Justice is the first to state his opinion. The idea of having the junior Justice vote first might seem to be based on the thought that, if he voted last, his opinion might be affected by those of his eight seniors in office. However, as he has previously listened to their opinions, there would not seem to be much logic in the procedure of his being the first to vote.

Before long, Cardozo's fluent pen was defending vital rights. One in which his vote made the fifth, and thus overrode the judgment of the four Justices led by Justice McReynolds, was a Texas Negro vote case. Nixon, a Negro, had sued the election judges because he had been refused permission to vote at a primary. He had lost his first case in the Texas Federal District Court, and again before the Circuit Court of Appeals on the ground that the State of Texas had not denied to him the right granted by the Fourteenth Amendment of the Constitution. He had been barred from voting by the executive committee of the Democratic party. A Texas statute had given to the Committee authority to decide on the qualifications of voters at party primaries, and in this manner the resolution to bar Negroes left the State itself in a position to deny that it had withheld from Nixon the protection granted by the Constitution.

When the case came up before the Supreme Court it divided the Justices into two groups. On one side were the more liberal-minded men and on the other side the more reactionary. Justices McReynolds, Van Devanter, Sutherland, and Butler contended that the executive committee was not composed of state officials and was not acting for any government. It was a question of an organization of whites who obviously considered themselves free to exclude Negroes. But Cardozo, writing the majority opinion, said: "We do not impugn the competence of the Legislature to designate the agencies whereby the party faith shall be declared and the party discipline enforced. The pith of the matter is simply this: that, when these agencies are invested with an authority independent of the will of the association in whose name they undertake to speak, they become to that extent the organ of the State itself, the repositories of official power . . . The test is not whether the members of the executive committee are the representatives of the State in the strict sense in which an agent is the representative of his principal. The test is whether they are to be classified as representatives of the State to such an extent and in such a sense that the great restraints of the Constitution set limits to their action . . . Delegates of the State's power have discharged their official functions in such a way as to discriminate invidiously between white citizens and black. The Fourteenth Amendment, adopted as it was with special solicitude for the equal protection of the Negro race, lays a duty upon the Court to level by its judgment these barriers of color."

Cardozo had found precedents and arguments to support in legalistic manner the opinion in which Hughes and Brandeis, Stone and Roberts concurred. But legality aside, how obvious it is to the man of the street that it would have been unfair to allow a subterfuge, almost a trick, to deprive the Negro of his rights. The more liberal-minded Justices here used their intellects to interpret law so that it might serve common humanity with greater vision and generosity.

The same point of view is manifested in other opinions concurred in or written by Cardozo during his first year in Washington. Almost invariably he is to be found on the same side as Justices Brandeis and Stone, and very frequently he was opposed to the group in which Justice McReynolds was the most intransigeant.

Among the decisions of the Washington period we find the case of the seaman who died on land of pneumonia contracted at sea. Was the steamship line to be held responsible for "personal injury" through "negligence"? "Approaching the decision of this case in a spirit of liberality, we put aside," wrote Cardozo, "many of the refinements of construction that a different spirit might approve. The failure to furnish cure is a personal injury actionable at the suit of the seaman during life and at the suit of his personal representative now that he is dead."

Cardozo's sympathetic protection of the individual is made evident in others of his decisions during the Washington years, but, of course, his attitude in questions of wider application were what brought him ever increasingly to the attention of the public. Though he was in most instances to be found on the same side with Brandeis and Stone, he was never afraid of standing alone in dissent. During his first session—his first court term lasted only six weeks—the Chief Justice asked him on two occasions to write the majority opinion. In the case of the Texas Negro, Cardozo eloquently showed his passion for the rights of the individual. A different kind of understanding was displayed in those cases where the New York, New Haven and Hartford Railroad was restrained from including its terminal facilities in valuing its railroad investment as the basis for transportation charges. So, too, Cardozo made use of his clear understanding of business in general when, in denying the right of meat packers to go into the grocery business, he set forth the dangers and the evils of the monopolistic system. He saw no reason for allowing Swift & Co., Armour, and the others to avoid the Sherman Antitrust Act. "Size and past aggressions," he wrote, "induced the fear in 1920 that the defendants, if permitted to deal in groceries, would drive their rivals to the wall. Size and past aggressions leave the fear unmoved today."

The American Tobacco Co. case in 1933 left Cardozo, Brandeis, and Stone in a minority that seems to do them exceptional honor. Without informing the stockholders concerning details of a plan involving 57,000 shares of the company's stock, the president and directors had made possible their own enrichment on a large scale. A minority stockholder, after unsuccessful attempts in the lower courts, had sought to have the plan voided by the United States Supreme Court. That tribunal decided it had no jurisdiction to interfere in the decision previously made and originating in New Jersey courts in the case of a New Jersey corporation. Technical considerations thus triumphed over basic ethical considerations. So, at least, thought Brandeis, Stone, and Cardozo and so, one surmises, would most men think of the Supreme Court's self-imposed abstention. Was there not then, to quote Cardozo's words, "the overmastering necessity of rebuking fraud or breach of trust"?

The same three Justices were in accord in dissenting from the opinion of their six colleagues when the Interstate Commerce Commission was frustrated in its attempt to have the Oregon-Washington Railroad Co. continue its transportation facilities into further Oregon territory. Cardozo's view was that the public interest outweighed the possible temporary loss to the railroad.

In Washington as in Albany, Cardozo continued to put a gigantic amount of energy into the work of preparing his cases, though, since the early heart attacks in Albany, his health was no longer able to stand the strain he demanded of it and was frequently overtaxed. His routine was similar in all cases. He prepared them in advance of argument. His law clerks and secretaries had looked up all the records and briefs, and the extensive memorandum was composed before the argument so that, after the case had been heard, Cardozo's opinion was quickly written. All the points had been investigated, summarized, and digested by the clerks and secretaries. Cardozo went through every case with the law clerks and in a charming way, after writing his opinions,

[245]

would say to them: "I'd like to put in your name. Really you have written it and not I."

After Cardozo's first breakdown, the Chief Justice never let him have his assignment of cases immediately after the Saturday conference. "We all knew," said the Chief Justice, "that if he had his assignment he would immediately set at work and probably work most of the night." So the assignment was sent over by the Chief Justice's messenger on Sunday morning.

While Cardozo had told Mrs. Hughes that he worked with difficulty, the Chief Justice doubted this. He "turned off his work rapidly."

Work seemed to be almost an obsession with him. He wrote to one of his dear friends: "The doctors found me in poor shape after the trying year in Washington, and they have condemned me to complete rest and quiet with countless unconstitutional restrictions upon fundamental liberties. They tell me that if I keep their commandments I shall attain—not heaven—but the privilege of immoderate labor here upon earth. For the present there seems to be no way of escaping from their tyranny."

And later he told the same friend: "I wake up often at night with nerves on edge as the result of worry about cases."

Yet later he wrote to another friend: "The new Court term is in full blast, and I am pestered with all kinds of insoluble problems. I hate work—despite the reputation to the contrary that I have gathered—and greatly prefer the summer when I can read the things I like instead of those I must. The primal curse of labor has been visited heavily upon this particular specimen of the bored and boresome human race." Here one realizes anew the sense of obligation the tragedy of his youth had imposed upon Benjamin Cardozo, and the profound sadness of his life.

Cardozo's first session at the Capital was a matter of

16 W. 75th St
Oct 13th 19

Dear Louise,

This is the sentence from the Holmes letter

"I always have thought that not place or power or popularity makes the success that one desires, but a trembling hope that one has come near to an ideal."

It was good to see you.

Faithfully
B.N.C.

Letter to Mrs. Stephen S. Wise

only some weeks, the Court term coming to a close toward the end of May. In those few weeks, while the Justice was living at the Mayflower Hotel, he made few acquaintances outside official circles. Now, as always in the past, he stayed aloof from social life, though he found that social demands on him were more pressing in the nation's capital. "Just a line to tell you that I still live," he wrote to his cousin Maud during that first Court term in Washington, "but that I am in dire need of a social secretary. The distribution of cards among the ambassadors and other dignitaries calls for rare finesse and expert knowledge. I am pretty homesick, but too busy to brood a great deal. I don't know whether I shall ever become accustomed to my new way of life. I hope so." A few weeks later he wrote: "I can't say that I have been happy in Washington but I don't believe it is the fault of the place. The fault is with me. I am never contented anywhere. What a horrible disposition! Social life in my new abode is pleasant if one has a flair for that sort of thing. The men and women that one meets are bright and entertaining. It is hard to keep pace with them."

In June, Court closed for the summer, Cardozo hastened back to the Seventy-fifth Street house, and wrote: "I am back amid my native skyscrapers, rejoicing in the dust and din. The satisfaction of home-coming makes me forget the horrid fact that vacation months go swiftly by and that in the fall I must return to Washington and leave the familiar scenes behind me. Nothing counts but the present. . . . I shall have a lot of things to attend to during the summer, arranging to move my belongings to Washington. I wish I had been left in my old court at Albany." The letter is signed "The exile."

That desolate note is sounded again and again during the Washington years, at the time when Cardozo had reached the peak of his profession. "It will be good if you will deign to look in on me," he wrote to a friend, "before the walls of the prison house at Washington swallow me up again."

Reference to Washington as a prison house or a place of exile appears time and time again in Cardozo's letters. Of his loneliness there can be no question, or of his more contented days at Albany when he could frequently run down to the beloved city of his birth.

The widest significance of Cardozo's years at the Capital lies in the public value of his work as a Justice. One hardly sets down a sentence of this kind before beginning to wonder whether it is not too obvious to be true. Perhaps the widest, the most profound significance of his life rested in what he essentially was; what he did, one feels, had its highest value in illustrating his character and personality.

At any event, history was in the making during those years. A revolution was in progress and Cardozo's place in it was important. The biographer cannot escape at least some discussion of decisions affecting the economic welfare and the more general social advance of millions of men and women.

Cardozo's attitude that law should primarily serve fundamental public interests when such benefit did not go counter to the constitutional rights of the individual led to his consistent support of the objectives implicit in the New Deal. In 1934 emergency measures planned to lead the country from its economic slough of despond were being increasingly presented before the Supreme Court for its judgment concerning the constitutionality of these various acts.

Could the police power of the state of Minnesota save countless farm owners and homeowners from losing their property by reason of foreclosures on mortgages? By a vote of five to four, the opinion of Chief Justice Hughes in favor of the hard-pressed debtors overrode the decisions of the four less liberal Justices, Sutherland and McReynolds, Van Devanter and Butler.

[248]

Did the act of the New York legislature which, after days of riot, was to take control of the dairy industry, run counter to the Fourteenth Amendment? Were the private property rights of the milk dealers to override the welfare of the farmers and the benefit of the public? Cardozo was, naturally, in these two instances, one of the majority to interpret the Constitution as a living instrument progressively devoted to the needs of the community.

We find him in the next year (1935) in lone opposition to his colleagues in connection with the "Hot Oil" case. The other Justices had decided that the section of the National Industrial Recovery Act granting President Roosevelt authority in connection with the interstate shipment of oil, was invalid. Congress, in their view, had no right to grant such power to Mr. Roosevelt. Cardozo took the stand that there had been no such grant. He saw no reason why the section in question should have been made more explicit when the intention was obvious in the statute as a whole. "The statute was framed in the shadow of a national disaster," wrote Cardozo. "A host of unforeseen contingencies would have to be faced from day to day, and faced with a fullness of understanding unattainable by anyone except the man upon the scene. The President was chosen to meet the instant need."

Cardozo in more than one instance found himself obligated by reason of his interpretation of constitutional amendments, to approve of the legality of statutes that seemed to him neither wise nor liberal. There was in 1934 the case of a California law obligating students at the University of California to follow courses in military science. When some of the students refused to obey, they were notified that they had been suspended from the University.

Cardozo concurred in the majority opinion written by Mr. Justice Butler, which found that the California law did not run counter to any of the provisions of the Constitu-

[249]

tion. However, he wrote a separate opinion in which he was joined by Brandeis and Stone. The paper made evident their belief that religious liberty was not being violated as "instruction in military science is not instruction in the practice or tenets of a religion" and "is not an interference by the State with the free exercise of religion." But Cardozo wrote that the kind of condition made obligatory in California "may be condemned by some as unwise or illiberal or unfair when there is violence to conscientious pupils either religious or merely ethical."

On December 8, 1934, Cardozo wrote to Dr. Stephen S. Wise: "I enclose the opinions in the California case—mine is annexed to the one by Butler. . . . I understand the feeling of the antimilitarists. Unfortunately it is not the function of the Court to pass upon the fairness or wisdom of the rule adopted by the Regents. We have only to say whether there is anything in their action which is in conflict with a provision of the Constitution of the United States. . . . I rather think you will agree with the Court that such a conflict is not made out."

The 1935 session at Washington was strenuous. Cardozo frequently found himself in the minority, sometimes with Brandeis and Stone, and sometimes quite alone, as when he contended that the New York State Superintendent of Banks was entitled to take action against New Jersey stockholders of the Bank of United States that had collapsed sometime previously.

In the Herndon case, Brandeis, Stone, and Cardozo maintained that the appeal of this Atlanta Negro, condemned to a long sentence, should have been heard. A technical question was involved as to the time during which the Negro's action might lead to insurrection. This question determined the man's right to appeal. In the words of Cardozo: "The protection of the Constitution was seasonably invoked . . . What the appellant is now asking is an opportunity to be heard. That privilege is his unless he has thrown it away by silence and acquiescence when there was need of speech and protest . . . Will men 'judging in calmness' say of the defendant's conduct as shown forth in the pages of his record that it was an attempt to stir up revolution through the power of his persuasion and within the time when that persuasion might be expected to endure? If men so judging will say yes, will the Constitution of the United States uphold a reading of the statute that will lead to that response? Those are the questions that the defendant lays before us after conviction of a crime punishable by death in the discretion of the jury. I think he should receive an answer."

The Herndon case involved Cardozo's deep feeling of fairness toward any individual, whether communist, criminal, or what not. In its direct application, of course, only one man was involved. Equally, of course, all the members of the Supreme Court were just as conscientious as Cardozo in their interpretation of justice. A letter from Miss Boardman says: "May I say one little word here, that I was much impressed with something that Mr. Justice Cardozo said to me the last time that he called and that was this: That he had been now a certain length of time on the Supreme Court bench and that he had been tremendously impressed with the absolute integrity of every member of the Court; that no matter how they differed, each man decided according to his honest conviction, and that no member was influenced by anything but his sense of justice and his honest interpretation of the law." But with him sensitive mercy, however unconsciously, played its part in all decisions.

The most important decisions of the Washington years had to do with cases of wider import, affecting the people of the United States as a whole. From 1932 to 1938 great social and economic questions held the forefront of the stage. The leading actor was President Roosevelt. One of his main supporters in the Supreme Court was Benjamin Cardozo.

In May, 1935, he had cordially agreed with the minority opinion from the pen of Chief Justice Hughes in opposition to the decision declaring unconstitutional the Railroad Pension Act. In January, 1936, he was one of the three "liberals" who regarded the Agricultural Adjustment Act as constitutional. He continued to dissent from various other opinions restraining the Administration's authority in various directions. During the 1937 term he voted in every instance in favor of enactments desired by the President. His entire record by that time showed that in twenty-seven cases he had sided with the Administration in all but five instances.

In maintaining that Federal insurance for aged persons was allowable by the Constitution, Cardozo wrote the phrases very frequently quoted from his opinions of the year 1937: "Needs that were narrow or parochial a century ago may be interwoven in our day with the well-being of the nation. What is critical or urgent changes with the times." Here, in brief, is the explanation of Cardozo's approach to interpretation of moot points in the Constitution.

Cardozo did not always support the President. In May, 1935, he joined his colleagues in their unanimous decision concerning the unconstitutionality of the NIRA. It had, in the opinion of the Court, taken away from Congress authority which belonged to Congress. It had given to the President authority to which he was accordingly not entitled. The enthusiasm wherewith the NIRA was greeted in the earlier years had now not only abated but had been succeeded by widespread opposition in the world of commerce and finance. America was recovering in considerable measure from the darkness of despair dispelled by Franklin

Roosevelt's optimistic courage. There was general jubilation when the NIRA was pronounced null and void.

With far greater excitement the nation awaited the decision of the Judiciary Committee of the Senate in respect to the President's attempt to reconstitute the Supreme Court. Here basic emotions and convictions of the American people were aroused. Party lines were forgotten and the verdict, in which Cardozo privately concurred, went overwhelmingly against Mr. Roosevelt's plan. This was in the year 1937.

In a brief note to his cousin Maud, on February 16, 1937, Cardozo said: "'Off the record,' and not for transmission, I am with you altogether in opposition and amazement." "These are exciting days for aged judges," he wrote a few weeks later. "I must try to prove my judicial quality by not writing all I feel."

The late Robert Marshall, a brilliant government official in Washington in the Forestry Division and a lover of fun, described to us a visit to Cardozo at this time. "When I entered Justice Cardozo's apartment, Miss Tracy met me at the door. She had been quite sick the last time I was there, so of course I asked her how she was feeling. She said she was fine. So I asked her if she was well enough to turn a somersault. She jokingly said sure, that she would do it if I would turn one first. Whereupon I promptly turned a somersault just as Cardozo came out of his study. He promptly said, 'It might be helpful if you would come down and teach some of my colleagues to do that in their judicial decisions.'" Mr. Marshall added that "eight days later Roberts and Hughes did that very thing in overthrowing the decision in the Adkins case."

During their talk Cardozo "was tremendously interested in the rise to power of the C.I.O. and wanted me to tell him a great deal about it. He didn't express any view of his own. He at first said he wouldn't talk about the Court, but later

[253]

said his main objection to the President's program was the unwieldiness of fifteen members which would ruin discussion of cases. He thought nine members was too many."

"'I don't worry any more,' said Cardozo, 'about whether I can influence the vote of the other Justices. I'm satisfied now if I can get myself to vote right.' Then he added: 'Anyone who knows anything about statistical probability realizes that a judge who's been on the bench as long as I have, for twenty-three years, has made a great many wrong decisions, but the consolation is that in most cases it really doesn't matter. The thing that really counts—of course, I assume that judges are honest according to their lights —is the attitude of mind, the desire really to render the best possible decision one is able to give in each case.'"

In discussing the "Hot Oil" case, Cardozo expressed the opinion that Justice Brandeis had voted as he did "because delegation of power didn't fit in his pattern." "Brandeis," Cardozo suggested to Marshall, "has thought out a pattern for the whole universe and he has a niche into which every fact fits . . . Holmes didn't see any pattern to the universe."

To his friend, Cardozo explained why he owned no stocks. He felt "that their value is too intimately affected by court decisions, even though the particular company may not be involved, to make it possible for a judge to avoid being at least subconsciously partisan in his decision. Bonds are not affected nearly as much."

Cardozo's final months at Washington found him an ailing man. There were no constitutional questions of major import arousing wide controversy to be decided upon. A comparative lull was taking place in regard to the Administration's measures in the sphere of economics and social security. The second term of President Roosevelt was launched. In what honor Cardozo was held at the White House is indicated by his selection to administer the oath of office to all the members of the President's Cabinet at the beginning of Mr. Roosevelt's second term.

The ceremony took place in the simple library on the second floor of the White House. The Roosevelts, a handful of friends, and a few close relatives looked on during what the President called "a strictly family party." To each of the incoming Secretaries Cardozo read the historical oath. Each answered "I do" to his query. Each swore to support the Constitution of the United States. No speeches, no addresses of any kind, beyond a few words of congratulation by the President. In the simplest of ceremonies Cardozo had been the central figure on an unprecedented occasion in the history of Washington. It was, to quote the leader of the New Deal, "the inauguration of another new custom."

How Mr. Roosevelt himself regarded—and regards— Benjamin Cardozo is set forth in the letter contributed to the present biography. "The late Justice Oliver Wendell Holmes," wrote President Roosevelt, "expressed so perfectly my feeling toward his successor, Justice Cardozo, that I can do no better in offering my praise of the jurist than to repeat the observation of the man whom he succeeded. In 1929 Justice Holmes wrote to a friend: 'Cardozo I am sure I should really love if I knew him better . . . [I have] noticed such a sensitive delicacy in him that I should tremble lest I should prove unworthy of his regard.' Three years later he wrote: 'I think you would love him as I do and have from the first moment I saw him—a beautiful spirit.'

"What more can be said of Benjamin Cardozo? Learned, beloved, courageous, saintly. I am grateful that I was privileged to know him, regretful that he was not longer with us."

In more public manner the President made evident his admiration for Cardozo when the nation listened over the radio to Mr. Roosevelt's address on December 5, 1938. He was speaking at the University of North Carolina. His

[255]

address began with the name of Justice Cardozo, and the Justice's philosophy was made the text essentially of the entire address. The address began with Cardozo's words: "We live in a world of change. If a body of law were in existence adequate for the civilization of today, it could not meet the demands of tomorrow." As the speech drew to its conclusion, "What I would emphasize," said the President, "is the maintenance of successful democracy at home. Necessarily, democratic methods within a nation's life entail change—the kind of change through local processes described by Mr. Justice Cardozo—the kind of change to meet new social and economic needs through recognized processes of government."

Modest and retiring as he was, it was inevitable that Cardozo, in his high position and with his charm which attracted people to him whether he would or no, should be much more in the public eye than he liked. "If I were to be wholly frank," he wrote to Mr. Beryl Harold Levy, the author of a valuable book on the Justice's opinions, "I should have to admit some regret at anything being written about me in these days when the Court and its members are so much in the public eye. . . . " Cardozo assumed that biography was beyond the scope of Mr. Levy's study and expressed alarm at an attempt thereof, as "such biographical notes as have been written about my colorless life have been so sadly erroneous."

Cardozo's own autobiography, in a few score of words, was written with his invariable alacrity in doing a kindness for young people. Robert H. Elias, a freshman at Williams College, was competing for a position on the college newspaper and had to have an interview with some person of importance. Cardozo's reply to his request follows:

"I am told you would like me to write you something about my life.

"There is really very little to tell beyond the fact that

[256]

I was born a great many years ago, and have been continuously alive since then. Perhaps even that isn't certain, for a palmist who looked at my hand informed me that the lifeline was broken, which indicates that I am already dead, though not in such a way as to be conscious of it, which really proves nothing, since death and consciousness are not supposed to go together.

"Well, waiving that objection, and assuming myself alive—I was educated at Columbia and practiced law in New York till about twenty years ago, when to my own great surprise I became a judge. I started in the Supreme Court of New York, and then after one month was assigned to the Court of Appeals, and later became Chief Judge of that court where I served till March, 1932, when Mr. Hoover appointed me a justice of the Supreme Court of the United States.

"You tell me you would like to know something about the difficulties of the office. It ought to be easy to answer an inquiry of that kind, for there is certainly no dearth of difficulties. They meet one at every corner. The difficulties are so great that very often the judges don't agree as to the proper method of disposing of them, and then we have a majority opinion and a dissenting one. The dissenting opinion doesn't constitute law, but the judge who writes it feels a good deal better after getting it out of his system, and wonders why the majority judges were unable to agree with him. Perhaps the next case that comes along will see him in the majority, with the judge who had the better of him in the earlier case the spokesman of the minority. So every one has his share of triumphs and reverses, though I ought not to use those terms, for the single aim of all, the undivided purpose, is to have the law and right prevail.

"There are a good many other questions in your list which I should greatly like to answer, but it wouldn't be the proper thing. A judge is not at liberty to express his opinion

[257]

in advance of the argument about a question of law which he may have to decide. He is under a duty to keep his mind open until both sides have been heard."

The Justice's attitude was not always so light in regard to majority and dissenting opinions. To the boy he replied gaily enough. But to a woman he spoke in far different fashion. Mrs. David de Sola Pool, wife of the rabbi of the Spanish-Portuguese congregation, was having tea with the Justice. She found him looking tired and careworn. "You look worried," she said.

"I am tortured," he answered. "I could not sleep last night. Tomorrow we have a decision to make. This majority rule! This majority rule! A single vote may turn the scales. The responsibility is awful!"

"I am tortured," said Cardozo. This was during the period when in various cases Cardozo's vote swung the Court into judgments favorable to the Administration. The liberals, as well as the conservatives, profoundly felt the far-reaching implication and effect of these contentions and determinations. Cardozo told his cousin Annie that he thought "the decisions the Court was making at the time were the most important to the country of any time in its history."

Determination and an imperial, though not imperious, will played their parts in some of Cardozo's decisions. For after he had painfully fought the fight in his own mind, his was an aristocratic will that could not bend to private cajolement or public pressure. We have already pointed out the fact that he did not hesitate to make unpopular decisions if he believed them to be just and to be best for the country. This is why he was profoundly shaken and gave way to one of his few outbursts of anger on reading an editorial entitled "Cardozo and Brandeis" which attacked their court decisions as being "un-American." "Un-American!" The man whose roots and traditions had been deep in

[258]

American life and thought from colonial days. The anti-Semitic bias shown in such an editorial grieved him deeply. With the growth of Hitler policies after 1932 he became greatly saddened, but his own attitude ever remained of inviolable dignity. One of the few times when he was known sternly to rebuke women to whom he was attached was over standards of justice which, in his mind, went beyond all questions of particular prejudice.

A New York magistrate had allowed an infraction of the peace, a disturbance directed against German sailors, to go unpunished in fitting manner. He found extenuating circumstances for his leniency in feelings aroused by the actions of the Nazi regime. His decision included a vehement attack on Hitler's methods. Politics and personal emotions thus invaded the bench, affecting the voice of justice. Cardozo was indignant. As an American he felt abashed; as a Jew he felt humiliated; as a judge he was angry and ashamed. In all Cardozo's courteous letters there is none that does him higher credit than one in which, brushing aside all gracious charm of words, he sternly records his own attitude. No two wrongs could in his eyes, make the slightest right. No violence of others could justify the violation of standards of justice.

"I am glad," he wrote to a friend, "you like me for myself and not for any supposed quality of greatness, which, alas, is nonexistent. All that I have accomplished in life has been the product of unceasing toil, and whatever greatness I have is the greatness of a drudge." Then he continued: "I am disappointed that you and she approve of ——— and his shameful utterance. What is the use of striving for standards of judicial propriety if you and she condone such lapses! It would have been bad enough if he had been a Gentile; but for a Jew it was unforgivable. Now our traducers will say—and with some right if you and she approve—that these are the standards of the race."

Only once in all his life did Cardozo forego the usual ways of courtesy as, in very telling manner, he let his own feelings for the German regime appear. When the card of the German ambassador was left at his house after Hitler had gone a long and cruel way on his road of persecution of the Jews, Cardozo left etiquette behind. He did not return his own card. With Hitler in full power, and Julius Streicher foaming in rabid rage, Cardozo was overwhelmed with sadness by the situation in Germany. Not so much as it related specifically to Jews, but because his whole nature revolted against hatreds of groups toward one another. "What can I say," he wrote to Dr. Stephen Wise, "what can anyone say about the speech of the Frankfurt ruffian? The crimes of violence are almost the least of the whole shameful business. One of the worst phases of it all is the widespread assumption—I think it is not unknown in our own land—that you may wound the souls of men with impunity if only you spare their bodies."

Cardozo's own soul had been wounded by the anti-Semitism of Mr. Justice McReynolds, and his frequent unhappiness at Washington is evident even in his gayer letters. For these were letters of gaiety touched by regret. To Aline Goldstone he wrote of "a girl, a bright girl too, who had cut my picture out of the paper and pinned it on her wall! At my time of life! A real romance! I was told of a little boy in a community center who was asked to write something about current events and evolved the following: 'Judge Cardozo had been put on the Supreme Court. He is 62 years of age. He is very old. *He is very smart for his age.*'" Then the letter ends: "If only I didn't have to go back to Washington in September!" And later, from Washington: "I was so glad to see you in my place of exile."

XVI

CARDOZO was never to lose altogether the sense of being
an alien in Washington, which he termed his place of
exile. Early in his first Court session I visited Washington and asked the Justice to dine with my daughter and
me. Gracious, as always, in his acceptance, Cardozo began
to speak of his loneliness in Washington. Of course, he was
besieged by invitations, but these were from comparative
strangers. The shy and modest man was overaware that all
these immediate letters and cards were due, not to the affection of old acquaintances, but to the high office to which he
had been called.

Washington was eventually to learn to love him, but as
yet he was a new figure at the Capital. A lonely man, still
longing for his beloved New York. A sensitive man, deeply
hurt by two or three letters wherein the writers had said
that he should not have accepted the nomination to the
Supreme Court. Justice Brandeis was already there. One
Jew, they said, was quite enough.

"But haven't you received hundreds of letters con-
gratulating you? Thousands, even, I fancy."

"Perhaps," answered Cardozo.

"And hasn't the whole country, through the press, shown unanimous satisfaction at your appointment? Are you going to let the opinion of a few prejudiced persons depress you?"

"Even if it's only two or three," the Justice replied, "I can't forget that some of my fellow Americans don't want me here." Then he added: "It's an experience I never had before. It was so different in Albany."

Cardozo had a custom, adhered to throughout his six years in Washington, of going out not more than one evening a week. The other nights were reserved for judicial work. On one occasion at a dinner given by Ned and Peggy Bruce the other guests were the Stones, Senator Robert Wagner, Sir Willmott Lewis, Washington correspondent of *The Times* of London, my daughter and myself. Even at comparatively informal gatherings in Washington, the usual etiquette is observed. As Justices of the Supreme Court take precedence over Senators, and as Stone had been on the Federal bench longer than Cardozo, it was, of course, to the former Dean of the Columbia Law School that the host turned with the request, "Mr. Justice, will you lead the way?"

Justice Stone smiled, and shook his head.

"I'm not so much interested in formalities," he said. "I recognize my superiors. Cardozo, *you* lead the way."

It was the junior Justice's turn to smile—that shy smile of his. Without a word he linked his arm into that of his associate, and together these two great jurists, these two fine friends, walked into the dining room.

Dean Bates of the Michigan Law School gives a vivid picture of Cardozo during these Washington years. "I called at his office in the Supreme Court Building," he relates, "and shall never forget the impression which he made on me at that time. He was seated at his desk, and part of the time, as he turned in his chair, his profile was presented to me, outlined against the dark wood paneling

[262]

in his office. His white hair and face made it a cameolike, striking picture. I recall his saying to me and my daughter, who was with me, that the year had been the most unhappy one of his life."

This unhappiness was not due to ill-health or to that sense of loneliness which was never wholly dispelled. It was due in part to sympathy for the outraged members of his own race and, in larger part, to his sense that justice itself, irrespective of race questions, was being violated as never before in the history of modern civilization. The nauseous plant of cruel intolerance had had its seed sown in Germany. In 1923 Adolf Hitler, backed by General Ludendorff, marched upon Munich during the unsuccessful revolt in Bavaria. Some of his companions were killed in the fighting. Hitler himself was wounded. Later in the year he was captured and imprisoned. Ten years later he was in full power at the head of the German government. The atrocities, the violations of human rights, the kidnapings, robberies, and all the other infractions of fundamental human justice so shocked Cardozo that he no longer wished to live in a world where such things were possible.

And here, perhaps, it is necessary to digress to indicate Cardozo's attitude toward the challenging yet irritating, the difficult and everlasting "Jewish question." He had, as we have already seen, given up synagogue attendance in early youth, but he had remained a member of the Spanish-Portuguese congregation. He had ever continued his association with Jewish cultural and philanthropic institutions. His social affiliations were with Jews as well as with Christians. He saw no reason to differentiate between them. If he did not feel at home with ostentatious and disagreeably mannered men and women whose ancestors had not believed in the divinity of Jesus, he was equally averse from association with similar individuals who followed the Christian faith. In a word, he disliked vulgar people.

[263]

Cardozo realized that there were not only historic reasons for prejudice against Jews, but that there were also excellent reasons for prejudice against individual Jews who had retained ways differing from the manners of their fellow citizens. He realized the historic reasons for some of these ways, and made the allowances that all broad-minded men should make. Hardly a century had gone by since restrictions on Jewish careers had been lifted and the doors of many European ghettos opened. Could one expect from immigrants of the first generation in America the manners of those who had a lengthier heritage of social contacts?

The cultural traditions of his race were ever cherished by Cardozo and one of the foremost gratifications of his last years came with the conferring of an honorary degree from Yeshiva College, an institution distinguished for its continuance of Jewish values finely worth preserving.

Ardent in his Americanism, Cardozo was not interested in the Zionist movement at its outset. But as time went on, and Hitler's persecutions became more rampant, Cardozo saw the value of Palestine, not only as a place of refuge but as a land where some of the finest traditions of his race might be continued to the increasing benefit of the world at large. As with other Jews, his heart strings were played upon by the cruel fingers of German enemies, and his loyalties refreshed and amplified. But above all this, there was for Cardozo, the servitor of justice, very special and very bitter humiliation at the eclipse of justice. Here, indubitably, was the profoundest cause of the sorrow which led him to say to Dean Bates that 1936 was the saddest year of his life.

His attitude in regard to the problems faced by the Jews was not always so tragic, however. In a letter to Mrs. Stephen Wise, referring to a translation which she had sent him, he wrote: "I think a good deal these days about religion, wondering what it is and whether I have any. As the human relationships which make life what it is for us begin

[264]

to break up, we search more and more for others that transcend them. Your book reaching me in this mood was doubly welcome, and I enjoyed it and admired its art, even if I did not share the fire of its enthusiasm. Some of its thrusts are delightful. The Jews have survived the Pharaohs, Nebuchadnezzar, Constantine, Mohammed; they have survived the Inquisition and assimilation; they will survive the automobile."

One of the rare flashes of bitterness appears in a letter to his cousin Maud. "*The Jews of Germany*," he told her, "is to my thinking a noble and beautiful book. I hope your ministerial friend will read and ponder it, though probably after meeting you he will not need to be convinced that at least there are some Jews who are not utterly uncivilized."

But for all his deep-seated sadness, his wit still flashed out, playing upon the subject which held pain to him, as it did on other facets of life. While he was in Washington, Dr. David de Sola Pool went to the Capitol to give an address on Zionism. In order to present an impartial picture, the clergyman spoke first for twenty minutes in favor of Zionism, and then for twenty minutes against it. The next day, Cardozo wrote to him: "The newspapers tell me that you were in Washington yesterday and had a triumphant discussion with yourself."

In spite of increasing ill-health and the pressure of work, in spite of the pall of gloom which the activities of Nazi Germany had cast over him, in spite of the inveterate shyness which made him shrink from social gatherings, Cardozo found himself leading a more social life during those last years than he had ever done before. When these social gatherings were of an informal rather than an official character, one suspects there were moments when Cardozo regretted that life had made him so much of a recluse. After his first Court term in Washington he spent the summer in Westchester County, New York, whence he wrote to his cousin Maud: " . . . the country is beautiful, and the change has benefited me greatly; I look and feel better than for many years past. The neighbors have been wonderfully kind to me, and the neighborhood includes not only Westchester, but all the counties near by. I have dinner engagements for weeks in advance, and have been given the privileges of so many country clubs that I repent more bitterly than ever of the misspent years which have left me ignorant of games of sport. It will be hard to settle down to work again, and harder still to move to Washington, away from all these old-time friends.

"On September 9 my lease expires. On September 14, the movers are coming to 75th to pack my goods and chattels, and on September 15, the van, laden with my belongings, moves on to the District of Columbia, followed, I hope and expect, by a procession of wailing mourners, who are to weep and beat their breasts at the thought of losing me."

And a little later: "There are some advantages in not being near such a host of friends as I have in Westchester. They are inviting me to dinners and luncheons at such a pace that my growing years and infirmities may be unable to stand the strain."

Nevertheless, when Dorothy Shubart told Justice Cardozo that she had used his name without permission as a reference in applying for admission of her young daughter into the Greenwich Academy, "Quite all right," the Supreme Court Justice replied, "but I'm not very well known in Westchester County."

He was always eager to arrive at his summer home in that attractive region. "Only about two and a half months more," he wrote, "and I shall be enveloped with the peace and calm of Westchester. To sit on one's porch at one's ease while the heathen rage in the legislative halls at Washington is surely a role for a philosopher." And, after the weeks had worried by: "The Court will sit on Tuesday to hand down the last decisions of the year, and Wednesday morning, bright and early, I set sail on a railroad car for White Plains. After all the strain of the last eight months it is a pretaste of heaven—or more accurately perhaps it *is* heaven or all of heaven I shall ever know—to have nothing in particular to make up my mind about."

In Washington Cardozo dined, as a rule, with Miss Tracy, who was the link between him and the past. Usually she addressed him as Judge and when others were present he always called her Miss Tracy, but when they were alone and especially when they had their slight spats—for Miss Tracy was very economical and also was very insistent about his not eating so fast and about observing his doctor's orders and not working too much—they called each other "Ben" and "Kate." On one occasion, she telephoned the Supreme Court office to find out whether "Judge Cardozo" was there. The reply came, "Mr. Justice Cardozo has just left." She was quick to grasp the implied reproof. Thus instructed concerning the proper mode of address, Kate at dinner that evening began a sentence with "Mr. Justice." "Oh, Kate," he interrupted, "don't be the old fool."

Once a week or thereabouts, Cardozo had guests. He went occasionally to the White House, where his presence was much enjoyed by the President and Mrs. Roosevelt.

During the last two years he hardly ever went out in the evenings though he did go out for tea. He was much sought after, particularly as people speedily came to feel his exceptional charm. One day in earlier years when he was taking tea at Mrs. Felix Frankfurter's, he met the English philosopher, Alfred North Whitehead, then a professor at Harvard. "I wasn't with that man more than five minutes," commented Whitehead, "before I knew I was in the presence of a great man." He often dined at the homes of his colleagues, where his hostess might be Mrs. Stone or Mrs. Hughes, Mrs. Brandeis or Mrs. Roberts. The wives of his colleagues in Washington were delighted with his company, as the wives of his colleagues at Albany had always been. Yet his happiest hours were those during which he was visited from time to time by old New York friends, or when he would be, to use his own phrase, "stealing a day or two off in New York." "The term of the Court is almost over," he wrote to me toward the end of his first session in Washington, "and my spirits rise at the thought that I shall soon be roaming among the skyscrapers."

It was pleasant, every now and then, to have a little group of never more than eight at his Connecticut Avenue home; his guests being at times his old Columbia teacher, Professor Seligman with his wife, or the Hughes and the Stones, or the Misses Solomons, or Senator Wagner, or Sir Willmott Lewis, or others in Cardozo's little circle of New York and Washington friends. The Judge himself took no liquor, but he served pleasant wines. Knowing little about vintages, he followed the advice of Justice Stone in their selection, and similarly submitted to superior judgment in the matter of cigars. There was nothing elaborate about the meals. On the other hand, there was no stinting of hospitality where the rarest food remained the conversation.

On one occasion, indeed, Cardozo took what he supposed to be fruit juice. It turned out to be some gin concoction. Hard liquor had rarely entered the field of his experience. The Judge, somewhat surprised at its effect, naïvely warned one of his law secretaries of the danger of its deceptive appearance.

In some other matters he proved to be equally without knowledge. He seldom went to see motion pictures and was widely ignorant of the screen heroes and heroines of the American public. One day the famous Swedish actress was being discussed in his presence. She was a star who had never swum into his ken. "But who *is* Greta Garbo?" Cardozo asked in bewilderment.

While he was fond of opera and concerts and occasionally went to the theater, the first movie that he saw was during one of his last summers in Westchester when he was much taken by one of Walt Disney's pictures. He was delighted by the screen presentation of the adventures of the poetically minded Ferdinand who led so retired a life—reluctant to be dragged as a hero into the arena. All his sympathies went out to the peace-loving quadruped. "I can understand his feelings," he said—he who, having been warned of the altercations which might enter into the Washington scene, had smilingly replied, "It takes two to make a fight."

Cardozo at Washington, Cardozo in his final summers, remained what he so long had been, a gentle Socrates, a witty and charming Plato—the practical philosopher rarified by idealism. If Socrates, in discussing justice, disregarded former conceptions and insisted on relevant facts as the basis of the law's edifice, did he not write to Plato of the leaping flame that would kindle the soul of the striver after justice? Did not Plato believe in these "voiceless discussions of the soul with itself"?

It was not merely problems of justice with which Cardozo concerned himself, but with the many aspects of philosophy as they affect the human soul. On one occasion he said to Judge Seabury: "I have never been able to get any satisfactory definition of liberty. It haunts me." Later, of course, he was to develop his relative philosophy which answered some of his problems.

Mrs. Winthrop Chanler, one of the Washington women greatly liked and admired by the Justice, has compared him with another philosopher of our own days—Henri Bergson. "There was," she writes, "a certain resemblance between him and Justice Cardozo—that high rarified atmosphere of the mind—a beautiful clarity of thought, of expression. But the dear Justice had a tragic depth to his soul that I did not find in Bergson—who had somehow achieved more spiritual

[269]

faith. . . . It will be difficult to convey that rare quality . . . something like a distillation of wisdom which made Justice Cardozo so unique."

Mrs. Chanler, in her engaging book of reminiscences, *Autumn in the Valley*, gives this picture of the French philosopher: "He is of the rare and exquisite type of Hebrew, a frail body, worn and spiritualized by thought, with eyes lighted by an inward fire. Charming in manner, responsive yet discriminating, appreciative with wakeful discernment. I seem to be describing our own Justice Cardozo. The two have a great deal in common. Some of the gentler prophets must have been like them."

In a later page Mrs. Chanler writes of Cardozo: "He avoids the gay world and is rarely seen where more than two or three are gathered together for social purposes. He comes to see me once in awhile and his visit marks the day with a red letter. No guest is more welcome to me. He combines all his knowledge and alembicated wisdom with such pleasant wit and modest simplicity, he has so many interesting things to relate, that the good hour flies far too quickly and he leaves me always to my regret, and to boast to my friends that he has come."

Others of the gracious and cultured women of Washington felt the honor of a visit from the shy, retiring man. Mrs. Roosevelt, now the best-beloved woman in America, has told us of her appreciation of Cardozo's "fine sensibilities and rare experience"; of the honor felt by Theodore Roosevelt's sister, Mrs. Douglas Robinson, when Cardozo called on her, and how Mrs. Roosevelt's aunt and the Justice thereafter sent books of poetry, each to the other. Mrs. Robert Woods Bliss writes: "His was one of the friendships we most valued and we are actively conscious of his absence and that we shall never again see him come in of a Sunday afternoon for a cup of tea and a talk about books and music."

What talks with Cardozo meant, whether to men or to women, is strikingly indicated by the fact that a friend of the Washington years made the trip from New York about once a month, just to visit Cardozo. Jane Perry Clark, now Professor of American Government at Barnard College, had idolized Justice Holmes. After his death she was eager to meet his successor. She was introduced by her father, John C. Clark, the distinguished New York Supreme Court justice. Miss Clark's admiration was immediate. As the acquaintance ripened, there would be Sunday luncheons followed by talks on law and literature and affairs of public interest. She has told us of his charming way of asking *your* opinion, even on constitutional points. Badinage would at times enter their serious discussions. His wit, she found, was sophisticated but always kind.

This kindness which all who knew him attribute to Cardozo was particularly evident in his graciousness to young lawyers. Now and then, it is true, he would express his regret at his inability to comply with requests from law students, as when one of them asked for an opinion as to the merits of his article in the *St. John's Law Review*. "If you reflect upon the matter," wrote the Justice, "you will see that there are many reasons why a member of the Supreme Court must lay upon himself a self-denying ordinance, admitting no exceptions." After this gentle admonition Cardozo closed his letter with the words: "I wish you success and happiness in the profession of your choice."

One of the Judge's cousins, Frances Cullman, asked him to receive a classmate of her son. Cardozo suggested that it somewhat embarrassed him to meet a law student. "He has the law at his finger tips while I'm a bit rusty at times." However, he wrote: "I'll see your young friend if he will call at my apartment, though it is against all the precedents and usages of the Court for any of the 'Nine' to give out an interview for publication. Perhaps the boy would like to have a talk with me anyhow," he went on, "and report that I'm old and ugly." So the law student came, "a pleasant lad who brought one of his friends with him. I didn't tell him anything worth repeating, but at least he could announce that he had entered the awful presence."

"While attending Georgetown University Law School," writes William Woodburn, Jr., "I was a member of a law club known as the 'Pierce Butler Law Club.' We held monthly luncheons and very often prominent members of the bench and bar addressed our group.

"In the fall of 1933 three of the boys called on Mr. Justice Cardozo and asked him to be our guest of honor and principal speaker at a luncheon in the near future. Mr. Justice Cardozo declined the invitation very graciously, saying he had made it his rule not to eat out since leaving the New York Court of Appeals. However, he said, 'Come in, gentlemen, and we will chat for a while.'

"He asked one of the boys, 'Do you young gentlemen study under the "case" system or the "text" system?' On being informed that the 'case' system was used at Georgetown, he said, 'You gentlemen are very fortunate; in my day at Columbia we used the "text" system and I feel that if I had studied under the "case" system I would really have been able to accomplish something worth while.'

"One of the young men, of irrepressible nature said, 'Why, Mr. Justice, I think you have done pretty well as it is!' "

With all the demands made upon his time, aside from the heavy and unceasing pressure of work, for speeches, for social activities, for the carrying on of a large correspondence, Cardozo with gentle firmness managed to maintain his privacy with the simplicity and aloofness he had always preferred. Chief Justice Hughes remarked that he never knew anyone who was so able to live his life as he wished in his quiet way, always making progress. Cardozo had, said the

Chief Justice, "a rare combination of restraint and capacity for felicitous utterance." He was "as charming a companion as could be." At the Court in Washington, Hughes said, "we sit around in our conferences, we meet at lunch where the conversation is general." These lunches were the occasion, by the way, of one of the few arguments between Cardozo and Miss Tracy. The Judge, it appears, was inordinately fond of cake and Miss Tracy made sure that every day a piece of cake appeared with his lunch. The regularity of this performance began to amuse the Justices, who adopted a bantering tone about it. Whereupon Cardozo told Miss Tracy that there was to be no more cake with his lunch. Miss Tracy, unable to see why he should forego anything that he enjoyed, ignored his orders, and the cake continued to appear. At length Cardozo gave his orders more sharply and the cake no longer arrived at the meal. It was one of the few times, Miss Tracy admitted, when he had been angry with her. It was not so much anger, however, as the self-consciousness which made the Judge uncomfortable when he became the butt of his colleagues' good-humored joking.

There was an occasion, however, in which he greatly enjoyed a joke on himself. Walking along the street, he had noticed a roll of bills on the sidewalk. His first impulse was to pass them by. After having done this, he retraced his steps and picked the money up. There seemed to be fifteen dollars in the roll. Deciding that the owner might return, he waited a moment or two. Then, from the house before which he was standing, a woman descended the steps. Cardozo asked her whether she had lost anything. "Yes," she answered, "some bills." "Here, madam," he said, "are your fifteen dollars." Looking at him sharply, "Sixteen," she said, in a stern voice. Greatly embarrassed, feeling almost as though he had been accused of theft, the courteous Judge handed the lady the money.

Cardozo told the story to a friend of his, Doris Webster, who in turn related the episode to the cartoonist, H. T. Webster—no relative—who thereupon made it, in somewhat varied form, the subject for one of his pictures of "The Timid Soul." For the idea the artist sent Doris Webster $10, which was invested in a new dress, and Cardozo wrote to her: "From time to time I have been casting timid glances at the pictures of the Timid Soul . . . I knew that 'Webster' was the author. Was it possible that the Great Doris Webster would be revealed when the veil of semianonymity was drawn aside? Was she an artist as well as a literary craftsman and a wit? Being a relative of Milk Toast, I was too timid to inquire.

"Your tale of the $10 will keep me henceforth in the path of rectitude. Honesty is the best policy. One may not grow rich oneself, but here is proof positive that one's friends will become opulent and will go about thereafter in fine and costly raiment."

Meanwhile the place of exile still weighed upon Cardozo, and his thoughts were often in Albany with the group of friends he had left there. It was with a pang, therefore, that upon answering the telephone one day he heard the words, "White House speaking." It was President Roosevelt, who, not wishing Cardozo to be distressed by getting the tidings from outside sources, had called to break gently the news that Cardozo's old friend and associate, Judge Cuthbert Pound, had died.

During all this time constant pressure was being put upon him for appearances at dinners, for speeches of all sorts. I was not guiltless of this myself, for I invited him to speak at the tricentennial celebration in New York of the birth of Benedict Spinoza. In accepting membership on the executive committee, "I cannot resist the temptation," he wrote, "of posing as a philosopher and patronizing Spinoza.

"But when it comes to making an address, that is a different matter. One trouble is that I don't understand my hero well enough to be able to tell an audience the secret of his greatness. Another difficulty is still more insuperable (for when did understanding become a barrier to utterance?). This other difficulty is due to the fact that I have abjured public speaking (at least till I have become more accustomed to the work of my new office), and that even if I were ready to forswear myself, the Court will probably be in session at Washington at the date appointed for the dinner, and its claim upon my presence will be stronger than Spinoza's. Now that I have disposed of that question, where, may I ask, did you discover evidence of the supposed fact that mine is 'the finest philosophic mind among American Jews,' or a philosophic mind at all? Flatterer; flatterer!"

And to his cousin Maud he commented: "That Spinoza dinner was a mere gesture on my part. I felt I'd like to compliment his ghost, and make his fame secure. George Hellman roped me into the affair a good many months ago, when I didn't know what the work of the Court would be at this season of the year. I shall be much too busy to be able to go to New York and must slave away at my opinions. Court will open shortly and I must be there."

His attitude in regard to his responsibility to the Court and his sensitive rectitude led him, at Christmastime, to refuse a valuable gift sent him by Judge Grossman, who had resumed the practice of the law. It seemed unacceptable to the Justice before whom the lawyer might someday be arguing a case. This may be thought of as following a principle too rigidly. It is inconceivable that any member of the Supreme Court could be affected in his decisions by a friendly gift; but that was Cardozo's way. It was followed, however, with the Justice's customary tact, a quality which stood him in good stead when at a reception of Mrs. Woodrow Wilson a guest was discussing her resemblance to her hostess. Mrs. Wilson did not seem enormously pleased. When Cardozo came up to them he was asked if he did not notice the resemblance. "The sun has many dazzling rays," he said promptly, "all too brilliant for me to differentiate."

How paradoxical that the days of Cardozo's highest office and widest renown were the days of his bitterest discontent, days in which he weighed his life and its achievements, uncertain whether he would find merit in them! A hint of this attitude is revealed in a speech he made at a Testimonial Dinner for Dr. Nicholas Murray Butler.

"Sometimes in hours of dejection," he remarked, "we say to ourselves that the travail has been wasted, that the good is not worth its cost in pain, that the world is blind, and dull, and unreceptive, and indifferent. Then, of a sudden, there comes a revealing glare of light. An illness, a misfortune, an anniversary, or some gathering like this, brings vividly before us the scores and the hundreds, and even indeed the thousands, who have perceived and understood, who have marked what we were doing through all the years of silent drudgery; and in that moment we know that our misgivings were uncalled for, that the life, toilsome as it may have been, was not an unnoticed spasm of effort, a futile pulse of motion in the midst of a merciless infinity, but that it counted after all."

The incessant labors in the Supreme Court did not, of course, prevent the Justice from being mindful of other obligations. Yet what meticulous conscientiousness the following note to Professor Seligman reveals!

"About a year ago I became a subscriber to a fund for the benefit of Dr. Fabian Franklin, the contributions to continue, if I recall aright, for a period of three years. . . . Has the time arrived for a second payment? Letters addressed to me at Washington go astray now and then, and I am fearful that some call has come from you to which I have failed to respond."

Dr. Fabian Franklin was a philosophic publicist whose

services were deservedly recognized in an editorial in the *New York Herald Tribune* after the aged scholar's death. In his last years a circle of admirers considered it a privilege to be of aid to this fine impoverished old gentleman.

Whenever he could escape from Washington, Cardozo returned for a few days to New York. In concluding its eulogistic editorial after the death of the Justice, the *New York Times* said: "If he belongs to the country and the world, he was our fellow townsman, a New Yorker born and bred." Indeed, so much did he feel himself a part of his city, and his city an integral part of himself, that he could call "blessed" its steaming pavements of July and win more content from its towers than any fields or woods could offer.

"How good of you," he wrote to Aline Goldstone, in a letter referring to Edwin Arlington Robinson, "to spare me a thought and a word during your little vacation among the pines! They tell me Robinson is extraordinarily shy; I should be drawn to him by that as well as by his noble poetry. You will make him feel at ease, however: that is one of your pleasant traits—not so rare, I suppose, for women as it is for men, but still rare enough to be worth noting.

"The blessed stone pavements are steaming hot and the divine towers of steel are soaring toward the brazen sky; and I am discontented and morose—but less so than I should be if shut up in a pine forest."

There was one noisy occasion in New York in the fall of 1933 which its son would have liked to attend. A struggle was going on, similar to that of twenty years earlier, when Cardozo was elected to the bench and Jack Mitchel to the mayoralty. Fusion candidates, headed by Fiorello La-Guardia, successfully opposed the cohorts of Tammany. But now Washington had become Cardozo's official residence. "I feel more than ever an exile today," he writes. "The great city election is on, and I am condemned to take no part in it. 'Hang yourself, brave Crillon,' said Henry IV

[277]

after a great victory had been gained. 'Hang yourself, brave Crillon: we fought at Arques and you were not there.' "

"I wonder," he wrote to Rupert Joseph, "do you miss the moorings to a settled home, or is there a greater joy in unattached freedom? Not for me, I fear, but then I am old, and too set in my ways to wish to change them if I could. I am to spend the summer at Rye, N. Y., close to my beloved city. Washington is my legal domicile now, but not the domicile of my spirit. If my heart is separately interred—I was interested in the clipping you sent me about 'Buried Hearts'— it will be in the old city that it will rest, wherever they put my body."

"Back to work," he writes to Rupert Joseph on another occasion, "the vacation only a dream! The fetters hurt at first: after wearing them a time I grow used to them, and forget that for a time I was free." And in the next letter: "I envy you your leisure and the capacity to read and study what you like, instead of being a galley slave as I am, chained to the benches of an ancient trireme. . . . But I have not the courage to break away."

And to Aline Goldstone, that longing for books, for time to read and savor them, appears again: "If only the Court year were over," he said, "I'd talk to you about the things that really count—about art and letters and the like. Never mind, I see the summer beckoning already. . . . The Court term is almost over. *Gloria in excelsis!*"

Cardozo and his sister Nell at Allenhurst

XVII

My library was dukedom large enough.

SHAKESPEARE

Tᴴᴇ things that really count," Cardozo called them "art and letters and the like." As a reader, Cardozo offers an opportunity it would be a pity to forego. Judges, lawyers, teachers and students of philosophy and of law will doubtless scan the footnotes of his various volumes, following thereby the vast range of his reading in his professional field. Holmes and Haldane, Learned Hand and Lowes Dickinson, Pollock and Lippmann, Whitehead and Wigmore. Dewey and Cohen, Beard and Giddings, Royce and Spinoza and Robinson, Blackstone, of course, and Hughes and Frankfurter—these are only a few of the authors whose writings Cardozo had studied. So many more besides—French, German, Austrian, Swiss, and Italian— contributed to the armory of Cardozo's implements at the bar and on the bench. But to the general reader, who from time to time is offered a list of the "best books" to be placed, it may be, on a five-foot shelf, why not give the titles of the books ordered by Cardozo either for himself or as gifts to friends during those last years of his life when he found more leisure—though never enough—to indulge his taste for writings not directly pertaining to his professional work?

[279]

But that, after all, would be too long a list. So let us give
the Justice's selection for merely the season of 1936–1937:

George Santayana—*Dialogues in Limbo*
Granville Hicks—*John Reed*
Irving Stone—*Lust for Life*
George Santayana—*The Last Puritan*
Henry W. Nevinson—*The Fire of Life*
Lewis & Smith—*Oscar Wilde Discovers America*
John Masefield—*The Letter to Pontus*
H. A. L. Fisher—*The History of Europe*
J. R. Commons—*Institutional Economics*
George Santayana—*Obiter Scripta*
John Gunther—*Inside Europe*
Beatrice & Sidney Webb—*Soviet Communism*
Clarence Day—*God and My Father*
Margaret Mitchell—*Gone with the Wind*
Claude G. Bowers—*Jefferson in Power*
Lord Haldane—*Autobiography*
Trevelyan—*Life of John Bright*
Van Wyck Brooks—*The Flowering of New England*
Desmond MacCarthy—*Portraits*
Desmond MacCarthy—*Criticism*
Desmond MacCarthy—*Leslie Stephen*
Victor Heiser—*An American Doctor's Odyssey*
Baudelaire—*Flowers of Evil*
Lin Yu Tang—*My Country and My People*
Sir William Rothenstein—*Men and Memories*
Mrs. Winthrop Chanler—*Autumn in the Valley*
A. E. Zimmern—*The Greek Commonwealth*
Allan Nevins—*Hamilton Fish*
The Letters of Mrs. Henry Adams
G. K. Chesterton—*Autobiography*
Virginia Woolf—*The Years*
G. H. S. Fifoot—*Lord Mansfield*
John P. Marquand—*The Late George Apley*
Odell Shepard—*Pedlar's Progress*
Carl Van Doren—*Three Worlds*

A. E. Housman—*Introductory Lecture*
C. H. Young—*Victorian England*
Herman Niernberg—*Einstein for Everybody*
Perry—*The Thought and Character of William James*
Winston Churchill—*Great Contemporaries*
Augustine Birrell—*Things Past Redress*
Theobald Mathew—*For Lawyers and Others*
Lord Lytton—*Antony*
The Journal of Eugene Delacroix
Duncan Phillips—*Giorgione*
Borghese—*Goliath*
The Letters of John J. Chapman
Benét—*The Devil and Daniel Webster*
F. J. E. Woodbridge—*The Son of Apollo*
Robert McElroy—*Jefferson Davis*
Irwin Edman—*Four Ways of Philosophy*
A. S. Eddington—*Science and the Unseen World*
Julius Lips—*The Savage Hits Back*

In this list of over fifty titles there are only five novels, including *The Last Puritan,* which might be classed, rather, as a work of disillusioned philosophy. Not easily affected by popular opinion in literature and the hullabaloo of advertisement, Cardozo was only after much persuasion induced to read *Gone with the Wind.* Mrs. Arthur Hays Sulzberger—wife of the president of the New York Times Corporation, a kinsman of Cardozo's, had told the Judge of her enjoyment of the Civil War story. "It may be a book for young romantic people," he said, "but not for an old judge like myself." Undiscouraged by this comment, Mrs. Sulzberger took the novel to Cardozo's near-by country residence at White Plains. Under these circumstances it seemed discourteous not, at least, to glance at the novel. Cardozo set forth on romantic miles of type. Soon Scarlett O'Hara began to exercise fascination. The "old judge" continued the journey with her to the end—almost without stopping.

Cardozo loved not only to read books, but also to be surrounded by them. In his apartment at Washington, as in his New York home, thousands of volumes were his sympathetic companions, speaking to him in many tongues. When he was in the Supreme Court he preferred, instead of having a book brought to him, to go in person to the library in search of the desired item. He was never a collector of rarities in any field. First editions and fine bindings meant little to him. Like Aesop, he thought more of the quality of the wine than the shape of the cask. But he loved to be among books. In all libraries he felt himself at home. His library in Washington was stacked to the ceiling and heaps of books were in the two closets off the library. On many of these books he made marginal notes or would write on scraps of paper which he inserted between the leaves. He had read almost all the books in his library and had, as we know, a phenomenal capacity for retaining what he read.

Moses Hadas, Professor of Greek and Latin at Columbia University, in a conversation with the author, spoke of Cardozo's love for the ancient classics, and how he kept up to date in connection with books referring to ancient civilization. Hadas remembers Cardozo told him that a lawyer in his court had quoted something from the Latin, but, Cardozo thought, had quoted it incorrectly. Something from Horace or Terence. When Hadas began to give the correct version Cardozo completed the entire quotation.

In Cardozo's preface to the volume issued in honor of Justice Holmes, he quotes from the *Iphigenia at Aulis* of Euripides. Cardozo knew the exact Greek wording but asked Hadas: "Don't you think it would be presumptuous if I used the Greek instead of translating it? Wouldn't it seem as if I were parading my little knowledge?" Hadas suggested that it would be more of a compliment to others if the Greek were retained.

Cardozo told Hadas how highly he had thought of Professor Merriam, his teacher of Greek in college days.

Merriam had made Athens alive to Cardozo, so much so that, in later years when he was walking on the streets of Albany, his thoughts would go back to walks and talks of the Greek philosophers. Euripides especially was often present in his mind. Cardozo and Hadas had enjoyed discussing the *Philosophy of History* by Toynbee, Gilbert Murray's son-in-law. Cardozo was impressed by its theory that in the study of history one should examine any and all developments as a response to a new attitude.

On one occasion when Hadas began to quote from Thompson's *Hound of Heaven* Cardozo finished the lengthy passage. Thompson's poems had been given to him by Kate Tracy.

Throughout his life Cardozo showed a thorough, intense intellectual interest in scholarship. He actually read the philological papers sent him by Hadas. Hadas tells me that he knows of only two other nonprofessional scholars who showed the same knowledge and interest in the classics. When Hadas expressed the thought that Sophocles, Aeschylus, and Euripides were three of the four greatest writers the world has known (Shakespeare, of course, being the fourth), Cardozo smiled and asked, "Do you really believe this?"

In his letters to Aline Goldstone—and his letters to women reveal in greater degree than any other source the gaiety of spirit and lambent wit of which he was capable— he spoke over and over of books he had read, sharing with her his enthusiasms. "*The Bridge of San Luis Rey* I had read in New York. I found it very wonderful; some of the sentences were so perfect I learned them—almost automatically —by heart. The transforming power of art is there exhibited to perfection. . . . The other volume, the essays by Yeats, I am reading now. I admire them, though being little of a mystic I find it hard to understand them. Also I resent some of my own feeling of admiration. Why should one love such meaningless obscurities? But there is a charm in the twilight even though it is the precursor of the darkness."

"The delightful little book [Edna St. Vincent Millay's *Aria Da Capo*] dropped into my lap a few hours ago, and I devoured it at once. That is the great thing about food for the *psyche* as distinguished from food for the body—one can go on devouring it again and again. So I mean to do with this dainty morsel, this recherché little tidbit.

"I do so envy the writers who can express the inexpressible. That is what we all try to do whenever we have anything to put into words, but most of us fail. Here comes along a new writer—new to me—though, I suppose, not new to the elect—and does the trick so blithely and gaily and deftly before our astonished and bewildered eyes. You have introduced me to some clever and charming people in your apartment, but now you have added to the benefaction by the introduction of a fairy sprite."

Later, the Judge is reading Galsworthy. *The Forsyte Saga* and *Swan Song* arouse his enthusiasm. "Nothing finer," it seemed to him, "has been written in our day. The *Saga* is perhaps the best."

The intellectual quality in Edwin Arlington Robinson's poetry appealed to Cardozo, and he found no difficulty in following the sometimes involved thought. But when it came to Joyce's *Ulysses*, "I'm too lazy," he wrote, "to force open these stiff rebellious doors when many a fine corridor lies beckoning before me. All the same I read the article on Joyce with interest."

Before sailing for Europe the Goldstones sent Cardozo a book that had interested them, Ortega y Gasset's *Revolt of the Masses*. "The book is here as if you had thrown it cityward from the dock . . . I'll enjoy *The Revolt*—of that I am sure. Is it an obscure something in the blood that wakens an extra thrill and tremor at the call of Spanish art? Who knows! At all events I feel quite certain that Señor Ortega's book will not suffer in my sight by reason of its Spanish origin. We have looked to Spain so long for gaiety and amusement. There is the charm of the unexpected in finding that she can furnish us with food for sober thought."

"Last night," he wrote later, "I sat in bed reading a new story—or the first installment of it—by Virginia Woolf. The title is *Flush*, and it is the biography of a cocker spaniel. Never was a dog soul more winsomely laid bare, but Flush was more than a cocker spaniel, he was the pet of Elizabeth Barrett Browning. So the story will tell us about dogs and poets. You will want to read it because of its poetry, and Harmon because it is written by Mrs. Woolf, and I because it tells about a dog."

Writing to these friends abroad, Cardozo for a moment puts books aside and talks of other things. Among the happiest memories of his life was his long-ago visit to England. He never forgot his days at Oxford and on the Thames.

"Your letter with its pen portrait of Devon, helped out by a picture of the hotel," he now writes as a man well past sixty, "filled me with a fleeting wish that I had gone abroad —only a fleeting one, however, for I love the comforts of home and friends; and it has stilled the pricks of my conscience to be told that a little of the same emotion takes hold of you at times. I know that I ought to love other things better—that I should have a more adventurous soul, but, alas! it is too late for the plastic surgery that might give a remodeled soul to a younger man, as it might give him a remodeled nose.

"There is a compensating peace here at Westchester. I think I told you that I called myself Gandhi—an ugly old saint—or at least a putative saint—to whom the faithful pay obeisance. They come here in great numbers, young and old, stupid and clever, some to stare and some to talk. Among the clever ones was Irwin Edman who called on me last night. What a delightful youth he is . . . He is to

[285]

lecture next week at Columbia on philosophy and poetry
. . . I was interested in the postcard with its picture of
Jeffrey's lodgings. I read a biography some years ago that
made me feel he had been a good deal maligned. The laws
of his day were cruel and he enforced them. Perhaps posterity will think little better of us. What a reward—if I can't
sell the 75th Street house—to have it reserved as a memorial
—the home of bloody Cardozo."

Cardozo never failed to answer a letter from a woman—
always with the exception of those hosts of women who had
besieged him with proposals of marriage at the time of his
appointment to the Supreme Court—and his vast correspondence was carried on in longhand. "An unanswered
letter," he confessed, "is for me a mosquito bite; it poisons
my blood till the virus is extracted and mingled with a drop
of ink. That is hard on my correspondents, but they are most
of them a forgiving lot and bear me no ill will."

In 1934 he wrote to Aline Goldstone: "You write so
charmingly to your friends—spacious, flowing letters giving
the reader a sense of intellectual abundance, a deep, rich
soil with only the thin upper surface turned, no end of
fertile earth below. Alas, I cannot vie with you. Perhaps it is
because I have grown only one crop, one kind of grain during the years. There must be a rotation of the crops—as the
scientists have taught us—if the soil is to keep its virtue.
Every little incident is foodstuff for your mind. You pass a
night at a wayside inn. My desire would be to take my leave
betimes. Behold, the inn when you rest in it is transformed
into a blessed haven of cheer and sweet repose. You meet a
group of travelers prattling of their own experiences. I
should forget to listen to their babblings. Behold, they talk
into your ears, and it is history, or romance, or poetry because of something you give out to it. I envy you the talent,
but still more the capacity for enjoyment. No drab world do
you live in, but one aflame with color."

Novels and verse, romance and poetry, continue to be discussed by the two friends. Cardozo does not admire Thomas Mann's *Joseph and His Brothers* as much as Aline does. He likes George Meredith more than what he calls "the present tribe of novelists." *Diana of the Crossways* had recently aroused his enthusiasm anew for the great Victorian writer whose intricacy of style necessitates contributory effort from the reader.

The closing months of that year saw politics creep into the letters. There was a deep satisfaction for Cardozo in the election of his friend Herbert Lehman to the governorship of New York. In the early months of 1935 there was grief at the death of Oliver Wendell Holmes. "Holmes was great. His lifework had been finished, but he remained a magnificent symbol. The world is poorer without him. I was the last person to visit him before he took to his bed." The jurist who succeeded Oliver Wendell Holmes then discusses with his friend the Supreme Court decision which disturbed so many Americans. Had not the good name of their country become slightly tarnished by the verdict releasing the government from adhering to a provision obligating the redemption of United States issues in gold? Cardozo's private sense of honor does not come into the picture, although it is suggested, when he writes: "As to the 'gold cases,' I don't wonder you are troubled by them. The difficulty is that most people fancy it to be the business of the Court to condemn as 'unconstitutional' everything that is unfair. Nothing of the kind! There is room for a lot of immorality within the confines of the Constitution and of constitutional law . . . The Court year has been a trying one." And later, "a cruel year—from the standpoint of courts and court terms."

In 1935, Cardozo wrote: "A great Englishman once said (I am fond of quoting the words): 'As I look back upon my life it seems to have been a series of miracles.' The consoling thing about it all is that in truth the happenings were not miracles; they were the fruits of patient and unceasing toil. I hope that the miracle-men will carry on to gladsome heights."

"Will Rogers's judgment upon mankind," Cardozo told Aline, "sounds fine when separated from its setting. What he really said, however—(at least, that is my understanding) —was that he had met many *prominent* men and had never met one he didn't like. That is not quite so magnificent, is it? Your tramp with the unshaven chin could hardly come in that category. Well, I'm willing to go pretty far in my love for humankind, but I can't have stubby chins around me. Fix me up, if you please, an epitaph to suit those sentiments."

Later Cardozo mentions Dr. Rosalie Slaughter Morton, a woman writer of our own day. Her book entitled *A Woman Surgeon* gives fine evidence of a life valuable and eventful. Cardozo had enjoyed meeting the author and reading her book. Less enjoyment, however, he seems to have found in *Poems* by C. Day Lewis, sent to him that September by his friend.

"The book by Lewis was slow in coming, and I have waited till I had time to read it before writing my thanks again. Dear child, it is too obscure and subtle for my dull and plodding mind. I found it interesting, just as I find the most modern music; I like to see the latest patterns that the thought and feeling of the hour weave, but it would be only an affectation to say that they give me the thrill and the lift that come from poetry as of old I knew it. Perhaps if you or one of your bright boys sat down beside me and we were to read it together, the missing tingle of the flesh—or is it the top of the cranium or the spine?—would come to me. Perhaps even alone I might get it if I were to dig the spade deep into the soil—but I am too old and weary for such toilsome work. I must skim my gold from the top layer. Also I like verse to sing, and there is little singing here.

"All this is not to say that I don't get illuminating flashes now and then. Still less is it to say that I didn't find a thrill of interest in learning the latest modes of art. Indeed I discovered myself saying that I must read Spender and Aiken and Jeffers and the rest of them. I have not lost my curiosity even if I lack the taste that ought to guide it."

"Dear Aline," Cardozo writes in a lighthearted letter, "do you really want to transform this world into one of stern-lipped discretion? Perish the thought. For judges, yes; but surely not for all. I am reminded of one occasion when I said to Nell that it was slander to repeat a tale reflecting upon someone though it were to be prefaced with a statement that the tale was only hearsay. 'I can't believe it,' she responded. 'What is there left of all our ancient liberties!' A good deal, I suspect, until the distant day when your ideal will be fulfilled."

"I am happy," he wrote the following summer, "that you are happy, and yet secretly a little pleased that you do not like the sea. I have been gathering extracts out of books that are on my vacation shelf—all hostile to that expansive element with its monotony and foolish waste. But my malice does not go far enough to cause me to lay upon you the curse of seasickness. I would have you say of yourself, as Galsworthy said of his fellow voyager Gilbert Murray—he is a good sailor, but not heartlessly good. There should be a little flutter now and then—abdominal, not mental, to prove the common humanity of good travelers and bad!"

Had Cardozo been in better health, "the curse of sea-sickness" would probably not have kept him from crossing the ocean a few weeks earlier that summer. Beginning toward the end of June, and reaching into July, the University of London celebrated its centenary. Nineteen distinguished men from many lands were then honored with degrees of Doctor of Literature, of Law, of Music, of Science. Albert Einstein, sometime of Germany; Emile Legouis, great scholar of France; the English novelist, H. G. Wells, and the English composer, R. Vaughan Williams; the Spanish poet and diplomatist, Don Ramón Pérez de Ayala—these among others. America received recognition through Benjamin Cardozo. In the citation, the Public Orator, addressing the Chancellor, the Earl of Athlone, said of Cardozo that he had been called "with unanimous approval" to succeed Oliver Wendell Holmes. "He is a worthy successor," the Public Orator continued, "for not only is he a judge of the highest eminence, but he is also a profound and illuminating writer on the province of law and its relation to the complicated structure of modern society. His reputation extends far beyond his native land, while his long experience and his brilliant gifts mark him out as one most admirably equipped to grapple with the difficult and far-reaching problems which come before a Court of such immense powers and responsibilities."

"My London degree," Cardozo wrote, "did give me a little bit of a thrill. Somehow it is exciting, and surprising too, to find that one is known abroad. And London University in its century of life has done more for the cause of liberalism than all the other universities put together. Indeed, by its precept and example it has molded the others to its form."

By the time his friend had returned from Europe, Cardozo was again in Washington. He took part in the second Inaugural Exercises of President Roosevelt. It was a bitter day of winter storm, dangerous for the multitudes in the open. His picture in the newspapers, standing bareheaded, the driving rain blowing his fine gray hair, was alarming in view of his never robust health. In reply to an anxious inquiry, he wrote: "I didn't catch cold, perhaps because I was fired with indignation at the folly of exposing thousands of onlookers to the vagaries of the weather at such a season of the year."

Cardozo was equally, or even more, "fired with indignation" by the quickly following attempt to add to the Supreme Court only Justices in accord with the presidential policies. However, in his next letter, the word "crusade" is suggestive, and his friends know that Cardozo, for all his sympathy with Franklin D. Roosevelt's fine social objectives, was opposed to that particular method of arriving at them. To his friend, who had broached the subject, he said: "I feel reluctant to write about the Court and the present crusade against it. There is no opinion you could express on any subject that I should regard as unforgivable or as anything but the revelation of a fine and high-minded spirit. So let us pass to pleasanter and safer themes."

So he went back to books. "Yes," he said, "I have read Carrel's book [*Man, the Unknown*] and found it stimulating and interesting, though, as so often is the case, he falls down when he suggests a remedy. I have no faith in his academy of superscientists. I have seen enough of the fallibility of super-judges generally."

To his cousin Maud Nathan, as well as to Aline Goldstone, Cardozo wrote openly, and with a gaiety and simplicity untouched by formal years on the bench.

"Please, ma'am," he wrote to Maud, "do you keep a swell establishment where a guy ought to bring a dinner coat, or will plain, ordinary garb suffice to gain admittance to the show? See what comes of inviting a guest who doesn't know the ways of polite society. The guy is looking forward to a pleasant time."

"I thought you were the favorite of a King's son," he remarked later on, "and behold! It is only a King's nephew! Pooh-pooh! Perhaps he is near enough to the throne to procure for you a jeweled order of merit or some such decoration. If he does, my awe-struck reverence will be reestablished. I am susceptible to the glamour of titles, but titles plus jewels and ribbands will make me grovel at your feet."

[291]

In a letter of January 9, 1933, the Justice refers to his cousin's book called *Once Upon a Time and Today*. In its pages there is an anecdote too amusing to omit. "The Consumers' League was circulating a petition for signatures in order to help secure some special legislation at Albany. There were two forms of petitions. One was headed 'We, the undersigned citizens,' the other 'We, the undersigned women.' Inadvertently, the secretary sent Judge Cardozo the latter form. He signed it, returning it to me with the observation, 'For *your* sake, I've signed away my sex!' "

Again he wrote, in regard to his cousin's request that he give an address at the Women's Forum. "My child—for child you are in spirit—I hate to say 'no,' but really I must. If you knew how I am driven and hounded by requests for speeches, you'd forgive me, I know you would. And the 'Women's Forum' of all places! Why, you have no idea of the inhibitions that hedge the soul—the pure and undefiled soul—of a Justice of the Supreme Court. He may not talk about events of the day. They may indicate his judgment as to problems that will come before him as a judge! He may not talk about the past. The past is the parent of the present and has given it its shape and mold! He may not talk about the future. The future is what we make it, and is here almost as we speak! And, of course, he may not talk about women. He is much too unsophisticated—especially if he is a bachelor—to have ideas upon a theme so charged with dynamite.

"Well, the result is that I don't make speeches anywhere —not even at bar associations. The American Bar Association sent me a letter the day before yesterday threatening extreme displeasure if I put their invitation aside. I defied the haughty monster. The only exceptions I have made have had their origin in the tender from universities of honorary degrees."

In March, Cardozo wrote to his cousin about the death of Justice Holmes. In this letter, there is reference to the case of the *Panama Refining Co. v. Ryan*. Cardozo, in his lone dissenting opinion, used the phrase: "There has been no grant to the Executive of any roving commission to inquire into evils and then, upon discovering them, to do anything he pleases." "I think," he commented to Maud, "I have had more glory out of my lone dissent than out of all my majority opinions. But lone dissents are not unusual. Holmes made them a habit, unless my memory is playing me tricks. The same day that I filled the solitary role, Stone was the sole dissenter in another case. The only difference was that mine was in the public eye."

In March, 1937, Cardozo finds himself unable to entertain his cousin in Washington. "The Court will be in session," he explained, "during the week of April 5, and my evenings during the session are given over to the vain attempt to rescue from destruction an ungrateful country.

"It happens that this week I made an exception to the extent of making an engagement to go on April 6 to the Philadelphia concert. If I were to deny the country the benefit of two evenings in succession, I don't know what would happen: I can only guess."

There was another correspondent of these Washington years, Doris Webster, who has been referred to before. She sent the Justice a copy of her book, *I've Got Your Number*, wherein the answer to a group of questions lead to key numbers of character studies. Cardozo reports that his key number is 1345. The analysis of character given for this number reads in part: "You like to think of yourself as an independent soul, complete and self-contained. Man, it is trying to be what you are not that makes you unhappy. You have a naturally faithful heart hitched up to a wide-ranging imagination—a difficult team to drive . . . A sense of insecurity has hung over from your childhood. Something has kept you from being one of the gang."

When he learned that a copy was being mailed to him,

Cardozo wrote: "I wonder, did you autograph it? Even if you didn't, I can paste your letter on the flyleaf of the volume where friends will be quick to see it when with premeditated carelessness I leave it in their way. Alas! What indiscretion—to give myself away by the revelation of this vanity! You will have my number, sure.

"The heading of this letter will tell you of my new abode in Washington, from which expressmen and porters have just been driven forth, leaving me happy in their going, but homesick for the scenes and faces that I have had to leave behind."

"So far as I can see," laments Cardozo, "1345 is not a very interesting sort of fellow, which confirms the estimate of my own qualities and powers that I formed long ago, though I have hesitated to communicate it to an unsuspecting world. If I feel too depressed at any time, I'll turn to the inscription on the flyleaf and find balm and solace there."

In return, Cardozo is informed that his "number" indicates a genius. "I thought your discernment was infallible," he tells Mrs. Webster, "but alas! you have made a slip. You have sized me up as a bit of a genius—admitting me into your own group—and, once more alas! I am nothing of the kind. As I told some college lads last spring, I am only a plodding mediocrity—a plodding one, please observe, for a mediocrity *simpliciter* stands still when a plodding one goes far if the road is not too steep."

Choosing a few phrases here and there from Cardozo's writings, Doris Webster had achieved a quatrain. Cardozo is much amused. "Many years ago," he relates, "when I was a struggling member of the bar, I tried a case with the euphonious title *State Bank v. Wilchinsky*. My client, the president of the bank, assured me in an outburst of gratitude, that the name of that case ought to be written on my tombstone.

"Now at last I have an inscription more dignified and

worthier. The poem that I wrote and that you deciphered beneath the palimpsest is to be carved upon the granite, bearing witness to my title as the first unwitting bard in history.

"Mathematicians tell us that Shakespeare's plays could have been written without an effort of mind if the letters of the alphabet had been shuffled long enough.

"I never really believed it, but now at last I do."

In 1935 Cardozo makes one of his brief references to the work of the Court. "No," he explains, "the opinion in the Gregory case wasn't mine. It was written by Justice Sutherland. It is a mighty good opinion, too, though taxpayers and accountants look at it askance.

"The alphabetical combinations are moving upon us next month. Pray for us all, I beg you, and most of all for your harassed friend, whose health, none the less, has improved unexpectedly since he came back to Washington to work harder than he should."

The reading of Mrs. Webster's next book provoked the following comment: "I have gone over the questions and know not how to answer them. 'Would you tell on a hit-and-run driver who did serious damage, if he were your best customer?' Well, I hope so, but how can I tell? If the response is to be an index to my moral aspirations, I am a paragon of virtue. Yet perhaps the very fact that I am hesitant is enough to show me up and exacts an answer 'no.'"

In 1937 he wrote, as summer drew to a close: "The summer is speeding by and I can descry in the distance the walls and the moats of my Washington prison house. Before the drawbridge is raised, the portcullis lowered, let me taste the joys of liberty." The letter closes with the famous refrain from Thomas Campbell's poem, "The Battle of Blenheim." " 'It was a famous victory.' Have you any notion of my meaning?" asks the Justice. One observes how guardedly

Cardozo refers to the outcome of the President's plan in connection with the Supreme Court.

In response to a laughing comment of Mrs. Webster's in regard to reincarnation, the Justice asks her not to wait for reincarnation "before saying nice things of, to, and about me. If I could think of other prepositions I would add them. Take a leaf from the government at Washington and be extravagant and lavish. Did you ever hear that a beneficiary of relief complained that he was getting too much?"

In a few days he had returned to Washington—"Back to the concentration camp!"—and here he turns to his favorite subject of books. "I haven't read anything by Otto Rank," he wrote, "but what you tell me about his writings makes me sure that I'll enjoy them. One of my favorite decisions is that the most enjoyable books for me are the ones I am unable to understand. They make up a library as big as the famed one at Alexandria. . . . " Later, after receiving the book: " . . . being wakeful, I tried to soothe my nerves by reading it. Soothing perhaps it was, but not intelligible. I haven't the slightest idea what the author is saying—not the slightest. Mr. Rank may be a wise and learned man, but as an author he is worthy of his name."

"To show you the kind of book I love—the classic spirit I adore—I am asking my booksellers to send you a biography of the Greeks. Put that on a shelf beside your incoherent Rank."

Cardozo received as much pleasure as he gave by his correspondence with these women with whom he could share his literary enthusiasms and with whom he could exchange lighthearted banter. There was need of such momentary escapes from the toils of work, for "These are tense days in Washington."

There was a foreign woman in Washington who, with her husband, afforded profound companionship to Cardozo during the final year at the Capital. Julias Lips and his wife Eva fled from the unrelenting Hitlerian attack against the freedom of the mind. In her book, *Savage Symphony*, the story is told. America restored them to the dignity of the human soul. In Washington they found peace again in the labor of the intellect. And they found in Cardozo not only a sympathetic friend, but the symbol of that justice whose torch had been extinguished in the land of their birth. What he meant to them, let the words of Eva Lips set forth.

She had been invited to deliver a Thanksgiving message on the Woman's Hour Program of the Jewish Theological Seminary. Her address concluded thus: "To me, belonging to a group of human beings which Hitler's insane terminology brands as Aryans, to me who refuses as my husband, a German scientist, refuses, to prostitute our souls, to submit to a sinister creed of hatred and barbarism—to us the 'New Quarter of Creation' is America whose proud citizens we will be in a few months . . . To us, the day of Thanksgiving means that God is given back to us, that we are allowed again to shield and cherish the truth for which we live. We have been reborn once more to a new knowledge of a higher freedom—freedom of the kind that means responsibility. But how could I ever celebrate Thanksgiving without remembering the name of the greatest man I ever knew! The name of the man who, last year, celebrated the peace with us. And since Thanksgiving means the expression of our gratitude to America, how could I end this short message but by pronouncing this one name, which to us embodied the soul of America! And thus, I say the name that made us forever devoted children of this great nation, the holy name of my Thanksgiving: Justice Benjamin Nathan Cardozo."

XVIII

He giveth his beloved sleep. PSALM CXXVII

SINCE that first heart attack in Albany, in 1930, the attacks had recurred occasionally. Perceptibly his health, never robust, grew worse. Resolutely he ignored his own waning forces, continuing to devote excessive energy to his work. His attitude toward his own health was in striking contrast with his solicitude toward others. On one occasion Professor Wormser of the Fordham University Law School acted as the assistant counsel of the New York Transit Commission. Suffering from a severe kidney attack, he appeared before Judge Cardozo to request an application for a stay. Cardozo did not limit himself to complying with the request. The next day he wrote: "I was sorry to see in your appearance yesterday the evidences of suffering and illness. I am writing to urge you to lay all work aside and give yourself exclusively to the task of getting well. I am sure that all my associates in the Court, as well as the whole profession, would echo this advice." After one of Cardozo's heart attacks, Justice Stone received a letter from Judge Lehman, asking Stone to suggest some physician in Washington who was a heart specialist, and have him call on Cardozo. Cardozo saw the physician but would not let up on his work. Stone, therefore, talked to

Hughes and between them they decided that no assignments should be given Cardozo until Sundays.

In 1935 Cardozo suffered his first serious illness. "The summer has been a failure," he wrote to Mrs. Webster. " . . . After my coming here from Washington, the doctor took me in hand and saw nothing in me but evil. For a time I was pretty sick with day and night nurses and many other restraints upon fundamental liberties. No autocrat like a doctor on all this regimented globe! Even after the worst tyranny was relaxed there was still an insistent demand for rest and quiet. Lunch parties were anathema, and the more interesting and enlivening the company, the greater the offense. Now, at the end of the summer, I feel pretty nearly my old self and ready to resume the cruel labors of the Court."

While Cardozo was convalescing at Rye, one of his few close friends, Judge William N. Cohen of the New York State Supreme Court, sent him a basket of fruit, "such," Cardozo told him, "as only a refined epicure like you could choose—grapes that were grown in the Garden of Eden; jellies that were preserved in the kitchens of Lucullus; peaches and other rarities known only to the educated palate. These have been left at the door of my humble dwelling for my consumption and delight in these days of pampered ease and leisure." Then, to reassure his friend, "There is nothing the matter with me," Cardozo adds. "The doctors are beginning to see this and are relaxing their restrictions. I sit up a good part of the day. The case is developing into a racket designed to extort baskets of goodies and other unmerited attentions from unsophisticated friends like you."

Writing to Rupert Joseph from Rye, Cardozo complained: " . . . confined to bed under the tyrannical sway of nurses and physicians. I was badly run down after the winter's work in Washington and the doctors, having put

[299]

me to bed for purposes of cure, are keeping me there, as they do hardened criminals, for the purpose of reformation. They'll have a hard time making over a tough old customer who has weathered so many years."

Friends were sending to the sick man not only books and flowers but also delicacies. A suggestion from Rupert Joseph led Cardozo to one of his rare references to eating. "I must not forget your recipe, which I have turned over to my cook. She happens to be an artist in her line, with an artist's joy in turning out a pretty job. She announced that she would have to think the thing over to form in her mind a conception of the *grand ensemble*. When it emerges in all its glory it will, I am sure, do honor to her and to me and to the friend who sent its formula from across the distant seas. Well, one becomes self-centered and egotistical when one is classified as sick with nothing special the matter with one. Anything is better than the work and worry that have been mine during the last year."

To another friend he wrote sometime in the fall: "You were good to telephone me during the summer, and it was a sad disappointment to be unable to see you. Tyrants rule a good part of the world today, and the medical tyrants had me in their grasp. I am still hopeful that you will visit me again in Washington—and relieve the gloom of my winter's exile. How I wish I could journey to New York from time to time! Alas, the prospect is not luminous."

"The President's reception to the Judges and his dinner next week to the Court will," he informed her, "represent the sum total of my adventures in the social life this winter. As you know, I was ill during the summer, and I am shielding myself this year from nerve-racking experiences, knowing that I have enough of them in the labors of the Court. What a grand excuse has been given to me by complaisant physicians!"

While he continued to work as hard as ever during the

winter, the next summer found Cardozo resting in an attempt to recuperate his forces. "I am glad that the summer has dealt kindly with you," he wrote to Professor Jane Perry Clark. "In me it has developed a shameless and shameful indolence, which none the less has been helpful to the body, though I cannot say as much for its effect upon the mind. I suppose I ought to rejoice in the prospect of an early end to this vacuity. But, alas, it is not so. I resent the flight of time when it speeds vacation to a close. How is it that neither of the political parties is proposing to place a curb on that abuse of temporal power?"

"Alas," he told her later, "the tyrannical doctors, intent upon returning me in good shape, have been urging me to be very quiet, renouncing evening engagements during the last week or ten days of the vacation. You must not understand from this that I am ill. I am in better shape than I have been for a long time. But tyranny is rife with us as it is with other Carrels, and doctors, like dictators generally, delight to show their power."

During that last year in Washington, Miriam Small, of the English department of Wells College, frequently visited the Supreme Court just for the purpose of seeing and hearing Justice Cardozo. But that was in the final months of 1937 and Cardozo was an ill man. She saw him sitting with head down. She heard him speak only once. A flustered lawyer was arguing a case involving water supplies in the state of Florida. He felt himself being heckled by one of the Justices who had grown impatient at the lawyer's floundering. Cardozo leaned forward. "Did you have any authority?" he asked. The question was the helpful cue, the embarrassed attorney then knew how to proceed. It was, he told a friend, "a raft to a drowning man."

Another friend, Bob Marshall, cheered Cardozo by taking a somewhat lighter tone in regard to his manner in court. Mr. Marshall knew that Cardozo loved fun. He had been delighted, for instance, when a picture taken of him going to the President's reception with his hat on crooked caused so many of his friends to ask him "what brand" he drank.

Mr. Marshall sent Cardozo the following:

Statistical Study of the Manual Support to the Heads of Supreme Court Justices in Action

"The head is generally conceded to be that portion of the body where the major part of most people's thought takes place. The Supreme Court is generally conceded to embrace those citizens of the United States who engage in the weightiest thought. It therefore seems of particular interest to observe evidences which have a bearing on the weight of Supreme Court Justices' heads. As an observable indicator of head weight, I have chosen for study the percentage of the times that different Supreme Court Justices support their heads with their hands . . .

Name of Justice	Number of times holding head	Percentage of times holding head
Hughes	11	73
McReynolds	11	73
Butler	8	53
Van Devanter	6	40
Sutherland	5	33
Roberts	3	20
Stone	3	20
Brandeis	2	13
Cardozo	0	0

"One extraneous feature which may have influenced these figures is the fact that Justice Cardozo slept more than any other Justice. He does not sleep with his head in his hand.

"Another extraneous influence may have been the fact that Justices Cardozo and Stone whispered more than all the other Justices put together and did not hold their heads while whispering."

"I feel proud," Cardozo assured Mr. Marshall, "of the demonstration that I have the lightest head of all the judges. I repel, however, as a foul slander, the charge that I slept upon the bench during the arguments of counsel. I was much too busy watching you. . . . Rather proudly and triumphantly, I said to myself, 'His scoffing and sardonic soul has been awed and impressed by the vision of the mighty nine. He knows us now for the great and inspired spirits that we are.' I shall never put my faith again in the physiognomy of innocence. Irreverent sir, I wish you happiness in the new year, and the opportunity for repentance."

There were other irreverent presents during holiday seasons from friends who, knowing him well, dared with affectionate understanding. There was, for instance, the box from two charming women in Albany, one of them the wife of one of Cardozo's old associates in the Court of Appeals. It contained a little Christmas tree rich in amusing toys. Dolls appropriately garbed represented the nine august Justices of the Supreme Court. Humorous verses—none too respectful—were attached to each—including, of course, the miniature China representative of Cardozo himself.

One of the Justice's secretaries helped with the unwrapping. The young man, somewhat taken aback by the caricaturing and the irreverence, anxiously watched Cardozo's expression as his mocked-at associates issued from the Christmas box. What would be the Justice's reaction to such impertinence? He saw Cardozo's smile grow broader and broader. He heard Cardozo say, "Those good people in Albany, *they* know I have the heart of a child."

Always he looked back regretfully to those days in Albany. "I have felt from my talks with him," writes

Governor Lehman, "that, while he recognized and appreciated the wider field of service that was his as a Justice of the Supreme Court of the United States, he never ceased to miss his friends in Albany and the associations which he had made as Chief Judge of the Court of Appeals of the State of New York."

On January 8, 1938, the blow fell which was to leave Cardozo partly paralyzed. The left arm and left leg were affected, and the right eye. Dr. Keating and later Dr. Daniels, with the heart specialist Dr. Worth Lee as consultant, sought unavailingly to restore their patient to health. Danger of pneumonia, and yet the necessity of soporific drugs, involved questions of worriment, and Cardozo's occasional spells of melancholia cast gloom upon the little household.

Nevertheless, the Justice fought hard against the advance of paralysis and on no occasion mentioned resigning from the Court. His consideration for those about him continued as of old. His last two law secretaries, Christopher S. Sargent and Joseph Rauh, have given many instances of his courtesy and thoughtfulness during those months of illness. He was so appreciative of every attention that on one occasion Kate Tracy said to him, "Don't wear yourself out thanking me for this glass of water."

During long hours the stricken man lay unmoving but with mind active. On his wall hung the framed letter from Justice Holmes. "I have always thought," read the sentence that Cardozo loved, "that not place or power or popularity makes the success that one desires, but the trembling hope that one has come near to an ideal." Whatever his modesty, his self-depreciation, there must have been hours when Cardozo knew that trembling hope. Offices and honors, fame unsought, won by what Cardozo considered the plodding virtues; but due, indeed, to the high endeavor were, at least, evidence of public recognition that an ideal had been approached. A shy and solitary man, by virtue of character and mind, and by the rare quality of charm, he came also to know what Justice Brandeis, quoting *Iolanthe*, called "the frenzy of love and devotion" of great numbers of people.

Cardozo had been warned of the danger of his condition, but had chosen to pay little attention to the warning. Several years earlier he had been told that unless he worked much less strenuously his life would be considerably shortened. But the lonely man in Washington cared much more for service to his country than for the prolongation of those years during which honors were continuing to fall upon his whitening head.

The heart tremors which did not cause Cardozo to desist from overwork led him, however, to give thought to the ending of life, and in 1936 he made his final will.

In it there is in miniature a picture of the man. After the preliminary words declaring this to be his final testament and revoking any previous wills, Cardozo directs, first, the "payment of my lawful debts." Next he bequeaths a sum of $2,000 whose income is to be applied "to attending and beautifying the burial plot in Cypress Hills Cemetery, Long Island, wherein I wish to be buried and wherein my parents, brother and sisters are already buried." He makes provision for the lasting beautifying of the grave at Woodlawn of his twin sister Emily.

He bequeaths $25,000 to the Federation for the Support of Jewish Philanthropic Societies of New York City, a corporation which benefits a large number of charitable institutions. He gives to Mt. Sinai Hospital the sum of $7,500 "for the endowment of a bed to be maintained and dedicated in perpetuity to the sacred memory of my sister, Ellen Ida Cardozo."

There was another woman toward whom Justice Cardozo felt tender gratitude, Kate Tracy, for forty-six years a member of the Cardozo household. She had known him before he reached the age of manhood. She was with him at the end. "I give and bequeath the sum of $70,000 to Kate A. Tracy, in grateful recognition of her devoted service during many years to my deceased sisters, Elizabeth and Ellen, and since their death, to me. . . . This gift shall bear interest at the rate of five per cent per annum from the date of my death to the date of payment."

Next follow bequests of $1,500 to Catherine Walsh, the cook; $750 to Anna Barthick, the maid; and $750 to Norvil H. Hayes, the chauffeur. In a codicil, Cardozo increased three of these legacies by the respective amounts of $6,000, $1,500, and $1,500, and added $5,000 to the legacy to Miss Tracy. It is interesting to note the sequence of the provisions that have thus far been noted. First, family love and loyalty; these took precedence above all others. Then the paragraphs wherein he showed his gratitude to the retainers who had served him devotedly. That was the way his heart and mind would naturally work. These provisions out of the way, he turns to his friends.

The first to be mentioned is George H. Engelhard, his law partner in early days and his dear friend throughout life. A money gift of $7,500 does not suffice. "I give him also my china and silverwear not otherwise specifically disposed of." In the home of George Engelhard he had many happy hours; at his table many delightful dinners. It was fitting that Ben Cardozo's china and silverwear should henceforth rest on the hospitable table of his lifelong friend.

"I give and bequeath to my friend William H. Freese of the City of New York the sum of $5,000." But this man, who had been a clerk in Cardozo's office, who took care of his affairs when the Justice was at Albany and in Washington, and in whom Cardozo had such implicit confidence, deserved more than a gift of money in token of their friendship. So we find him receiving also "my jewelry and other articles of personal adornment."

"As a memento of our friendship, I give and bequeath to Irving Lehman of the City of New York the sum of $2,000." Then he continues: "I give him also any books in my library that he may care to own, the other books, if any, to form a part of my residuary estate."

The bequest to Mrs. Lehman was, "as a memento of our friendship, the silver loving cup that was presented to me by the Judges of the New York Court of Appeals when I retired from that court."

The residue of his estate was given to Columbia University—the gift of a loyal alumnus and an honored trustee. Without making it a mandatory direction, Cardozo expressed the wish and hope that the gift should be applied to "the foundation and maintenance of a chair of jurisprudence in the Law School of the University, to be associated with my name and to perpetuate the scientific study of a subject which has been one of my chief interests in life." Here there is evidence that the Justice was not averse to fame—that he would be glad to have the name of Cardozo remembered.

The Justice, frugal in his manner of living, and with none of the expensive tastes of the collector, was careful also as an investor. Almost half of his estate was in United States Treasury issues, the other half mainly in New York City mortgages. The total reached a sum of between three and four hundred thousand dollars. In round numbers, $189,000 was devised to Columbia.

In his report for 1938 Professor Young B. Smith, Dean of the Columbia University School of Law, said that the purpose of the course to be established by Cardozo's bequest was to "open the minds of students to those vast fields of thought embraced within the sphere of jurisprudence and philosophy which strive for greater understand-

[307]

ing of law as a social institution, its process and its limitation and its true functions in the social order." And here, in connection with the will, it is a pleasure to record that when Judge Lehman received the check from the Cardozo estate he immediately endorsed it over to Columbia University, his Alma Mater and that of his friend who had died.

During the months while Cardozo's health was waning, Judge Cohen, anxious about his friend, sent this telegram to Washington: "The old Judge wants to know how the baby is getting on. Is the crib comfortable? If not, let me know, and I will fix it up for you. Love. Judge Billy."

Cardozo answered: "I don't sleep in a crib any more. I'm a big grown boy. When I'm twenty-one, like you, I'll make things hum. Thanks, dear boy or man, for your thought of me."

The afternoon before the serious heart attack Cardozo had insisted on going to the home of Justice Brandeis, the man whom he had characterized as one of the great judges not only of his country, but of the world. Kate Tracy had urged him not to go. She had asked him to come right back home after his work at the Supreme Court was over. But— Miss Addie Cardozo has informed us—her cousin was insistent, saying that "Nobody is going to keep me from going." That was the last time he ever left his Washington room, except to be taken, some months later, in an ambulance to the railroad station, to be met at Port Chester by another ambulance which brought him to the home of Judge Lehman. Critically ill during the first part of December, he was made very uncomfortable by an ailment which led him to remark that "the road to hell is shingled."

During the latter part of December there was some progress. The Justice was allowed to read. *Northwest Passage* was his first attempt. Gifts were coming in from many friends, but he was too weak to acknowledge them in person. He was visited daily by his regular physician and twice a week by Dr. Lee, the heart specialist. Cardiographs showed that a marked depression of the heart had taken place.

But with the new year came the really tragic calamity— the stroke on the eighth of January. Sinking spells had preceded it, and a severe heart attack the day before. Kate Tracy telegraphed to Addie Cardozo. She came immediately to Washington to be at her cousin's bedside. January was a month of decline, of artificial feeding, of more difficult breathing, of hours of unconsciousness caused by morphine. February showed improvement, and early in March, Cardozo was able to sit in a chair now and then, and to get more pleasure from the tulips and roses and other flowers, from the books and other gifts sent by his friends. He especially appreciated the attentions from young people. When a young Washington girl—Kate Meyer— sent him an orchid, he insisted on having it placed in a vase on the table next to his bed so that he need but turn to see what for him was a symbol—the devotion of youth.

April found Cardozo more apathetic, more drowsy. He was losing strength. Those who loved him were losing hope. President and Mrs. Roosevelt, Chief Justice Hughes, Justice Stone, and many others came to visit him, to bring flowers. But only the most intimate friends and relatives were admitted to the sickroom. Prayers were offered for his recovery in Washington, in Albany, in New York. Said one woman, "I hope for God's sake he gets better. I pray day and night for him." This was Mrs. Alice Williams, the last nurse of Cardozo's sister Nellie. When, after Nellie's death, Alice Williams fell ill, Cardozo aided her to meet the hospital bills. On her recovery he helped to set her up in earning another kind of a living, as severe arthritis had left her incapable of her former profession. At her newspaper stand at Eighth Avenue and Forty-second Street Alice Williams, if you ask her, will tell you that Benjamin Cardozo was "a marvelous man," and the only man who ever helped her.

Dr. Anson Phelps Stokes, similarly considered Cardozo "a marvelous man."

"I shall never forget two delightful, long talks I had with him, once when he came to take tea with us on the afternoon of a holiday—I think quite likely the first of the year; the other when I called to see him at his house. On both occasions I was specially impressed by his culture, his spiritual attitude toward life, his keen mind, his breadth of interests, and with them all a most charming and lovable personality. I can truly say that during the fifteen years that I have lived in Washington I have known no one who has been more admired and loved by those who knew him well than Justice Cardozo. Members of the Supreme Court have repeatedly told me of the deep devotion of all of their members to him. They considered him an ideal judge in his temper of mind, his devotion to high ideals of justice, and his power of lucid presentation."

During the last summer of Cardozo's life, Dr. Stokes could not refrain from telling the Justice what he thought of him. Cardozo lay stricken in the home at Port Chester of Judge and Mrs. Lehman. Only a few weeks of life remained. Letters expressing hope for recovery, flowers, and books were pouring in from many friends and admirers whom the Justice was never again to see. "I wonder," Dr. Stokes wrote, "if you realize fully how you are honored and loved by all thoughtful people in the community? If you do not you certainly should have the satisfaction of knowing it, for I have never heard more unanimity of opinion among thoughtful people as to the real contribution which you have made through your thinking and your character to our nation."

2101 CONNECTICUT AVENUE
WASHINGTON

Thanking for a novel entitled "Persian Conqueror"

After Cardozo's death, Canon Stokes, speaking in the pulpit of Washington Cathedral, referred to the Justice as "a man of exalted character and ideals, who had rendered his country conspicuous service as a great judge." Later, in November, Dr. Stokes gave a radio address entitled "Message of a Christian Minister to the Jewish People." In it he dwelt on the Fatherhood of God and the brotherhood of man. "We Christians feel profoundly grateful to the Jews for helping to keep alive in a mad and skeptical world the fundamental truth of the existence of a righteous God and the vital importance of the moral law." The Canon expressed gratitude to the Jewish race for having given to the Christian world the Founder of their religion who had been "brought up in a consecrated Jewish home." Then, as the address proceeded, Dr. Stokes urged self-examination on the part of Jews "with a view to removing causes of friction and antipathy." "Every individual of every denomination and every race" should do this, but quite fittingly the Canon suggested its special value to Jews at this time of rising prejudice. Then again he paid a tribute to Benjamin Cardozo. "The American nation," said Stokes, "has in a great Jew, whom I had the privilege of calling a friend, a striking example of what I mean, namely, the late Justice Cardozo, who consciously and with noble success devoted his life to overcoming the record of a near relative guilty of dishonorable conduct as a judge in New York City. In the same way we should, as Americans, examine ourselves so as to overcome whatever is amiss in the temper and disposition of our lives."

The last time Chief Justice Hughes saw him in his apartment in Washington, the man whom he had known as a boy was brought into the room in a wheel chair. There were tears in his eyes. When Hughes took his hand, "They tell me I am going to get well," Cardozo said, "but I file a dissenting opinion."

May, 1938, and the Justice has left Washington forever. He is at the lovely country home, on Ridge Street, Port Chester, of Judge and Mrs. Lehman. They have made it more his home than theirs. A few—very few—visitors are allowed to see him. His health appears to have improved in the quiet country surroundings. His last birthday comes May 24, devoid of any excitement. The Justice is deeply touched by all the letters, by the many gifts, that speak their messages of affection. A wheel chair takes him on the lawn and into the garden.

In June he is well enough to see a few more friends—well enough to be taken on an automobile ride around the beautiful country of Westchester. But the doctors are not deceived. Cardozo's strength is waning.

He died on the ninth of July.

"I have watched," the words are those of Cardozo's cousin, Annie Nathan Meyer, "I have watched by the side of many upon whom Death, that mysterious visitor, has laid its hand, but never had I seen it take on so breathtaking a beauty. The noble silver-crowned head, the delicate spiritual features, the long slender form clad in silver silken pajamas, lay there as some knight of old encased in shining armor."

At Cardozo's funeral there was no word of eulogy. He did not wish to have it. He had so requested. Passages from the Scriptures were read—some of the Psalms, some of the Proverbs. The ancient ways were followed—the traditional Hebrew prayers of the Spanish and Portuguese Jews. The commitment services in the chapel—the prayers and the chanting—were all in the ancient Hebrew. No word of English for this master of the English tongue. Far away were the days since he himself had departed from orthodox religion, but his sister Nell would have wished her brother to be buried according to the custom of their ancestors.

We saw the coffin lowered. From the hands of cousins earth was cast on the blanket of flowers. Finis to what was mortal in the man who understood so well the words of Portia—who knew, moreover, not only that mercy should temper justice, but that mercy and justice are one.

A gentle rain was falling.

EPILOGUE

.

EPILOGUE

As was said in the Foreword, the primary purpose of this biography has been to portray a personality. The philosopher and the judge have, of course, been kept in mind but it was the lovable man who, foremost, has invited attention. If, as a consequence, this book is regarded by those who did not know Cardozo personally, as a work however permissibly biased by affection, let the voice of associates in the law and the voice of the wider public speak the final word.

For days after the death of Cardozo the press of America contained column after column of accounts of his life. Such immediate eulogy as poured forth has had no parallel in all our history since the time of George Washington. This is no exaggeration. Not even Abraham Lincoln—in whose praise the South would not join. Go through the alphabet of the states—call their roster from Alabama to Wyoming—and they reply with articles and editorials in which sounds the note of such unqualified admiration and, above all, of such reverence as seldom is offered to any man. For days these tributes streamed from every part of our land. And then for months, and during the succeeding years, addresses in Cardozo's honor and memorial meetings in city courts, state courts, the Supreme Court at Washington; tributes from the pulpits of churches of many denominations; essays in magazines; tributes at memorial meetings of bar associations; essays and addresses written by famous judges and lawyers and printed in pamphlet form for distribution to American universities and libraries.

In the months succeeding Cardozo's death the most

important law journals in the country were vying with one another in their testimonials. A characteristic example appeared in the December issue of the *Cornell Law Quarterly*. On the editorial page this tribute written by the former Dean was printed within mourning borders:

BENJAMIN N. CARDOZO

1870–1938

Judged by the highest standards of culture, professional learning and technical skill, and by a sensible practical wisdom, Justice Cardozo ranked with the most eminent judicial minds, not only of his own generation but also of our American and English judicial history. All of his rare qualities were unmarred by glamour or ostentation. The expressions of his great mind were clothed in a quiet beauty of style unexcelled in judicial opinions and expected only in pure literature. In the construction and interpretation of the law he was ever aware that "The letter killeth but the spirit giveth life." He was indeed a remarkable legal genius.

EDWIN H. WOODRUFF

The law journals of Harvard, Yale, and Columbia published a special joint issue devoted in its entirety to articles in honor of Cardozo, wherein jurists of Europe, Asia, and America gave tribute. Turning to the West for a typical example, we come to the article in the *California State Bar Journal*. There Professor Charles Fairman of Stanford University writes: "Of Cardozo as of no other Justice who ever sat upon the Supreme Court, it may be said that he was chosen by acclamation." Speaking of him as "one of the greatest of our Americans," Professor Fairman gives "as an evidence of Cardozo's greatness the respect in which he was held abroad. The citation of American decisions has never been encouraged in the English Courts; quite the contrary. But exceptions have always been recognized, and Judge Cardozo was one of the very few American judges whose names have been known and honored among English lawyers."

A law journal that belongs, as its name implies, to both the East and the West is the *National Lawyers Guild Quarterly*. Its first issue after Cardozo's death had as its leading article a paper by Professor Morris R. Cohen. Here we shall find a discussion of the main features of Cardozo's philosophy— the emphasis on law as "an essential part of the process of adjusting human relations in organized society." Then, too, is stressed Cardozo's conviction that "to meet his responsibility for making the law serve human needs the Judge cannot rely on legal authorities alone but must know the actual facts of the life about him, the psychologic and economic factors which determine its manifestations, and must thus keep abreast of the best available knowledge which those engaged in various social studies, researches or investigations can supply."

In this stimulating paper there is one comment on Cardozo which, one way or another, has been made by many other writers: "He was not merely the Chief Judge of New York State, he was also the intellectual and spiritual leader of the legal profession."

It would be tempting to quote from many other law journals and from publications—monthly and weekly magazines read by the general public. But even if space did not disallow, reiteration tends to a loss in effect. It may even be thought that this danger has already been ventured upon in the pages of this book. Even so, one paper will be drawn upon from the *Journal of Social Philosophy*. There its editor, Dr. Moses J. Aronson, discusses at great length "Cardozo's Doctrine of Sociological Jurisprudence." He quotes Roscoe Pound, one of America's greatest writers on law, as saying: "In the American sociological jurisprudence the outstanding work is that of Mr. Justice Cardozo." The writer himself states: "It remained for Cardozo's genius to bridge the chasm between private and public law, and to demonstrate that the process of judicial law-making is fundamentally identical in all its branches. In so doing Cardozo effected an original systematization of the view which his brilliant fore-runners had emitted in fugitive flashes of intuition. . . . By uncovering the subterranean passages which lead from the social sciences to jurisprudence, Cardozo helped to invigorate legal theory with renewed life, disclosing to it visions of novel perspectives and larger horizons."

The two gentlemen whose words have just been quoted are Professors of Philosophy in Eastern universities. Another two with whom Cardozo enjoyed discussing philosophy, and who have testified to the profundity of his knowledge and the beauty of his character are Horace M. Kallen and Irwin Edman. The greatest of living American philosophers, John Dewey, corresponded with Cardozo. One of the greatest of all time, Albert Einstein, has informed us that his "precious talks" with Cardozo "belong to his most beautiful memories."

A volume of a thousand pages could not contain all the tributes. Here let us add excerpts from one address, one pamphlet, and one editorial to indicate, nutshell-wise, the forest of praise.

[320]

At the last session of the Supreme Court of the United States in the December succeeding Cardozo's death, Attorney General Homer S. Cummings, representing the bar of the Supreme Court, followed the reading of its resolutions with a eulogy wherein he dwelt on the greatness of Cardozo as a constitutional jurist. "No other Judge of his time," said the Attorney General, "was so deft in weaving the precedents of centuries into a new shape to govern a new society. . . . No one saw more clearly than he that the imperfect rules of today may stir equities that become the law of tomorrow."

In responding to the presentation of the resolutions, Chief Justice Hughes delivered an address of high admiration and tender affection. Speaking for all his colleagues—save Mr. Justice McReynolds, the only one absenting himself from the occasion—the Chief Justice said in part: "We, his brethren of the Court,—still awe-struck by the fate which brought his career to such an untimely and tragic end—receive this tribute with hearts burning by the sense of loss of that personal association which was to us a price-less privilege. . . . In the field of the common law, his learning gave him the freedom which comes with mastery, as he utilized its processes to secure its intelligent adaptation to the needs of his time. Modest, sensitive and retiring, he was still a mighty warrior for his convictions and in his expert hands the pen became a sword wielded with devas-tating power. . . . No Judge ever came to this Court more fully equipped by learning, acumen, dialectical skill, and a disinterested purpose. He came to us in the full maturity of his extraordinary intellectual power, and no one of this Bench has ever served with more untiring indus-try or more enlightened outlook. The memory of that service and its brilliant achievements will ever be one of the most prized traditions of this tribunal. . . . Mr. Justice Cardozo was devoted to our form of government and to him our Constitutional guarantees of essential liberties constituted a heritage to be defended at all costs. With rare insight into our social problems and with vivid imagination, what he thought and sought to enforce was built upon the foundation of profound study. . . . In his view the competing demands of stability and progress pointed to an essential compromise,—'a compromise between paradoxes, between certainty and uncertainty, between the literalism that is the exaltation of the written word and the nihilism that is destructive of regularity and order.' . . . For Justice Cardozo, the distrust of a concept was the beginning of wisdom and he was constantly on guard against the tyranny of labels. . . . In conference, while generally reserved and reticent until it was his duty to speak, he then responded with an unsurpassed clearness and precision in statement. His gentleness and self-constraint, his ineffable charm, combined with his alertness and mental strength, made him a unique personality. With us who had the privilege of daily association there will ever abide the precious memory not only the work of a great jurist but of companionship with a beautiful spirit, an extraordinary combination of grace and power."

George R. Farnum, former Assistant Attorney General of the United States, has published three pamphlets devoted to the great trio of Supreme Court Justices in recent American history—Holmes, Brandeis, and Cardozo. The paper on Cardozo, originally appearing in the publication entitled *The Lawyer*, is headed by excerpts from two letters to the author. Judge Julian W. Mack wrote: "I know of no man more respected, admired and loved—nor anyone who deserves it more than he. One is at a loss to decide in which he excels the most—learning, modesty, charm, literary grace, character. In each he is on the heights." Frederic R. Coudert, the very distinguished New York lawyer, wrote: "He is one of the noblest souls I have ever known." Mr.

[322]

Cummings's own tribute includes the following, among other passages of similar admiration: "He was inspired and dominated in his work by the faith, as he once expressed it, 'that all our precedents and principles and procedural regulations must be revivified by constant reference to the ever-shifting needs of life.' . . . His conduct in life was governed by a high moral purpose. He was moved by deep mystical feeling. . . . He unconsciously permeated the science of the law with his own spirit and he consciously strove to transform its principles and precepts into more vital aids in promoting right standards of conduct and a happier ordering of social existence. . . . The tolerance of his judgment, the sympathy of his nature, and his innate gentleness and humility breathe in all his free compositions. There is an unmistakable grace and lyricism about them that identify the poetic instinct. . . . As his predecessor Holmes once said, 'If a man is great he makes others believe in greatness; he makes them incapable of mean ideals and easy self-satisfaction.'"

The tributes by Hughes and Farnum and Cummings were from men who knew Cardozo. Now let us listen to one who did not know him personally but whose words epitomize the opinion of the American press. The choice falls not on a writer of Cardozo's native city or native state, but on a Nebraskan, Mr. J. E. Lawrence, editor of the *Lincoln Star*.

"America sorrows because Benjamin Cardozo died; died when he was needed so badly; died when he was a tower of strength to a country which has need of all the strength it can summon in readjusting its institutions to the uncheckable currents loosened by mighty forces. Justice Cardozo lived a quiet life of retirement. The public did not know him because of his deliberate habit of secluding himself. But he was a great man of unimpeachable integrity; of dauntless courage and faith; of accumulative wisdom, a

[323]

wisdom that was not 'bookish' but human and virile. . . .
The American people have suffered a great loss. The Court
has sustained an irreparable loss. In its own transition, a
modification of court view along social and economic lines
that is more pronounced than in any other similar period,
Justice Cardozo gave to that transition a confidence it
could not otherwise have enjoyed. . . . His influence was
profound, and so well established was his place that men
appreciative of his sound scholarship eagerly watched to
see what Justice Cardozo thought of these grave constitutional questions confronting the Court. . . . The high success of his life, the honors which came to him, issued from
the continuance of the most sacred of American traditions.
In mourning his death, America can say she has made
good on the ideals of racial equality. She can think of him
and think of this magnificent contribution which he made
to America. She can think of the life of Justice Cardozo
and renew the vows this shall be a land of the free—a land
in which there shall be no racial discrimination, no class
distinction, and no limitations upon the right to worship
as the heart may dictate, or to think and speak as the mind
orders."

Such, then, was this American judge. Such was his contribution to the land of his love. Yet if Benjamin Cardozo,
as his life was ending, had been asked:

"Shall thy heart's answer be: 'So far, all well'?"

the reply of this self-searching torchbearer might indeed
have been:

"No, to the brave never 'All well, so far,'
While in the soul's deep heaven shines one elusive star,
Wherein the hope of mankind lies:
The bright ideal flame which ever beckons on
And lights anew desire for higher skies,
And makes us not content with acts already done."

[324]

ACKNOWLEDGMENT

ACKNOWLEDGMENT

THE first word of thanks goes to the President of the United States and Mrs. Franklin D. Roosevelt, whose admiration for Justice Cardozo is manifest in the foregoing pages. Others of his friends who have proved preeminently helpful are Chief Justice Charles E. Hughes, Justice Harlan F. Stone, Judge Learned Hand, Rev. Dr. and Mrs. David de Sola Pool, Rev. Dr. and Mrs. Stephen S. Wise, and, very especially, Dr. Nicholas Murray Butler.

Without the interest and generous aid of Justice Cardozo's family, on both the paternal and maternal sides, this biography would hardly have been possible. Here are named with gratitude Miss Addie Cardozo, Ernest A. Cardozo, Mr. and Mrs. Michael H. Cardozo, IV, Sidney Cardozo, Mr. and Mrs. William B. Cardozo, Miss Adah Marks, Mrs. Annie Nathan Meyer, Mr. and Mrs. Harold Nathan, Mrs. Maud Nathan, Robert Nathan, and Mrs. Julius R. Wolff. Other kin who have been more than kind include Mrs. Joseph F. Cullman, Mr. and Mrs. Lafayette Goldstone, Rupert Joseph, Honorable and Mrs. N. Taylor Phillips, Miss Aline E. Solomons, and Colonel and Mrs. Arthur R. Wolff.

To Miss Kate Tracy, in the most devoted sense a member of the family, separate lines of thanks are due. Other women who have graciously aided the author include Miss Carrie Bijur, Mrs. Nathan Bijur, Miss Mabel T. Boardman, Mrs. Sidney C. Borg, Mrs. Louis D. Brandeis, Mrs. Robert Woods Bliss, Miss Blanche Content, Mrs. Winthrop Chanler, Professor Jane Perry Clark, Miss Elinore Denniston, Miss Hettie Goldman, Mrs. Alfred Hess, Mrs. Walter

Hirsch, Mrs. Alexander Kohut, Mrs. Eva Lips, Mrs. Arthur Strasser, Mrs. Arthur H. Sulzberger, and, in rich measure, Mrs. Samuel C. Webster.

Among clergymen, the Rev. John J. Cloonan, the Rev. Dr. Elbert Floyd-Jones, the Rev. Dr. Thornton B. Penfield, the Rev. Dr. Howard Chanler Robbins, and the Rev. Dr. Anson Phelps Stokes have very kindly contributed. So, too, with artists—Jo Davidson, Kenneth Hayes Miller, A. Vincent Tack; and with authors—John Erskine, Fannie Hurst, William Lyon Phelps, Norman Thomas.

Among men holding or having held high public office who have courteously responded with valuable aid are the Honorables Homer S. Cummings, Abram I. Elkus, George R. Farnum, Stanley M. Isaacs, Herbert H. Lehman, Robert Marshall, Charles H. Tuttle, and Robert F. Wagner. Educators in great number have been similarly kind. To mention but a few—Dean Henry M. Bates, President James P. Baxter, III, President Robert C. Clothier, Professor A. L. Corbin, Dr. Frank W. Crane, Professor Thomas H. Fiske, President Frank Pierrepont Graves, Professor Moses Hadas, Dean George W. Matheson, Professor George C. D. Odell, the late Professor Edwin R. A. Seligman, and Professor E. H. Woodruff.

Justices and judges, active or retired, all of them devoted to the memory of Cardozo, have talked or written to the author. In this group figure the Honorables Frederick E. Crane, Moses H. Grossman, Henry J. Kellogg, Julian W. Mack, John F. O'Brien, Joseph M. Proskauer, Samuel Seabury, Thomas W. Swan, and Irving Lehman, who as Chief Judge of the Court of Appeals of New York State now holds the high office formerly so brilliantly adorned by his dear friend.

The phrase just used leads to probably the dearest of Cardozo's friends—George H. Engelhard. He and William H. Freese were closely associated with the Justice since the early years of his legal practice. These two gentlemen belong to the host of lawyers who have shown helpful courtesy to the biographer. Among that large group of Cardozo's admirers young and old are John Bogart, Charles C. Burlingame, Melville Cane, John Kirkland Clarke, Frederic R. Coudert, John W. Davis, Emanuel Hertz, Edgar J. Kohler, Beryl H. Levy, Edmund McCarthy, Charles T. McDermott, H. H. Nordlinger, Nathan Ottinger, Walter Pollak, Henry M. Powell, Louis H. Robinson, Eustace Seligman, Abraham Tulin, Henry A. Uterhart, George F. Warren, Jr., W. Arnold Weissberger, and, notably, Dr. William Draper Lewis.

Of course, important aid was obtained from men who had served as Cardozo's law secretaries at New York, Albany, or Washington. The author offers his cordial thanks to Ambrose Doskow, Charles E. Hughes, Jr., Joseph Rauh, Percy H. Russell, Jr., Christopher S. Sargent, and Allan Stroock.

One would think that here might end the list—so long a list—of those to whom thanks should be tendered. Not so. Notations of conversations, letters received, reveal further obligations. They are the due of Arthur J. Cohen, Rodman Gilder, Richard Hillman, E. H. Hornbostel, Henry Hurwitz, Remsen Johnson, Willard V. King, Thomas P. McKenna, John Dynely Prince, George Stevens, David Rosenblum, Leonard D. White, Frederick Willets, and a large number of Cardozo's college mates.

Officials at Cardozo's alma mater, with President Butler at their head, have shown most valuable courtesies. Harvard, Yale, Princeton, the University of London, and all the other distinguished institutions of learning that conferred honorary degrees on the Judge have been similarly courteous in their aid. Thanks are likewise due to The American Law Institute, The Association of the Bar of the City of New York, Columbia University, *Harvard*

Law Review, the Jewish Institute of Religion, Oxford University Press, St. John's College, and Yale University Press for permission to quote from writings and addresses of Cardozo. Bruce Rogers and the Oxford University Press have kindly allowed the inclusion of a few verses from T. E. Shaw's translation of the *Odyssey*.

Among the Justice's male cousins, his favorites seem to have been Edgar J. Nathan, Jr., recently a nominee for the New York Supreme Court, and Michael H. Cardozo IV, a brilliant young lawyer. A very special word of thanks goes forth to the latter for his interest and aid.

In conclusion, the biographer allows himself the privilege of naming, in love and reverence, his mother, who is no longer alive. She it was who gave him recollections of the Cardozos when they and her parents had their country homes in close proximity. She it was for whom the Justice of the Supreme Court inscribed his photograph: "To Frances Hellman, my own and my family's friend for many years. With the good will and gratitude of Benjamin N. Cardozo."

Here, then, acknowledgment has been made to more than a hundred men and women who have been greatly helpful. And yet this is only a fraction—far less than half—of the persons who have so kindly afforded information of use to the biographer. If such a vast group is not individually named in its entirety it is because too long a list—like Homer's catalogue of ships—becomes tedious to the reader. The gratitude of the author remains none the less sincere to them all.

G. S. H.

INDEX

[332]

[333]

H

I

J

K

L

[337]